D1432784

A World of Men

Polar Plateau

A World of Men

Exploration in Antarctica

Wally Herbert

G. P. PUTNAM'S SONS · NEW YORK

Contents

Foreword		*page* 9
Introduction		13
1	We sail	17
2	Ice-floes and sea lanes	24
3	A moment of glory	42
4	Two strong men	53
5	Contented castaways	65
6	Hair-shirt and stone age	72
7	Self-imposed cruelty	86
8	Vaguely like bodies	94
9	A grey, desolate world	106
10	Sea sounds and liquid ribbons	126
11	Walls of sliding water People, people everywhere	134
12	A different polar scene	140
13	Sons, daughters and dogs	146
14	Scarcely a moment to shudder	158
15	The whisper of discontent	167
16	The thunder of the elements	174
17	With a feeling akin to awe	182
18	The forbidden journey	193
19	In the footsteps of Amundsen	203
20	Epilogue	228

Plates

COLOUR

Polar Plateau   *Frontispiece*

1   R.R.S. Shackleton at Pitt point   *facing page* 48

2   Mt Erebus – the end of winter   112

3   Mt Don Pedro Christophersen   168

4   The Axel Heiberg Glacier Region   200

BLACK AND WHITE   *following page* 96

1   Blade Ridge and Mount Taylor, Hope Bay

2   Hope Bay

3a Seal – 'Come on in, it's lovely!'

3b Penguins – at sixes and sevens on the pack ice

4   Antarctic explorer – a drawing by Wally Herbert

5   The northern tip of the Graham Land Peninsula

6   Perspective view of the Graham Land Peninsula
    north of latitude 64°50′ S

7   The Base leaders
    (a) Ron Worswick
    (b) Lee Rice
    (c) Dick Foster

8a Dr Hugh Simpson

8b Dennis Kershaw

8c Hosts and guests at the Reclus hut

9   An aerial view of the McMurdo Sound and
    Scott Base area

10   A cup of boiling water exploding into ice
       at an air temperature of —80° F. *following page* 96

11   A sledging team 12 ft from the tongue of the
       Barne Glacier

12a Scott's hut at Cape Evans on his second expedition

12b Shackleton's hut at Cape Royds

13   Captain Roald Amundsen

14   Camp near the Polar plateau

15   Retracing, in reverse, Amundsen's route to the
       Pole along the Axel Heiberg Glacier

16a ⎱ Part of the Queen Maud Range and Axel
16b ⎰ Heiberg Glacier region

Plates 1 COLOUR and 2 BLACK AND WHITE were taken
by Dr Hugh Simpson. Plates 4, 5, 6, 7, 8 and 13 BLACK
AND WHITE were all drawn by the author. Plate 9 is re-
produced by courtesy of the Department of Land and
Survey, New Zealand.

DRAWINGS, BY THE AUTHOR

1   Wandering albatross   *page* 21

2   The hut at Hope Bay   34

3   The hut at View Point   66

4   Nordenskjöld's hut at Snow Hill Island
      as it appeared in 1957   98

5   The Reclus hut   130

6   Husky   152

MAP

The McMurdo Sound–Scott Base area, including the
Queen Maud Range and the Axel Heiberg Glacier *page* 204

Foreword

The Antarctic Continent, which only ten years ago was the last great blank on the map of the world, has now been generally explored, and the planet on which man has lived for some half-million years is about to become his base for exploration into space. The thought of space travel has fired man's imagination for centuries. The Antarctic, on the other hand, has attracted universal interest during only two brief periods of history.

This apparent oversight was not without good reason. The Antarctic is isolated in the centre of the earth's oceanic hemisphere, surrounded by seas and a barrier of pack ice; and the idea of a fertile Southern Continent had been proved wrong by Captain James Cook in 1773, who concluded that 'no continent was to be found in this ocean but must lie so far south as to be wholly inaccessible on account of ice'.

It was not until the 'heroic age' – a decade heralded by Captain Robert Falcon Scott in 1901 – that the Antarctic caught the imagination of the man-in-the-street, and it did so then only because the exploration was spiced by national prestige and the challenge of the Pole. However, this interest in the Antarctic died with the First World War and did not fully revive until the commencement of the International Geophysical Year of 1957–8.

It was my good fortune to go to the Antarctic for the first time just before the wave of science broke. Our voyage South twelve years ago was an escape for long-imprisoned dreams, and the blizzards that beat our backs like whiplashes sang with a cheer in each sting. We saw a paradise in snowscapes and heard colour-music in the wind. For two and a half unforgettable years we were a world of men in harmony with our environment.

I am, undeniably, a romantic – the appeal of the South for me was the adventure, and only indirectly the quest for knowledge. With that same spirit I returned to the Antarctic after an absence of two and a half years, only to find, on the fiftieth anniversary of Amundsen's and Scott's heroic race to the South Pole, a very different atmosphere. Five years after I had first stood on the Antarctic Continent I stepped down from an aircraft on to the ice-runway at Mc-Murdo Sound, an alien among a new kind of polar man. Gone were the ascetics and self-provers and the characters of old – men attracted by the challenge, by the beauty, by the rigours of the polar way of life. Man the scientist had come and his retinue of servicemen with their thundering machinery. No longer was there one major glacier that had not been seen by the eye of the camera, nor a mountain range that had escaped notice.

Most of my new comrades were ordinary men, not explorers, adventurers, or aesthetes. They scorned the romantic conception of a continent ablaze with heroic deeds, and saw no sense in challenging the elements, for they were being handsomely paid to run a geophysical observatory, and could do so better if they were comfortable. However, being an alien intensifies one's perception, and it is with deep feeling for the material that I have endeavoured to build this picture of two different ways of life.

To the men with whom I shared these experiences, particularly to Dr Hugh Simpson, Roger Tufft, Lee Rice, Dennis Kershaw, and Peter Otway, I owe a deep debt of gratitude. Each man who goes South sees a different Antarctica, but what it stirs in the heart I have tried to re-capture. This effort would have come to nought without the encouragement of a few close friends and the faith of my parents to whom this book is dedicated. I thank them all.

Here then is a book that will answer no questions posed by a man of science, nor will it objectively tell what the Antarctic is like; it is written because the feeling needs expression, and adventure needs its advocate.

October 1967

                                                        W. W. HERBERT

Postscript written from the Arctic Ocean, Latitude 81°30′ N, 163° W,
June 1968

We are now over seven hundred miles north of the Alaskan coast and have sledged farther from land over the Arctic Ocean than any other travellers. The pessimists predicted that we would get no farther than the mush ice belt, the southern limit of a zone of shearing ten miles off the coast where the moving pack ice grinds past the land-fast ice.

During the first few weeks, on a treadmill of drifting floes, my three companions and I were carried almost fifty miles off course and many were the times we broke camp in a hurry to get ourselves and our four teams of dogs out of the path of advancing ice pressure or to escape from open water. But we escaped north, not south, and set for ourselves targets which always seemed just beyond our reach.

Unlike Scott and his companions who, during their trudge to the South Pole in 1911, used as a pacemaker the log of Shackleton's South Pole attempt of 1909, no one before us had set out from Barrow with the intention of sledging via the Pole of Relative Inaccessibility and the North Pole to the Arctic Island of Spitzbergen. Even the Eskimos seldom intentionally sledge farther north from Barrow than twenty miles, and cash bets on how long we would survive were still changing hands in the village when we were more than 300 miles north, and in an environment which to them is almost totally unknown.

For reasons of the supposed hazards and uncertainties of the pack-ice environment and the extreme isolation of the party during all except the initial and final few weeks of the sixteen-month trek, it was no easy task to raise support for the first surface crossing of the Arctic Ocean. Often during the four years of preparations, criticisms were raised that the proposed journey was no longer justified. I had argued that the urge in man to respond to a challenge is one of his finest attributes and to scorn or discourage these attributes is to ignore his innate sense of curiosity which throughout the history of human endeavour has resulted in discovery.

In each of the great explorers of the past was a spark of what today is called the spirit of adventure. One can sense this still in the atmosphere of the historic huts in McMurdo Sound – the huts from where Shackleton and Scott set out on their South Polar trek. It is present also in the remains of Nordenskjöld's Antarctic hut and no doubt now – impregnates every nook and cranny of the old timber hut at Hope Bay. It was there I spent my formative years living a monastic life – in a world of men without religious discipline. We were twelve men around a bunkhouse fire, or two men in a drumming tent, spinning yarns or planning journeys, or one man in the solitude of summer-warmed hills. It was a hard but carefree way of life, unreal, isolated, over too soon.   W.W.H.

Introduction

Above the mud banks of the estuary I lazed away my free hours painting, smoking, always dreaming. Seaward with my hopes went matchsticks, whirling downstream, past seagulls pecking at their plump reflections. Shoreham-by-Sea bustled not far away. A church bell clanged the hour of day, marking the passage of wasted time. I was alone; a morose, bearing the weight of frustrated ambitions.

I got up and walked through the boat yards to the road and five miles eastward towards the white and cream sea-front of Brighton. I unlatched the door to my landlady's home and climbed the stairs past prints of flowers and pictures of cats with lugubrious eyes to my poky room, lace-curtained and bare but for the bed and the ornately-framed picture of Jesus Christ. My warder was a spinster, and there was no escape from her religious mania save by a thrust of devilry. She sneered at my ambitions and at my friends – the harmless bohemians who hung around the cider bars and back street pubs of Brighton. We wore strange-looking clothes to distinguish ourselves from 'normal' folk, but in our wakeful hours we were all dreamers, and only truly honest when we were depressed.

After three years' military service I had wandered back to England from Egypt, with only £30 in my pocket. I had taken a job as a surveyor in Shoreham, but, as summer warmed my discontent, I felt once more the breeze of adventure blowing past me out to sea.

It was a blustery day, and the lurching bus taking me to work was dank with the odour of steaming raincoats. I had paid my fare and lit my pipe. I closed my eyes, felt a rush of wind, and there in my lap a newspaper lay that had fallen from the luggage rack. It was open at the 'Public Appointments' page, and as I wrestled to turn the page over, two advertisements caught my eye almost simultaneously: 'Surveyor required in Kenya' one said – 'Expedition to Antarctica' said the other!

... THE FALKLAND ISLAND DEPENDENCIES SURVEY which maintains isolated land bases in the Antarctic, requires

SURVEYORS. Candidates, SINGLE, must be keen young men of good education and high physical standard, who have a genuine interest in Polar research and travel, and are willing to spend 30 months under conditions which are a test of character and resource. They must be competent to carry out survey operations in the Antarctic, including plane tabling and astral fixing. Unqualified candidates who have had experience with the Ordnance Survey or Royal Engineers Survey would be considered for training. Salary in this case would be £330 rising to £420 a year – Write to Crown Agents, 4 Millbank, London, S.W.1. State age, name in block letters, full qualifications, and quote: M3B/35407/DA.

I jumped off the bus, ran past the boat yards, over the bridge and along by the mud banks. I arrived at work in a glow, borrowed a pen, secluded myself in the smallest room and wrote an application for each of the jobs. It was an agony of excitement.

Two months went by. I had no reason to feel despondent – I had been sent official application forms which I had completed and returned immediately. But I could not believe that I stood a chance, and so sought consolation in a round of parties which were to prove almost disastrous, for with only three days notice, I was summoned to London to attend an interview at the Crown Agents' building.

'Mr Herbert?'

I stood up apologetically. The commissionaire cast me a quizzical look from below a pair of bushy eyebrows. 'Follow me,' he said in a commanding tone.

He bounded up three flights of stairs, and following his example I took them all two at a time. I reached the top exhausted, but there was not time to regain composure or to pull my shoulders back, for the commissionaire had already thundered my name.

'Good morning,' I panted – and three speechless men glared up at me from behind a huge polished table.

I could feel myself sweating – so I waved my arm limply in the direction of the door and intimated that they took the commissionaire instead. I smiled wryly at them – and met the rebuff:

'Sit down Mr Herbert – we haven't much time.'

For all the questions they asked I should have had answers – simple questions I should have guessed they would ask.

'Why do you want to go to the Antarctic?' A searching question if ever there was one, and yet all I could answer on the spur of the moment was, 'Because I want to.' I felt very foolish.

'If you were tent-bound for ten days or more, how would you keep your tent mate amused?' That beat me.

'I'm sorry, Mr Herbert, but we really don't think you are very suitable,' the professional interviewer kept saying, and I became fidgety. What fools they are, I thought. Surely they can see I deserve a try.

But they just sat there twiddling their pencils, and when they were on the point of drawing a line through my name, I suddenly realized they were in earnest.

'Why do you think I am unsuitable, sir?' They all looked up from their pads, surprised, but their expressions softened in due course, and the man in the middle explained in a gently reprimanding way:

'Well, Mr Herbert, it's like this: we are interested in what a man has done – not in what he says he would like to do. You haven't done very much with your life so far, have you?'

'No, I suppose not, sir.' I was about to remind them of my first letter in which I had mentioned my hitch-hiking journey from Egypt to England, but thought better of it and, instead, stood up. I tried to say 'Good morning' but the words stuck in my throat. I turned and walked slowly to the door.

I felt numb at first – then slightly sick, until I returned to the waiting room to collect my coat. There I met a sun-tanned man. He was tense and full of apprehension and I was pouring out the reasons why I thought I had failed, so that he might avoid falling into the same sad traps, when the door burst open and a voice bellowed out:

'Mr Orford! Follow me.'

We had been talking like conspirators hard-pressed for time. Suddenly he had gone. I put on my duffle, pulled on my beret and, ambled in a daze out of the building.

How dare they sit in judgement! How could they think I was not tough enough for the sea voyage south – had I not come through a nightmare steerage passage from Cyprus to Turkey? If only I had told the interviewers how forty of us were locked in the forward hold for three days, so that we would not disturb the nostrils of the sweeter smelling passengers, they might have thought differently!

I had come through that ordeal as I had with so many others

during my wanderings, with no more than a shaking of my pride. I was ready (my ego told me) for the sterner test of polar exploration.

''old on a minute, sir!' I stopped and looked around. It was the commissionaire, 'Blimey, sir, I thought you'd never stop. They want you to go to Harley Street for a medical straight away.'

I assumed that it was just a formality, for the interviewers had made it painfully clear that they were unimpressed by me, but Harley Street had a certain magic about it which transformed a mundane medical into a ritual of great interest.

'Ah! – you're one of the potential explorers, I see' said the pretty nurse who handed me a perspex jar graduated in centimetres.

'You're not very big as explorers go,' said the doctor, prodding me with his stethoscope.

'But you say the Antarctic appeals to you. . . . Say "Ah" . . .'

'Ah . . . It does, sir.' Then, coughing to order, I performed before him a zombie-like dance around the room; crouching, stretching, reflexing – sitting with one hand over an eye and listening intently.

It was soon over. I caught a train back to Brighton and for three weeks plodded through a miserable routine almost in a total daze, until one evening after work when I had arranged to go up to London. I had as usual left myself very little time to catch the train, and was in the street shouting for a taxi when my landlady caught me up in a flurry of excitement. She gave me a letter and a telegram, both of which had arrived that afternoon, but I hardly had time to open either of them before we reached the station.

In the first envelope I found a short letter offering me the job in Kenya. I jumped forward, slid back the partition window, slapped the driver on the back and shouted:

'Cabbie – I'm going to Kenya – I'm going to Kenya!' But he just spat out a round oath and grunted, while I bounced up and down on the seat like a boy, laughing each word of the letter out loud. Then I tore open the telegram, stopped bouncing, and read what seemed too incredible to be true.

'Cabbie – I'm going to Antarctica. What do you think of that?'

'Look, mate. Which is it to be – Africa or Antarctica?

I tumbled out in a fit of madness, put a pound note into his hand. 'Antarctica of course!'

By the skin of my teeth I caught the train to London.

CHAPTER ONE

We sail

A bagpipe played a lament as the Royal Research Ship *Shackleton* inched away from berth 37, Southampton Dock. It was 27 December 1955. A fine drizzle was falling. We were about to cast off. The moat that only a moment before had been bridged by a gangway from ship to shore had widened to a swirling broth. Two thick ropes smacked the water. Limply they sank, then coming to life they wriggled towards the ship and were hauled aboard bristling and dribbling.

I was standing among a herd of healthy-looking men, their faces beaming. We were following a few weeks in the wake of the Commonwealth Trans-Antarctic Expedition's ship, the M.V. *Theron*, but the sounds of a sea port paid us no attention: no sirens or church bells bade us farewell; only a few friends and relations on the quay mirrored in puddles of water they stood in were waving handkerchiefs tearfully. They knew who we were and where we were going, but the sea mist must have stifled their cheers, for we heard only a soft moan in the rigging and the throbbing of the engines as our ship's wake trailed away from those tiny specks huddled close on the quay.

The R.R.S. *Shackleton* was a trim looking ship of 978 gross tonnage – a Norwegian coastal vessel originally, with a large forward hold which obliged the superstructure to sit squatly at the back; but she had grace and was tastefully painted in two tones of grey. Her fittings were too good for boisterous men – we felt constrained by the polished wood. We ran our fingers over the tables and nodded approvingly to each other, but felt uncomfortably like guests in our own expedition mess, until all twenty-nine men had squeezed in.

The atmosphere was polite – almost reverent. It was as if we had assembled after burying our old way of life, and were about to hear someone read the will of the dear departed from which we knew we would all benefit. Eager faces smiled shyly across the room. Sweating men, their hair windswept, their clothes dishevelled, sat with steam

rising from their trousers, each man asking himself if he was at last
breathing the atmosphere of a polar expedition.

We chatted quietly in threes and fours, our heads inclining together, and each man taking his turn to say his name – but no one
shook hands for fear of attracting attention. Mike Orford was there.
We had become friends, he and I and Jim Madell, for the three of us
had done a refresher course in astro-navigation at University College,
London, and had only completed it a few days before joining the
ship at Southampton. But I knew very few of the others for it was the
first time our full complement had been gathered together.

They were a surprisingly mixed crowd. Instinctively we listened
for traces of accent, and signs of breeding. We studied each speaker –
his clothes, the nervous movement of his fingers as he fumbled for a
match, the contours of his face moulded in the glow of a leaping
flame as he lit his pipe. We looked for an apology as his pipe gurgled
and his audience choked through clouds of smoke and took notice of
the choice of oath as the smoker burnt himself.

'Not a very nice day to be sailing,' someone said. We nodded in
agreement.

'It's a nice little boat isn't it,' the big fellow offered, and we all
answered in unison, 'yes, it is.' Our ears were tuned into everyone
else's conversation, while our eyes wandered around the mess missing not a gesture. The man I was scrutinizing suddenly looked up –
we grinned at each other and looked away. Then a slightly built,
innocuous-looking fellow in the middle of the gathering opened a
beer can the wrong way. A jet of alcohol squirted over everyone.
Roars of laughter dispersed the fug of good behaviour and among
twenty-nine potential Antarctic explorers the ice was at last broken.

The voyage was a delight from that moment on, and day by day
the sun rose higher until at last we passed directly beneath it. Every
day at local noon thereafter, our shadows pointed due south, and the
Shackleton chugged leisurely through a sleepy swell at a lazy ten knots.
There was time to think. Time to talk. Time to lie in the sun and
wriggle our toes, rub our chests or scratch our perspiring scalps.
There was time to smoke and daydream – time to reflect on our old
way of life and measure our new-found companions against those
we had left behind. There was time to wonder if we had done the
right thing – and we all marvelled at our good fortune.

We would hang for hours over the stern rail watching the wake trailing away, while the ship's log ticked off the sea miles and the engines softly rumbled, vibrating the flesh on our bellies; or we stood barefoot on the hot forecastle deck where we could feel the lazy sea motion and hear the breeze in the stays and rigging – and there we would gaze out ahead and talk of our hopes and ambitions.

We planned expeditions years in advance, and in our flights of fancy voyaged the world. We travelled the old Inca trails through Bolivia and Peru, and into the Amazon Basin; we had expeditions to the Himalaya and across the Gobi Desert; we even planned to follow Shackleton's route with dog teams up the Beardmore Glacier to the South Pole. Only those who knew in their hearts that our Antarctic adventure was their goal and not the start of their active life avoided falling under the spell.

Each day was a discovery. Men we had not noticed at first out-shone the coarser ones in the sun. Roger Tufft was one: a lean and powerful Welshman with a degree in economics and a passion for historical biography. He had been a paratrooper, but they were two a penny on that ship – he was an athlete, but there were others keener to exercise than he. And yet it was Roger, with no professed ambition to be a great traveller, who was later to spend three years in Ant-arctica, voyage 28,000 miles under sail in the sub-Antarctic and Greenland waters, make first ascents in Spitzbergen and man-haul a sledge across the Greenland ice cap. Dennis Kershaw was another. He was a deep-voiced Lancastrian who had spent most of his working life in a textile mill, and was content enough to play cricket for the local village club and go out for a few pints on a Saturday night. He was one of the most unpretentious men in the *Shackleton*: and yet it was Dennis who, at the end of his time in the South, took the long walk back to England through South America.

For six weeks we were suspended between the past and the future. It was like a dream separating a yesterday from a tomorrow – a period of rest in which we were aware of our companions and of the ideals which bound us together, but without the reality of action and apprehension we had conditioned ourselves to meet.

For hours we lounged or sprawled in a circle around one or the other of the two men in our company who were going to the Ant-arctic for the second time. Like disciples round a prophet, as 'the old

Antarctic explorer' spoke of mundane base chores, we would trans-
plant ourselves in our imagination among the grinding icefloes or
into the cold blue depths of enormous crevasses, while hanging for
safety on to his reassuring words. Sometimes a query of ours would
either raise his eyebrows or the corners of his mouth, for our conception of the Southern continent was very elementary.

From those two men we learnt a great deal, but like all individualists
we treated their advice only as an incentive to prove them wrong.
The best advice they gave us – as we were only later to realize – were
which places to avoid in Montevideo. This wonderful city was in
effect our last contact with civilization for over two years, for the
bleak, windswept Falkland Islands are only an outpost to civilization
– neither one thing nor another.

From Montevideo we sailed together in the confined space of a
single thought – 'Antarctica'. We were committing ourselves to
isolation and hardship in a part of the world about which we knew
very little. We had severed all ties, had renounced feminine company,
and some men had seriously hindered or entirely abandoned their
careers to join the enterprise. What kind of impulse can start such a
fire burning inside a man?

Some insisted that they had always wanted to go to the Antarctic,
but surely a man cannot have 'always wanted to go' anywhere? It
seems to me that a man can only want something badly enough the
moment before he gets up and goes after it. Most people say they
would like to go to the Antarctic, while tacitly cloaking their dreams
in reservations. And why not! Dreaming of far away places can be a
most pleasant pastime. No one can go and see the whole world for
himself. But no amount of dreaming will shift a seated man.

I do not believe that any of us consciously thought of our adventure as a voyage of personal discovery, but the psychological need
for esteem and success perhaps went deeper than we were prepared
to admit. No doubt there were a sprinkling of escapists in our
company, but enthusiasm for the venture was the uniform disguise
of each man's personal motives.

We were not even a complete expedition. We were just a number
of bodies who would be shuffled like cards around the existing bases
in Graham Land – the relief for men who had already spent two years
in the South. Our enterprise offered us no large financial rewards,

nor even prestige, which we were tempted to assume fell as a pleasant precipitation on all polar men, but which we later discovered fell in excess over some areas of the Antarctic while the remainder suffered drought. But it did offer each man a challenge for which the reward was satisfaction, and this satisfaction was, by the very nature of the task, as big as the effort each man put into it. Add patriotism and you have a most potent force. Our heritage from Scott and Shackleton had implanted in us an image so stimulating that, without a second thought, we were driven to renounce everything that represents comfort and security to our society, and join an enterprise from which there were no guaranteed rewards. That was not a motive for going South – that was what fired the motives, which were themselves washed out of all discussion by the anticipation, and then by the alarming experience of ploughing through the turbulent South Atlantic towards Port Stanley in the Falkland Islands.

Wandering albatross

There was more than a breath of Antarctic air in Port Stanley – one either leaned into it, or was swept along by it; but we convinced ourselves that it was invigorating, and our gooseflesh was excused on the grounds that we were still unacclimatized. We spent a few days there stevedoring cargo from the *Shackleton* to the old *John Biscoe*, and we were issued with our Antarctic kit. It was all rather like a dress rehearsal for a school play; although we tried to disguise our delight, and went to considerable trouble to avoid being caught looking at ourselves in the mirror while trying on our gear for size.

We were interviewed again, and with great delight I was transferred to the old *John Biscoe* for passage to Hope Bay, Graham Land. Roger Tufft and Dennis Kershaw were less fortunate for they were to spend their first year on islands where travel would be restricted. There was no base to which I would rather have gone, and no way of getting there that pleased me more than a passage on the *John Biscoe*, despite the old tub's legendary performance in heavy seas.

She was a strange-looking craft of 870 tons, but so sturdy and squat that she seemed to symbolize the invincible spirit of John Biscoe himself, who, after circumnavigating the Antarctic, discovered and annexed Graham Land for King William IV in February 1832. Her sheathing of greenheart bore a few scars from her battles with the ice, and she had left a good many years in her wake; but there was something about her which settled the minds of landlubbers – even though she violently upset their stomachs. Perhaps it was the old salty smell she had about her; perhaps it was the soothing green-grey of her timbers; perhaps it was nothing more than the comforting thought that she had safely done the voyage to the Antarctic so many times before.

But for four days I lived through a delirium; a prolonged anguish from which the only respite was fitful sleep. My innards slopped from one side of my abdomen to the other – I could actually see and hear them moving – even when I strapped and wedged myself into the bunk. A thousand times I was convinced that the *John Biscoe* would not roll back again, and sometimes we seemed to hang on the point of capsizing for so long that nothing short of a miracle could save us. Nothing I had experienced in my life up to that time alarmed me as much as when the screws came clear of the huge seas and the ship leant right over and shuddered.

On the fourth morning I awoke to find that the engines had changed pitch and the *John Biscoe* was holding an even keel. At first it was positively eerie; for all around the other men lay curled up in their bunks like corpses, with their mouths hanging limply open, and the fluff from their hairy pullovers matting their stubble. The air was fouled with sweat and vomit, and over the deck lay a debris of kit and broken crockery. But there was no mistaking the tone of the engines and the gentle motion – we had found the shelter of a harbour. A little while later the roar of the anchor chain running out brought all of us back to life and we tumbled out of our beds.

'I think we have gone back to Port Stanley,' someone said – and we all agreed that it was a possibility, for it was hard to believe that much progress had been made towards the Antarctic over the past few days. Then Roger climbed aloft and opened the heavy hatch door.

'We're in Admiralty Bay,' he shouted down to us – and a draught of Antarctic air wafted into our den.

There was a frantic fumbling for kitbags full of unfamiliar looking clothing, and the store-scent of new woollens and anoraks. We clattered aloft, bunting and flapping against one another in our baggy garments, and in single file we ducked through the door out on to the slippery deck. The crisp air stung us and we gasped a deep breath – a smell tainted only slightly by an old wet ship, the 'smell' of ice!

The sun was obscured by thick rolling layers of cloud, but their base captured some of the reflected light from the icescape, and the blue-grey sea was dotted about with great chunks of ice which lumbered up and down in the gentle swell.

We gazed over the scene as if we already owned it. We lit our pipes and filled our chests with pride. Then a tiny dinghy caught our attention: it was rowed by three burly men. They came alongside, secured the boat and pulled themselves up the rope ladder. Their big beards bristled and their seal-stained anoraks stank; their mukluks were patched with canvas and string. Our skipper appeared on the bridge and smiled down at them without losing his dignity, and their faces broke into broad grins as they spotted him; then as we stood back they swept past us with an air of amused tolerance and disappeared into the Wardroom, leaving us all with the impression that we had just seen, and smelt, for the first time, the ripe fruit of maturity in polar men.

CHAPTER TWO

Ice-floes and sea lanes

There is something to be said for going to the Antarctic for the first time as a young man. His first impressions will not be profoundly reverent, and he will lack the ascetic discipline which is so satisfying to his more mature companions; but he is more likely to be emotionally swept off his feet. You have only to watch a group of men standing together on the forecastle head of a little wooden ship, as it enters the ice for the first time on its voyage to the Antarctic, to realize how differently the same scene affects each man.

They stand feet apart in a seaman's stance – hands in their pockets like off-duty cooks. They lurch a little as the ship crunches into a bergy bit, and mutter mild profanities as they look up at the bridge. They talk quietly. Move casually. Some are dressed in dirty old clothes bartered from the old hands, the rest wear shiny new anoraks and baggy battle-dress trousers. They appear embarrassed with a pair of binoculars in their hands, and pass them on to the next man still out of focus. Occasionally one of them will raise a new camera to his untrained eye and take yet another over-exposed picture. They light their pipes; they point at circling petrels. The sun is warm on their backs and they squint in the glare off the ice ahead. They show no impatience. There is no excitement, except in their eyes.

The older men take in the whole scene slowly. Their deepest satisfaction comes from the overall experience, whereas the younger men are intensely interested in each piece of ice to be rammed. They fidget, fighting a desire to run from one side of the ship to the other. Their glances dart around the scene. They hear the tinkling and popping of loose brash ice, and the gurgle of the swell as it rushes into the smaller caverns and undercuts of the nearby bergs; while astern, the throbbing of the ship's engines beats a gentle rhythm. There is no polar sound more soothing than the music of a wooden ship gliding slowly through loose brash ice on a dead calm day.

The ship unexpectedly grazes a bergy bit which plunges below the surface, the water rushing in after it. The bow lifts and glides to one side, and the ice scrapes and rams the tough greenheart with a grinding noise that rends the still air. Men are thrown off their feet. Older men are conscious of their loss of dignity. Their suspicious minds conclude that the Captain deliberately directed the helmsman to ram the ice, and they grin weakly up at the bridge, like good-hearted victims of a practical joke. But the younger element stagger to the rail, and peer into the dark depths at the green monster that is rolling, lurching, and thumping the ship as it slides by. Never, never again will they have quite the same powerful impression of this new world of ice.

The sky at the zenith is a soft blue which pales towards the horizon where a few wispy clouds hang over a distant headland. Towards the Weddell Sea quarter, an ice-blink reflects off the long hazy cloud-rolls and every detail and tint of the ice-islands is mirrored in the glass-like surface of the sea. The ship glides across lakes surrounded with fields of ice, lakes that seem too small for the vessel; and with the engines cut off the only sound is the soft lapping of water against the bow. At the far side of the lake the prow pushes against the white bank of ice, which moves ahead creaking and groaning as it rubs against the other floes. It splits into a lead with a biscuit-like crack, then a sigh and a rush of cold sea. The ship's engines chug again and press the bows into the split, which keeps opening ahead a roadway of deep water ruffled on the surface with eddies and splinters of ice.

The lead opens into a field of small brash ice, dotted with glittering white crystals and stained with the pastel greens of the submerged pieces. They knock on the ship's bows as she moves slowly through, they jingle as the bow wavelets sweep them away – a flotilla of sparkling sea gems, riding out a gentle swell and left far astern softly chattering. The tiny ship glides by a berg. The men marvel at its grotesque form, with its caverns like enormous yawns; and peering into the water they see its body, green and slippery, gnarled by the currents. Its root sombres into indigo and plunges deeper into awe.

We sailed all day through the pack ice on our voyage around the coast to Duse Bay where we were going to land the building stores at View Point for a four-man hut we would erect later in the year. It was not a long voyage in sea mileage, but it had to be taken slowly, and even lunch in the mess that day was something of a novelty. The reflected light from the floes and bergs shone like a torch beam down the steep steps into our sea-level cubby hole. Up on deck we could anticipate a collision with the ice and revel in being part of something big, about to crush something weaker. But below deck we listened wide-eyed to the creak of timbers under pressure from the ice, as crunching, scratching, massive 'growlers' attacked our ship down both sides. Suddenly the engines stopped. We froze. Without vibration the ship became a wild animal, crouched for the kill – holding its breath for ten seconds or more before the mighty blow was struck. Then . . . crunch! The ship lurched. Crockery crashed to the deck. Men fell cursing in a heap. The cook had wasted his time that day: we could not eat in that turbulent cage while outside a new world was drifting by.

Late that evening a curtain of low cloud was drawn slowly across the sky, leaving only a chink of brilliant light along the western sea-board which caught the frayed cloud base in waves of crimson and purple, and was reflected in the sea lanes between the ice-floes. The faces of the beautiful bergs blushed a delicate pink. The shadows deepened and turned mauve, tarnishing the floes as they crept along like sin in search of a virtue to stain. To the east, night had already settled, and the sea, of deepest indigo, was dabbed gently with lighter shades of blue. By the time we reached Duse Bay, it was dark.

No ship had ever been in that bay before, so the Captain was disinclined to break a channel through the old bay ice towards the previously-chosen site of the new hut. The site was difficult to see from the ship even with the searchlight but we were told by the men who had sledged there many times that it was a low outcrop some twenty feet above sea-level, and only about thirty yards from the sea-front of the ice-field through which it protruded. A small wooden hut had been built there some years before, and extended a few feet by the ingenious use of old packing-crates – but as a permanent residence it was inadequate, and even as a temporary one it was not much more comfortable than a tent.

The area was well known for its winds, and in the summer season the strong sea-currents often choked the bay with icebergs and brash captured in the Erebus and Terror Gulf. All things considered, it was not a healthy place for a ship to linger.

The crew and passengers were divided into two working parties. One, which would be ship-bound, would work the stores from the hold to the scow, while the other group would work ashore, offloading the stores on to a rocky headland about a mile and a half from the hut site. I was detailed to go with the shore party after the first load of stores and timber had been piled into the scow. The night was almost pitch black by that time; but we had a thin shaft of light from the Bosun's torch, and an occasional flash from the ship's searchlight (operated by someone with a sense of humour) from the bridge of the *John Biscoe*. It was my first landing on the mainland of Antarctica, and was both romantic and dramatic, for each man was obliged to make a leap from the motor-boat on to the slippery rocks of the headland.

The scow bucked in the swell and scraped on the rocks. The mooring lines slackened, then tighted and tripped men as they struggled with cumbersome loads. We crawled like ants over jagged rocks, supporting each other, or formed a chain to pass sandbags and crates, or crowded around an extra big load to haul it across the slippery planks, precariously bridging the surging tide between the scow's gunwale and the sea-sprayed rocks. The ship's searchlight would feel its way along the coast, find us, then wander away. Each man for a moment was recognized. Then in darkness again we fumbled about, far more aware without our sight of the things we would normally have taken for granted.

Eventually the first load was landed successfully; then the motor-boat took the scow back to the *John Biscoe* for a second load of stores, and we were given the choice of either staying on the coast or going back to the ship for a short break and a cup of cocoa. I stayed ashore; even though I had another two and a half years to spend in Antarctica. I was driven by the same kind of impulse which makes a boy polish his brand new shoes as soon as he takes them out of the box; but I never regretted it, for the only other fellow who remained ashore, Major Ellery Anderson, had just completed his time as base leader of Hope Bay, and had made a very fine sledge journey of just over a thousand miles down the coast and back, mapping a considerable amount of new country.

Within a couple of weeks he would be back in Port Stanley where he knew he would be rudely jolted back to the civilized world; so he

intended making the most of his last few days in the Antarctic. It
was the first time I had met a real explorer in his own environment
and, not wishing to break the spell, I said hardly a word, but just
stood and listened to tales of blizzards and crevasses. His hooked pipe
burned brightly and bathed his face in a macabre glow – a moving
mask with the highlights shifting all the time and occasionally catching
his eyes which sparkled with the fire from his own story-telling.

Beyond lay a sombre backdrop of deep grey hills, very faintly
outlined against a bleached horizon while overhead I was vaguely
conscious of the closeness of cloud, tumbling slowly in an almost
imperceptible breeze. The sea was a pool of ink, lapping around the
rocks below us, and the *John Biscoe*, with its well-deck ablaze with
yellow light, lay off the headland contentedly purring to itself. It was
a magic night, and the wizardry of it worked through those strange
stories, told softly in the unfamiliar language of a polar man.

It was a long time before the next scow-load of building stores
came across, but only then did I realize how long we had been standing there, and how cold I had become. But I was soon warmed by the
exercise of lifting and dragging heavy weights and stumbling over
slippery rocks, and by the time we had finished unloading the scow
and fastening the heavy tarpaulin over the building materials, the
next day was dawning. In the weak light of early morning the *John
Biscoe* sailed out of Duse Bay, and after a hot mug of cocoa I turned
in to sleep off some of my fatigue and excitement. I did not wake until
the anchor dropped in Hope Bay – my new home.

Our long voyage to the Antarctic had been a kind of inverted mass-
hypnosis. Our ultra-receptive minds had absorbed a confusion of
facts and fiction about the Antarctic – the latest information always
cancelling out what had gone before it. But at Port Stanley we had
been told to which bases we would be going, and from that moment
on other parts of the Antarctic were relegated to the backs of our
minds.

From Hope Bay great sledging journeys had been made in the past
and tens of thousands of square miles of the east coast of Graham
Land had been explored. I was expected to uphold these great
traditions by making a sledging journey down the central plateau of
Graham Land and completing the last blank on the map within reach

of the base. It was to be a four-man party, the leader of which would
be Ron Worswick, the base leader. He was just starting his fifth year
in the Antarctic, having spent two years at Signy Island, one year as
the leader of the base at Admiralty Bay (where Roger Tufft had disembarked), and the last year at Hope Bay under Ellery Anderson.
But I was awe-struck more by tales of his phenomenal strength than
by his Antarctic record. He was six feet seven inches tall. He had
bent a steel HALT sign in Port Stanley and could pick up a fully-
grown husky dog under each arm.

Dr Hugh Simpson was another certainty for the plateau journey.
He had come South a few months earlier on the *John Biscoe*'s first
voyage that summer. The man was renowned for his incredible feats
of endurance in the Scottish Highlands and his high-pressure enthusiasm. Jim Madell was to be the other surveyor. We had spent a
few days in Port Stanley reading up the sledging reports of our predecessors at Hope Bay, but we were less comfortable with that extra
knowledge than we were in ignorance, for it spelt out a legacy of
standards we felt sure we could not maintain.

The first British hut had been established on 12 February 1945 as
part of a British naval expedition under the wartime code name of
Operation Tabarin. The leader of that expedition was Major Andrew
Taylor of the Royal Canadian Engineers, and their experiments with
sledging techniques and the many arduous journeys that they made
from base made fascinating reading. At the end of Taylor's year
Captain V. I. Russell took over the base leadership: it was he who
discovered the route to the Graham Land plateau which we were to
follow in 1957, and many of the maps we were to use for local journeys were from his original work. In 1947, Frank Elliott had become
leader and during his first winter he had made a 700-mile sledge
journey with three companions down the east coast of Graham Land
to Three Slice Nunatak, then over the peninsula to the British base at
Stonington Island on the west coast, from where he had been shipped
back to Hope Bay. His reports in particular had interested Jim
Madell and me, for Frank Elliott had been on our interview board,
although we had not known who he was at the time. The Hope Bay
tragedy we also first learnt about from Frank Elliott's reports. On 8
November 1948, while Elliott was away from base on a sledging
journey, a fire had started in the generator room, trapping Oliver

Burd and Michael Green, and the hut was burnt to the ground. The graves of the two men were dug at the summit of a small rocky outcrop within a stone's throw of the old base.

On 4 February 1952, exactly three years after Elliott's party were evacuated from Hope Bay, the new base, Trinity House, had been established; but only after delay caused by a most extraordinary incident. The Argentinians had established a base themselves at Hope Bay on 14 January of that year, and on 1 February, as the British landing party from the *John Biscoe* were working ashore on their first load of stores, the Argentine shore party fired a few bursts of gun-fire over the heads of the British, who were then surrounded by armed Argentinians and forced to withdraw. Subsequently the Argentine Government informed the United Kingdom Government that the commander of the Argentine Naval Detachment at Hope Bay had acted with an 'excess of zeal in the defence of the National Territory of the Republic', and that the shots had been fired by accident and not in any offensive spirit.

On 8 February 1942, the Argentine expedition aboard the *Primero de Mayo* had taken formal possession for the Argentine Government of a sector of the Antarctic lying between Longitudes 25° W and 68°34′ W, to which the northern limit of the territory was the 60th parallel south; and the claim was extended in its western limits to Longitude 74° W in 1946 by an Argentine Government decree. However, this claim conflicted not only with the British Letters Patent of 21 July 1908, which consolidated earlier territorial claims dating from 1775, but also with a Chilean Presidential Decree of 6 November 1940, proclaiming sovereignty over a sector of the Antarctic lying between Longitudes 53° W and 90° W. The respective governments took those conflicting claims to sovereignty of an apparently barren and climatically hostile territory very seriously indeed at the time. Ships' commanders, as well as base leaders, were directed to act with extreme politeness, dignity, and decorum, as hosts to any foreigners who came into their respective territories; which, since they all overlapped, became a battleground for etiquette!*

---

* It was, at the time that I first went to the Antarctic, a serious farce, in which protest notes were exchanged like cards in a game of snap. Refuge huts were razed to the ground by patriotic vandals, and ships escorted each other up and

George Marsh had been the leader of the party which had run the gauntlet to build Trinity House, and for two years he and his party carried out long-range surveys down the east coast and mapped James Ross Island. He was later to join the Ross Sea Party of the Commonwealth Trans-Antarctic Expedition as medical officer and dog expert at Scott Base, and two other ex-Hope Bay men, David Stratton and Ken Blaiklock, were with Dr Fuchs' party which had officially established Shackleton Base a few days before we sailed south from Port Stanley, so we felt proudly represented even before we had become Hope Bay men ourselves.

I scampered up the steep steps from the dungeon mess and ducked through the door out into the crystal air. I made for the bow down the shaded side of the ship, plunged into sunshine in the well-deck, ran across the tops of popping fuel drums, up ringing steps to the forecastle deck, leapt over chains and snakes of rope and reached the blunt-nosed bow of the old *John Biscoe* out of breath. Jim Madell and Ken Hill were there already.

What a scene to delight the eyes, that first glimpse of Hope Bay: an ambush of towering pyramids, blade ridges and scooped snow corries; a sky slashed by frayed ribbons of cloud flung by an invisible hand; a pool full of inverted mountains jostling for space to expand amongst the chattering chunks of ice.

Mount Taylor dominated the picture, and small wisps of cloud drifting out of its shadow puffed alight in the sun like silent shell

---

down the coast like devout nuns. Antarctic summers in the Graham Land area became known as the 'silly season', and remained so until the International Geophysical Year of 1957–58, when a refreshing breeze of scientific bonhomie blew all Antarctic endeavour towards a sensible goal. That goal was the Antarctic Treaty which was signed in Washington on 1 December 1959 by the twelve countries that had participated in scientific activities in the Antarctic during the International Geophysical Year. In substance they all agreed that '. . . it is in the interest of all mankind that Antarctica shall continue forever to be used exclusively for peaceful purposes and shall not become the scene or object of international discord'. It went on to 'ban the bomb' in Antarctica, and to 'freeze' all territorial claims for the duration of thirty years. Antarctica is at present the only place on our planet where (quoting from the Treaty) 'there shall be prohibited, *inter alia*, any measure of a military nature, such as the establishment of military bases and fortifications, the carrying out of military manoeuvre, as well as the testing of any weapons'.

bursts above Depot Glacier; while Mount Flora, majestically crino-lined in scree, preened herself in the mirror at her feet. On either side of us, like gigantic waves, smooth snowfields dipped steeply into the bay, staining their waterline almost black with a tidemark of bare rock. The floating ice was drifting imperceptibly. It was jingling and knocking against the sides of our ship, and the dust of sun-beams played on the water in pricks of light amongst the chunks of brash.

The rumble of the generators at the Argentine base drifted across the water. We could see their base clearly with the naked eye, but it was a while before we spotted the tiny speck that was Trinity House. It was 150 feet above sea-level, on the last outcrop of rock below the wave of ice which rose 300 feet. It looked like a tiny boat about to be engulfed.

'There are two men scrambling down the rocks from the hut to a small snow valley. I can't make out why they're in such a hurry . . . here – what do you make of it, Ken?' Jim Madell handed the field-glasses to eager hands.

'They've reached the snow now. They seem to be waiting for someone . . .' The roar of the winch motor started up, and the First Officer shouted to us from the bridge to get our gear ready. We waited until the scow was lowered over the side, then made a dash for the mess and struggled with our bulging kitbags and rucksacks up to the deck. The currents of the bay had by that time swung the *John Biscoe* to a new angle with the shoreline and to an unobstructed view in the distance down the small valley of four dog teams in single file sweeping silently over the snow. I had never dreamed their movement could be so graceful.

The launch had come alongside. The men hanging over the rail were more interested in the man who was climbing the rope ladder than in that thin line of movement ashore. I reached them as they stood aside and a pair of giant hands gripped the rail to haul into view a bespectacled, bearded face. The hulk of a man grew until he slapped a boot on the rail and vaulted on to the deck with a thud. He stretched himself to his full six feet seven like a beaming monster bellowing for his dinner, and said – 'Well – where are my men?' My companions pushed me forward, and I stood before him with a bottle of whisky in my hands intended as a small present for the men on base.

He stepped forward and took it, and without a word, strode off to visit the Captain.

The launch taking us ashore threaded its way around small bergs and jammed in the floes. We poled ourselves free and slowly closed on the Argentine's floating jetty, where some forty of Hope Bay's 150 huskies were waiting to be deported to other bases. They were piled one by one into the scow which soon became a seething mass of hair and snarling muzzles. The pent-up power in that scow was an alarming sight – how on earth would I ever learn to control such vicious creatures, I wondered aloud.

'Oh, you'll soon get used to them,' Derek 'Derro' Clarke said.

We walked through the Argentine camp along what was almost a road, but its only traffic were men and dogs, and occasionally a stray penguin. Friendly black-haired men in navy blue blouses and baggy windproof trousers shouted their greetings. Derro seemed to know them all – a bit unpatriotic I thought.

'Ah, they're a great crowd the Argies . . . Buenos Días Rodriguez! . . . don't believe any of that political nonsense . . . Hey Bempo! Cómo está? . . . in Antarctica there's no problemo.' Derro was to be our diesel mechanic. He was just starting his third year in the Antarctic, and had spent the last year at Hope Bay. He was what I later discovered the Argentines called 'muy simpatico'.

We were about thirty yards from the hut when a stocky man emerged, covered the ground in a burst of energy and said –

'Let's take your bags, man,' in an almost English accent – grabbed two kitbags, and swung off into the hut. I was speechless for a moment by the wind of his movement.

'Oh, by the way,' said Derro, 'that was Dr Hugh Simpson.'

No building has ever meant so much to me as that timber hut at Hope Bay. It was steeped in character. Its traditional design of the bunk-house living quarters resembled the system instituted by Shackleton in his Cape Royds hut at McMurdo Sound. Like Shackleton's hut, our bunkhouse was one big room full of atmosphere, with the beds head-to-toe around the walls and a fireplace near the middle; but unlike Shackleton's men we were not permitted to build partitions, and so lacked even the modicum of privacy. This did not upset us – on the contrary, I believe it was partly responsible for strengthening our expedition spirit. What inspired us, or challenged us, more, however, was the legacy of intrepid journeys that had been made from it by our predecessors.

The hut at Hope Bay

How well I remember it, coal black against a big white hill, with its flag stiff and drumming and its chimney rattling in a gale. It was a shell of pine timbers that creaked and groaned, with big double windows down either side and guy wires that passed right over the roof every ten feet throughout its length and anchored the structure to solid rock. It would not have been a handsome hut in any other setting but it had a certain majesty in its stark simplicity, and the rows of upturned sledges neatly parked down the leeward side gave it the distinctive character of a British polar base.

There was a door at either end, the more pleasant entrance of the two being the downwind or north-east door below the tattered flag. It opened into a narrow room aromatic with sledging smells of raw linseed oil and tautening dope, beeswax, ropes, and lampwick harnesses each marked with the name of a dog and reeking with its sweat. To the left in racks against the wall were sets of skis and bamboo sticks, while to the right hung alpine ropes and oiled ice-axes, crevasse probes, dog-whips and centre-traces. Sledging chattles filled the shelves and littered the benches at the far end of the room, evoking an impression of a ship's chandlery store stocked with such a diversity of gear that only initiated men would have known what each strange item was for. It was the workshop where Roger Tufft was usually found re-lashing sledges or splicing dog traces, and where our jovial neighbours from the Argentine base stamped snow off their boots and embraced stray Englishmen on entering or leaving Trinity House. It was a room full of atmosphere, off which to the left went a passage, three paces long, like a tunnel between one cave and the next.

Blood-stained anoraks grisly with seals' hair, and felling axes greasy with blubber hung on either side of that passage-way while on a low shelf in one corner was an open bucket which served as a urinal when the weather was foul.

It was not the sweetest-smelling part of our hut, nor was the room to which that passage gave access, for the carpenter's shop with its boiler stove roaring was next to the throbbing generator room with its smell of oil and diesel fumes. That generator room was the domain during my first year at Hope Bay of Derek Clarke, a kindly, peace-loving man who with infinite patience and understanding had taught the new men how to handle the dogs. His successor, by contrast, had been preceded South by his alarming reputation as an entertainer with a talent for enlivening a party by eating a wine glass or swallowing a cigarette that had been broken in half and set alight at all four of its ends. Johnny Walsh was his name – a man of simple tastes who had been a courier before joining our enterprise as a diesel mechanic.

The carpenter's shop was the preserve of no man in particular, although I cannot think of that room without picturing a lean and intense ex-sailor by the name of Pat Thompson, and Ken Brown, a black-bearded Welshman who had been a navigator with the R.A.F. bomber squadron during the war. Pat was the more skilful craftsman of the two, and he had a talent for model-making and was passionately fond of classical music. It was, I suppose, the unlikely combination of these two interests which had induced him during our second winter to make a violin – an ambitious piece of carpentry that had very soon become the focal point of Trinity House. Even our friends from the Argentine base had filed like pilgrims through the sledge workshop to pay their respects to the mute musical instrument that, like a small dismembered body, lay for weeks on the workshop table. But in time it had become the bane of our lives, and on the day that its belly peg slipped we dared not even glance in its direction as we hurried through the workshop to and from the tiny washroom. As for the dramatic end to Pat's plywood violin – that came a few days later when in a moment of intense frustration he had smashed it to smithereens.

Such moments of high emotion, however, were rare in our society. I can recall only three occasions in two and a half years when voices were raised, and only one occasion other than the violin incident when a man for a moment went berserk. It had occurred on my last night at Trinity House, when we were having a farewell party. Being unaccustomed to liquor several of the company, which included our Argentine neighbours, had become very merry and were dancing around the bunkhouse with one another. With the exception of Ken Brown who had put an empty fire bucket over the head of Colonel Mendez, the Argentine Commandant, and was vigorously banging it with a soup ladle, the general conduct was exemplary. Suddenly a thunderous roar came from the kitchen and, barging through the door, three or four of us were just in time to see a fellow roaring hysterically at the far end of the room and throwing the weighing scales and kitchen weights through the double glazed windows. Strewn on the kitchen floor were about four hundred tins that a moment before had been neatly stacked on the shelves. His eyes were wild and his face contorted. He looked like a trapped animal in the far corner of the kitchen, and with his escape cut off, he had picked up a carving knife and stumbled towards us across the sea of coloured tins. He fell and lay quite still. We pounced on him but he was unconscious, and feeling embarrassed and somewhat alarmed we had rolled him out of sight under the kitchen table and quickly restacked the shelves. He remembered nothing of the incident the following day, and was so deeply disturbed when we told him the story that he secluded himself in a room and wept.

Many polar expeditions have been less fortunate. I have heard alarming stories that, for obvious reasons, will never be published, but no doubt it is significant that most cases of psychological unbalance and degeneration occurred at the static bases – those isolated meteorological stations manned by five or six men. Careful screening before the men go South will eliminate some of this risk, but interaction of personalities can seldom be predicted so there must inevitably be an element of luck in the selection of a party. Nor are these problems necessarily decreased by having a larger expedition, for the men invariably split up into cliques. The most enjoyable expeditions are therefore those that have some definite goal – preferably a physical one which is so demanding on each man that there is no time to incubate a grievance or to feel confined. Ours was just such an expedition. The hut was our temporary refuge – a haven from which we set out on long sledge journeys and to which we returned to rest, recuperate, repair our gear and prepare for another trek. It was a minute shell of comparative warmth in a vast and hostile environment, each room of which now evokes memories of the men who gave it atmosphere.

The inner sanctuary was protected from the noise and smells of the generator room and the carpenter's shop by two doors and a short corridor. Off this corridor to the left was a tiny office in disuse during my two years at Hope Bay except that it served as entrance to Hugh Simpson's surgery which, with its roaring stove and shelves full of books and coloured bottles, was at the far end of that office through a door frame draped with a heavy curtain. There Hugh spent his days rapt in research. It was a sacrosanct world from which he emerged only for meals, base chores, or sledging journeys – and one into which we were seldom invited.

On the opposite side of the corridor was an office where Jim Madell and I prepared our field sheets and computed and plotted our surveys. Maps covered the walls and on shelves were stacked the reports of our predecessors with detailed accounts of every journey that had been made from Hope Bay. It had not the mystique of the surgery, but was a cold, stark, odourless room in which during the winter our drawing inks froze, and in which even during summer we were obliged to work in thick duffle coats. Nor was it such a peaceful room as Hugh Simpson's den for the thoroughfare to or from the heart of the hut passed within one pace and the crunch of footsteps, the slamming of doors and the jocular shouts of 'get on with your work' were an almost constant distraction.

The heart of our hut was the bunkhouse next door – a room of crude charm and character. Exposed to everyone's view twelve bunks were ranged head-to-toe around the walls, separated one from the other by headboards from which hung a bulging assortment of personal gear. All the bunks, or 'pits' as they were called, were the same height from the floor, and from the base of each hung a red and white chequered curtain which hid an unsightly chaos of clothing. But in this respect alone were they alike, for each alcove was one man's domain. The improvized shelves with their books and nicknacks and pictures pinned on the walls and the headboards, even the way in which the beds were made were so characteristic of each individual that even when the bunkhouse was empty one had the sensation each alcove was occupied, and that not a movement of sound would go unnoticed or unheard.

The pine-timbered walls were stained and varnished, and the white painted ceiling, sloping gently up to a gable, glowed in the light of the fire. There were two long strips of coconut matting on the cold linoleum floor and three worn rugs curling at the corners. Around the dining-room table to one side of the room, eight cheap and functional tubular chairs stood side by side with their seats tucked away out of sight, while the remainder, together with two stained coffee tables, were in a circle around the anthracite stove.

Like the rest of the rooms in Trinity House, the bunkhouse was an irregular shape. It was narrowest at the end we entered from the survey office, where to the left a small door opened into a tiny photographic darkroom. On the flat roof of this there was an alcove below the hut ceiling where in a pocket of warm stuffy air new sledging gear was stored. No other alcove in Trinity House had such a strong fascination, for it was the only part of the hut forbidden to us. Only our base leader, Ron Worswick, ever went up there, and as he sorted amongst piles of new socks, pullovers, and anoraks, or fished out of boxes marked 'The Hudson's Bay Company' pairs of mocassins, mits, and sealskin boots, we would gather below in anticipation that he would pitch something down to us – a new pair of socks perhaps, or a store-scented pair of windproof trousers to replace those so greasy with seals' blood and blubber that they 'perspired' when we stood near the fire.

As base leader, Ron had been sworn in as a magistrate and justice of the peace. In addition to this he was the Postmaster, and all outgoing mail from Trinity House bore the stamps of the Falkland Islands Dependencies. Our base, therefore, (along with the nine other British bases in the Dependency) demonstrated an effective colonial administration, which would have been one of the arguments in support of the British claim to territorial sovereignty had the conflicting claims of Argentina, Britain, and Chile ever been taken before the International Court of Justice at The Hague. The nerve-centre of this outpost of the Empire at Hope Bay was a converted food storeroom which was next to the bunkhouse. Code books, a dictionary, a diary, a tin box and a volume called 'Operational Instructions' were the only items on the shelves. The room had one chair, a table and a threadbare rug.

The kitchen, to which Ron's office had access, was equally simple. Down one side was a table flush with the wall, above and below which were shelves heavily laden with tins. On the opposite side was an anthracite-burning stove with two ovens, a copper tank in which snow blocks were melted, and a slop bucket. There was a small pantry next to the base leader's office in which was stored two months' supply of provisions and boxes of plain flour in which were packed the penguin eggs.

The main thoroughfare from the bunkhouse to the exit at the nasty end of the hut passed through one end of the kitchen into a corridor cluttered with swill buckets and fire extinguishers, to the left of which was a radio workshop and storeroom, and to the right the radio shack. It was a short, dark, smelly corridor which opened into an airy passageway where the pup pens, bunker and toilet were situated. Three paces and a tug at a slightly jammed door and we were once again outside and leaning into the biting wind.

An Irishman by the name of Sam Blake ruled over this end of the hut, or so at least it seemed, for from his window in the radio shack he overlooked the corridor and saw or was seen by every man who passed by throughout the day. Sam had knocked about the world trying his hand at several odd jobs – he had sold encyclopaedias in Sydney and worked on a chicken farm – but so sad were the endings to his stories he would have had us all in tears had we ever taken him seriously.

Sharing Sam's radio shack, but separated from the radio equipment by a low partition, was the meteorological office. It was sparsely furnished, and except for two wall barometers, met code books, shelves full of graph rolls, and a wind-speed indicator connected by a cable to the anemometer tower over by the dog-lines, there was little to see. Even the met observers, of whom we had no fewer than seven, were seldom to be found in that room for weather reporting was not a time-consuming job. The short walk from the hut to the met screen outside was, however, not made without risk when a hundred-knot wind was blowing and fragments of rock were being hurled through the air. Even sixty-gallon fuel drums were sometimes blown over and rolled a quarter of a mile down to the sea. But in such conditions, as well as in fine weather, the routine three-hourly observations had to be made, coded and transmitted to Port Stanley, for we were part of a network of manned weather reporting stations – it was one of the reasons we were in the Antarctic – although this, like our 'presence' in Graham Land which at that time undoubtedly had a political significance, meant little to us, and few of the met observers took more interest in the job than was demanded by their conscience. The great open country to the south had for each man a far stronger appeal.

These met observers were a motley crew, and none of them were professionals. There was Mike Reuby, an intense man in whom we suspected a touch of Romany. He had been an assistant keeper of bears at a zoo before he had heard the call of the South. There was George Larmour from County Down, a padded pillar of a man, gentle, slow moving and quite unlike my preconceived picture of an Irish chartered accountant. Pat Thompson and Ken Brown were also met observers – so was Ron Worswick, our base leader, and Dick Walcott, a powerful New Zealander with a sharp intellect and a short temper, who had abandoned a degree in mathematics at Auckland University and worked his passage to England in the hope of finding a place on the Commonwealth Trans-Antarctic Expedition. So keen was the desire of each man to get to the Antarctic they would have gone South in any capacity and foregone the meagre salary for the privilege of joining that enterprise, and since such men could not be ignored by the administration, they had been given a short course at the Met Office training centre and sent South to record the weather. Reading thermometers, however, had soon grown tedious, for each met observer at heart was a sledger, and none more instinctively intrepid than the lean and muscular Roger Tufft.

Fortunately at Hope Bay there was an outlet for this energy. We were part of a systematic survey that had been going on for years and would be continued by others after we had gone. Our small part in that great enterprise was the survey of the north-east coast and the central plateau – the last unexplored region within range of our base, and to the achievement of this we had dedicated our efforts while competing with each other for a place on the plateau party. This competition extended into every field of our endeavour, but was particularly noticeable in the operation of chopping up seals to feed our one hundred and fifty hungry brute huskies or on Saturday mornings when everyone, including the base leader, tried to do more of the chores than was his rightful share.

The hard work of shifting stores, handling the dogs, chopping up seal meat, and the hundred and one smaller tasks that we had to do about the base tired our unfit bodies; while the new routine and one's general feeling of incompetence for a new way of life grew out of all proportion. There seemed to be no end to all we had to learn, no end to the mistakes we made, and the aura of experience that surrounded the old hands was like a wall separating them from their greener companions. But we could not have found a kinder or more sincere fellow than Derro Clarke, who patiently taught us how to handle dogs, or Laurie Catherall and John Noble who always seemed to be around when we had a heavy box to lift. They were never sarcastic; they were never intolerant, and always with a ready explanation, a short demonstration and a word of encouragement to carry the new boys through another experience. Eventually, and almost unnoticed, we developed and became a part of a closely-knit little society – a world of men.

CHAPTER THREE

A moment of glory

On 3 April 1956, at 3.30 p.m., I crawled in through the double sleeve entrance of a polar tent for the first time, singed my hair on the primus stove roaring away in the centre of the floor space, jerked myself away from it, stiffened with severe cramp, fell in agony on the thick pile of the sheepskin covering my area, and broke my pipe stem. A blizzard blowing through the entrance snuffed out the candle and the primus stove which hissed in rage and filled the tent with fumes. My tent mate fumbled frantically for the matches, while I, still writhing with pain, dragged in more snow with my oversized mukluks and caught the handle of the billie which flooded the floor of the tent. A match spurted and was blown out by the wind. A foot shot out and pinned down the billowing sleeve entrance and the tent was plunged into total darkness. The second match scratched alight and moved towards the primus, but it had ceased to vaporize and was shooting up a fine jet of neat fuel: the match caught it and the tent filled with orange flames which licked hungrily at the anorak, socks, and gloves hanging in the apex. A tense face glowed momentarily a few feet away, and a hand in a flash unscrewed the safety valve on the primus. Once again the tent was a fabric dungeon. Fumes and the smell of singed socks stung our nostrils, and all the time the blizzard outside whined in the guy ropes and drove the snow against our shelter with the noise of pelting rain. The candle was lit. Its yellow glow filled our little home and I looked across to my tent mate who was gazing spellbound at the havoc I had caused; then in a reprimanding tone his high-pitched voice said, 'Bloody hell, man!'

I could hardly have made a more chaotic entrance into the double-jointed art of polar camping, and it was Dr Simpson's twenty-fifth birthday – I had been wondering how I could give him a surprise. We were on our first sledging journey, the first of many polar journeys we were to make in the years that lay ahead.

We mopped the floor with toilet paper, moved the primus, brushed the snow off the sledge ration box and set it between us on the floor of the tent. It was like a tuck box. We snapped the wire bands, knelt beside it and opened the lid. On top was a layer of flattened wood shavings, which we lifted off gently and set to one side. The box was packed tightly with dull-looking tins, but it was a delight picking them out: tins of New Zealand butter; cardboard boxes of cube sugar; packets of Symbol Expedition Biscuits (which could only be broken by strong molars or a mallet); khaki tins of pea flour, dried onions, and oats; a squat tin of fat bacon; tea, cocoa, and milk powder. We found thick tiles of pemmican – the traditional staple in the polar man's diet and bars of milk chocolate – marvellous! The food of adventure lay strewn about us as if the box of tins had boiled over with joy.

In the years ahead, experience robbed us of many simple delights, but on that first night together in a polar tent, as our candle snuffed itself out in a pool of its own juice and we snuggled into our sleeping-bags, only good times could be seen on our horizons, and we laughed ourselves to sleep.

Ahead of us lay a long stay at View Point where we were going to help build a new hut. To guide us on our first journey was Ron Worswick who, with all his Antarctic experience, had elected to camp in another tent to avoid the direct and gushing enthusiasm of his two new boys. Jim Madell and Pat Thompson were already at View Point. They had made the first sledge journey of the season a few days before under the guidance of Ron and Derro, who had returned to base as soon as Jim and Pat were established. The new hut we were going to build at View Point would eventually be manned as a climatological station, with the men at Hope Bay taking it in turns to occupy it. Jim's task was to make a detailed map of the View Point peninsula.

Our eighteen-mile journey took us three days and, on arriving at View Point, Hugh and I pitched our tent a few feet from the hut, while Ron moved in with the two residents. For the next thirteen days we laboured hard, shifting the stores by dog sledges from the headland where we had landed them from the *John Biscoe*. Slowly our new hut began to rise and take shape. We killed seals with ice-axes (for we had no rifle) and felt the warm blood on our hands with the tingle of pride. The black meat became our staple diet, being served almost ritually every evening and with less conscious attention for breakfast. We worked a simple routine, lived a basic life. The only highlights were when Hugh made fudge or when Pat baked some bread in an oven made from a dog pemmican tin. The squalid little shack, with its odour of stale smoke and dank mattresses, was dark, poorly ventilated, and overcrowded, but it was, nevertheless, a fug of warmth at the end of a hard day's toil.

On our thirteenth evening at View Point, Hugh and I decided that we would dine in the tent and as a perquisite we put on a pot of dehydrated apple rings to simmer for dessert. Camping was no longer the novelty which had first captivated us; we had matured along with the smell of our clothing and the wetness of our sheepskin mattresses. We were going through the period in the life of sledging men when we considered it was more intrepid to live in filth – which indeed it is.

The heat from our bodies had sunk the snow beneath our sheep-skins into smooth pits almost a foot deep, and the rubber sheet which followed the contours of the icy ground was wrinkled and inclined to slip; but we were always too tired in the evenings and too busy during the day to level off the surface, so we just shaped ourselves to fit it.

Our tent that evening was a contented scene. We were both strip-ped down to our long woollen underclothes. Hugh was stirring sugar into the apple rings while I was frying seal steaks which were spitting hot fat. Steam, smoke, and fumes rose in billowing clouds from the cooking area in the centre of the tent, obscuring our view of each other. The steaks done, we started our meal and, to save time, Hugh put the pot of apple rings back on the primus for a final burst of boiling. They bubbled and slopped around like vests in a washing machine.

Suddenly the groundsheet slipped. The pot of boiling apple rings slithered off the primus stove, gurgling, spitting and belching steam, and poured over Hugh's foot. His foot shot out and knocked the primus stove over; the sheepskin sizzled and sparks rose in swarms up to the apex. The tent became a frantic place of steam and fumes. Hugh, berserk with pain, was struggling to peel the sock off his scalded foot. I was beating the smouldering sheepskin and feeling each sound he made. Then suddenly the poor fellow threw himself at the sleeve entrance and burst his way through it into the night. A blizzard was blowing, but above the sharp crack of our flapping tent and the hiss of drift I could hear him groaning in agony. It was an awful sound that went on and on. It was a terrific relief when he went out of earshot.

Jim moved into the tent that night to make room for Hugh in the dingy little shack, and for the next few days the scalded foot grew bigger and Hugh became weaker. Then the blizzards started in earnest, and Hugh's foot turned septic. The medical kit was without any strong antibiotics and the constant bathing of the foot was nauseating. He could not bear the water too hot or too cold, and it would never be just right for more than a minute. He had us distraught with his agonized cries of 'more snow', or 'more hot – for God's sake man – Quick!' We would rush into the blizzard to gather a cupful; it had to be clean and freshly fallen. Then came the business of ladling water at exactly the right temperature and just the right flood. He would almost faint if we poured it too fast – he would howl with the torture if we poured it too slowly, and he had no sympathy when his nurses felt sick. One after the other we would make our excuses to go into the blizzard to check on the dogs. There we would breathe deeply and feel dizzy in private, while 'the foot' was demanding three men to watch it swimming around the chipped enamel basin. It was soon decided that two fellows from base would have to sledge over with penicillin, while Jim and I would sledge back to base to relieve them. The hut by this time was almost completed. Only the finishing touches were left to do, and since there were only two hammers – both being wielded by better craftsmen – we started preparing for our journey back to base.

For the next ten days the blizzard raged. Enormous drifts piled up. Visibility was seldom more than ten yards and often less than two. Five dogs died during the third night. They had allowed themselves to be drifted over and had for a while a natural shelter, but the wind packed the snow like iron that night and the buried dogs had suffocated. One pair had died locked in a fight and were frozen so hard we could not tear them apart. We dragged them away, their stiff bodies scratching tracks in the snow, and heaved them by their tails to slide them the rest of the way on their own, to their grave – a breath gash in a smooth face of snow which opened and shut with the action of tides. When its lower jaw sank and the blue split gaped open, we fed it with refuse – tins, boxes and crates, seals' heads and slops. As the tide rose so the lower jaw creaked and the mouth closed on our offerings. It crushed them with its lips pressed shut and gaped open for more at the next low tide.

On the fourth day of the blizzard we let all the dogs off the spans so that they could move freely wherever they liked. Under normal conditions they would fight and perhaps seriously wound one another, but some of the dogs had reached a very low ebb and had to be massaged before they could stand, while others jumped up and scampered away as if such conditions meant nothing to them. I have never known a blizzard last so long without a single break. We had to gasp to draw in breath and rope up each time we left the tent to feed the dogs or visit Hugh. The smell of decay in the shack grew stronger, but as the days dragged on Hugh's condition improved a little, and his turning-point was significant – he dragged his Leica from his personal bag and photographed the septic foot in Koda-chrome, 'just for the record, man!'

At last on 6 May the wind abated slightly, and, following a fairly regular pattern with the tail of a blizzard, it would come in violent gusts then die away almost to a calm. Visibility was no more than a quarter of a mile; but Hugh was joking, his foot was healing, his camera was clicking – our little world was getting back to normal.

At 5.30 a.m. the next morning the alarm went off: two right hands reached out in the dark, fumbled across the pots-and-pans box, knocking pipes and boxes of matches into the remains of the previous night's cocoa, and eventually crashed on the jumping clock. The arms retracted into the sleeping-bags like snakes' tails disappearing into a hole, and early morning coughs filtered from the warm interior of two shapeless sacks which wriggled a little, then lay still. Everything was still, quite still. Suddenly the two sacks convulsed, then sat upright; a head appeared from each and plumes of vapour rose from their nostrils and mouths and moistened their brows. Hands came up from the depths of the bags and wiped the moisture evenly over their faces. Fingers poked their ears. They looked towards each other their eyes wide open but seeing nothing – and in unison two voices exclaimed:

'It's stopped!'

I dipped my grubby fingers into the tin mugs and fished out my pipes and sodden boxes of matches, while Jim fumbled with the sleeve entrance of the tent which had been tied with thin lampwick cord, shook it open, and poked his head out.

'I think it will be O.K.,' a voice said from outside the tent, as a spurt of light died on the end of my first match. The second match spluttered and caught alight, casting a pale glow with shadows that chased around the tent as I moved towards the candle and lit the wick. Everything came into focus as we shivered and waited for the primus to warm up the tent. No matter what happens during the day – any day – that first five minutes of each morning in a polar tent in the Antarctic is the worst.

Breakfast consisted of porridge, with lump sugar that could not be crushed with the spoon without splashing some of the precious goo; so each lump was hidden beneath the surface where it would dissolve in due course (we had extra lumps that morning to give us energy; at least we hoped it would); and as second course, we fried some bacon. Finally we had the usual Symbol Expedition Biscuits, on each of which was balanced a lump of frozen butter and a square of milk chocolate. This filling meal we washed down with two cups of cocoa and a brew of tea, then we took a short siesta. We smoked a while and felt fortified for whatever the day might bring.

It was still very dark when we crawled outside, so together we worked in the light of the lantern to dig our tent out of the drifts. By the dawn we had broken camp and had only the sledge to find. This took longer than we had expected and it was a very strenuous task digging it clear, but the weather promised a cloudless and wind-free day. Neither of us spoke – there was no need – we knew where everything had to go on the sledge, and we felt quite confident that we could handle the dogs, for we had sledged over 300 miles in moving the hut materials from the headland to the site; but that eighteen-mile journey back to base was to be the first we were to make without being under the watchful eye of an expert sledger.

At eleven o'clock we were ready to go. The dogs were yapping and lunging forward in their harnesses, and the only thing holding us back was a short line to the back picket driven into the hard-packed snow. With both feet on the brake and one fist around the handlebar, I held the team while beating the picket out of the snow with a heavy sledge hammer. Three or four strokes and it shook loose: the sledge shot forward, towing the bouncing iron picket; the dogs stopped yapping, the sledge runners squeaked, the steel prongs of the foot-brake scratched two deep furrows, and the huskies left behind howled farewell. Our team leaped the tide-crack and the sledge thudded on to the sea ice. Jim, who had run a little way ahead to get the dogs in the right direction, let them overtake him, then sprang aboard the travelling sledge and put on his sun glasses. We were away!

For the next eight miles our route round through a chaotic icescape so diverse in character, texture, and hue, that it would have been impossible to find any two beset bergs that caught the sun alike. The bay was a labyrinth of grotesque, tortured shapes, frozen the instant the fang-like pinnacles had pierced their writhing bodies. Our dogs raced around them, occasionally casting quick glances over their shoulders to see if we were still following, while the sound of their panting and the creaking of our moving sledge, rebounded off the ice walls which towered on either side. We raced up snow ramps and side-slipped around the lips of wind-scoops, or went right down into them and trundled across the flat hard ice close in by a berg, bumping over the ice flowers which grew like little white mosses on the frozen moat. We twisted the sledge on summits of steep mounds, skidded down the other side, across frozen blue pools criss-crossed with cracks that were filled with snow – and we stopped at twelve o'clock for a 'smoko'.

There was not a breath of wind and the sun poured its warmth on us, while over the stretched-out bodies of nine resting dogs hung a thin pall of vapour, dissipated now and then as an animal got up, stretched, and looked towards us to see if it was time to go. We drank cocoa from a thermos flask and ate our brittle chocolate. We smoked a while, and marvelled at the perfect calm that had descended on the chaotic icescape all around. Icebergs that had been a battleground of vicious shapes while we were moving, had transformed, when we had stopped, into a frieze of gently heaving ice-forms, towering majestic-ally. No one else would ever see that icescape from just where we stood; for in the day an icescape changes, bergs are polished and eroded, and the smaller splintered pieces, like our sledge tracks, would soon be covered.

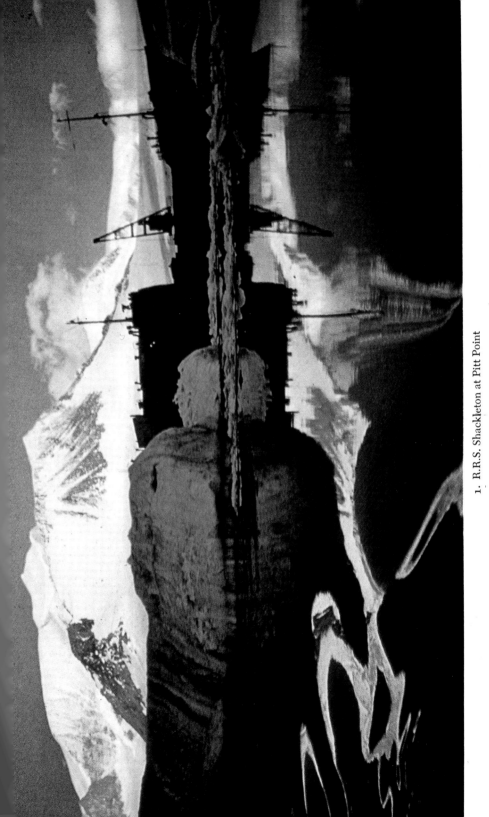

1. R.R.S. Shackleton at Pitt Point

It needed no more than a change of pitch in the voice and the dogs were up and away. The leader answered commands well enough to avoid major obstacles, but occasionally he cut off a corner, which would oblige us to jump off the fast-running sledge and give it a sharp skid at the rear to swing the front of it clear of the ice knobbles and back on to a smoother course. We had become so confident in our ability and so sure that we would get to Hope Bay before dark, that we started choosing routes which took us on the sunny side of the bigger bergs, where the refracted warmth from the dazzling white towers and buttresses soaked us through to the skin. But sometimes our route was barred to the sunlit side, and we would have to drive our team in the shadows down the cold side. The dogs would glance up and yap vigorously if we drove past quickly, but if we stopped our team, they would quietly talk to the ice – a gruffing, growling, whining talk – grumbling very softly. The dogs would never look directly at the piece of ice they were talking to, but would move around uneasily, slumping down, stretching, casting furtive glances at the monster. Our brute huskies became timorous rag dogs in the shadows of those ice-world creatures, warped by the sun's rays, their bodies perspiring the juices of green ice, ugly with pots and holes, majestic with crowns of light – breathtaking monsters, veils blowing out above their shoulders – blades of translucent ice, through which the sun's beams broke into a spectrum and tinted the firm snow at our feet in a scatter of gorgeous colours.

By the time we reached the far side of the bay, the huge rock buttresses supporting the icecap of the peninsula were glowing a reddish brown, and the ice cap and the spectacular icefalls which split between the buttresses were bathed in a pink alpenglow. Clouds forming at a high level were catching the blood of a dying sun, and low stratus were developing over Last Hill, which was on our route. At the junction between the bay ice and the piedmont we met our first obstacle, a six-foot ice cliff. We waited for a while to see which way the tide was moving, but even as we stood there contemplating the cliff, the bay ice creaked and lowered itself. The tide was going out and it would be many hours before it had risen enough for us to sledge straight on to the piedmont. However, a little farther along the tide crack we found a snow ramp banked up the cliff to within a few feet of the top, and took the dogs along to have an attempt at it.

Jim tied a climbing rope to the front of their trace, climbed the cliff, and one by one dragged up the whining animals after him. The surface of the piedmont at that point was glazed blue ice, on which the dogs and Jim kept slipping, so he got down on his hands and knees and started crawling at an angle across the slope towards a patch of snow, while barking encouragement to the dogs who were sitting in a huddle shivering and crying. One by one they started sliding back very slowly towards the edge. The inevitability of the situation was painfully funny and I stood on the snow ramp shaking with laughter – for nothing is more diverting than seeing someone else lose their dignity. There was Jim, stiffened with dog-like disdain for gravity, slipping nearer and nearer to a five-foot ice cliff. The whining of the dogs echoed off the nearby bergs as they flopped one after the other over the edge and erupted on the bay ice in a glorious fight. Into the middle of that seething tangle of teeth and fur Jim fell with a dull thud, and the dogs spread out like a wash from beneath him. I have seldom seen a dog fight stop so dramatically. Jim picked himself up and announced that he was determined to beat the ice cliff. We did – but it took a long time.

Dusk settled while we were still seven miles from base – but we sledged on. By the time we were only four miles away an opaque layer of cloud hung just above our heads and the night was almost pitch black, but still we sledged on. It was all downhill from that point and a compass bearing gave us a general direction, so we both rode the sledge and directed our team by watching the swing of the compass needle. All went well for a while. Then the ominous rattle of the sledge skidding across blue ice began to worry us, and I was having difficulty in checking its pace. We went faster and faster until by chance we ran across a patch of snow – the foot-brake bit in and we stopped. Jim shone the torch on the mileometer that had been ticking off the distance travelled by the bicycle wheel we towed behind the sledge, and found that according to dead-reckoning we should have been in the neighbourhood of a small nunatak, from where the ground falls away at a moderate pace towards the crest of the 300-foot escarpment above the base. It seemed prudent to both of us to make a reconnaissance.

As a precaution, and to help me check the pace of the sledge on the downhill slope, we fastened four thick pieces of hemp rope under the runners to lift them off the ice. The plan we devised was very simple: I would let off four dogs from the back of the team, so there was less chance of the runaway sledge crushing any of the animals, then Jim would go off on his own, while I held on to the remainder of the team if possible until he flashed a torch. That was to be my signal when he had located some object on the route which he recognized. So, followed by four big dogs slipping and sliding, he disappeared into the night.

With all my strength on the foot-brake I was just able to hold the rest of the team as they lunged at their harness. They yapped till my nerves frayed and jerked the sledge inch by inch nearer to the edge of the snow patch. With a concerted pull they could have had the sledge moving, but they tugged out of time as I 'cooed' to them softly. I started to tremble, and from two miles away the dogs back at base set up a faint wolf-howl. At that very moment in the distance a pinprick of light flashed on and off. The sledge trundled on to the ice with the clatter of an old hand-cart and we were soon gathering a frightening speed. The steel prongs of the foot-brake, pressed hard on the ice, sent jarring vibrations right through my body, and, as I weakened, the sledge ran out of control. The friction of the rope-brakes under the runners gave off a strong odour which sent a chill up my spine. If they wore through and lowered the sledge to the ice nothing but a miracle would save us from disaster.

It soon became obvious that the dogs were not going to run towards Jim, for as we approached we had come in sight of an Argentine navigating beacon which was flashing on and off down on the coastal rocks, and the dogs decided to run for that instead. Faster and faster we went – past Jim who was slithering and shouting in an attempt to cut off the dogs and draw their attention, and on towards the crest of the escarpment. I can only remember thinking how cowardly it would be to abandon the sledge while there was a slight chance of saving the team from plunging into the sea. But I was terrified, and so too were the dogs who whimpered as they heard the sledge so close behind them. They galloped for their lives while I hysterically screamed at them to stop. Then ahead of me, against the deep blue-grey backdrop of the northern horizon, I saw the faintest outline of a boulder embedded in the ice, and judged that we were going to miss it by no more than a few feet. As we closed on it, the dogs chose

their course, and with a mighty swing I managed to set the sledge
sliding across the ice to pass the boulder on the other side. With a
sickening sound of animals and sledge colliding, we wrapped ourselves around that boulder like a chain shot, and I lay stunned for a
while among crying, trembling dogs.

As Jim caught up I let off the frightened animals and, abandoning
the sledge, we all set off together to slither the rest of the way to base.
We had been no more than a few yards from the crest of the escarpment when we had stopped, and as we reached it all the huts came
into view way down below, with their lights blazing like the carriages
of trains in the night. It was a strangely beautiful and comforting
sight. We were so very nearly home. We could see torch beams flashing as men caught the forerunners of our team and chained them up;
but they could not see us, the night was too dark, and we were more
than thankful for that. The rest of the team we sent on ahead over
the crest and down to the base. They slid out of sight on their bellies
with their legs outstretched like dog-skin rugs. We could hear their
claws scratching ice all the way down, and so reluctantly we eased
ourselves inches at a time over the crest on our behinds!

Gathering speed we rode down towards base and a heroes' reception. Men crowded around us in the kitchen and pumped up our ego
until we swelled with pride. No one was tactless enough to notice
the clouds of steam that rose from our windproofs as we stood backs
to the fire in our moment of glory. Perhaps all they could see were
two weather-worn men with a fund of adventurous stories to tell.
But I think their perception went deeper than that. One by one they
slunk away with cloudy expressions in their eyes, until Jim and I
were left alone. Their turn would come to go sledging.

CHAPTER FOUR

Two strong men

The best time to get back to base from a sledging journey was on a Saturday afternoon when everything smelt fresh. Saturday afternoon was the end of the week, and any man who worked on a Sunday did so for the good of our little society or in the cause of science, and glowed with smug virtue beneath a disguise of discontent. Saturday was pay day. Saturday was feast day.

A grumbling cook started it by getting out of his bunk; and an eye or two would open as he scratched himself and yawned. He would clatter the poker and liven up the fire; pad across the bunkhouse and look at the thermometer – shiver – poke the fire again and start to make his bed. The night-watchman would come in and the two men would pass the time of day in whispers, like old ladies in a cathedral; then, tittering irreverently and hushing each other reproachfully, they would both head for the ablutions. A few minutes later the night-watchman would come back and climb into his bunk, and the cook would pass through to the kitchen and quietly close the door. We who were awake would hear him filling up the kettle and muttering the formula as teaspoons rattled in the cups: Derro two with milk, Nick two and a half strong, Hugh no sugar medium – on and on it went until eleven separate prescriptions had been made up – all under the general heading of an early morning cup of tea. Then the door would fly open and into the bunkhouse would come the cook on the last day of his duty, and the ritual would begin. He would go quietly up to each sleeper, place the cup of tea on the little shelf, then shake and wake him up. Around the bunkhouse the cook would stroll, leaving behind him a trail of disturbance which erupted below the blankets, and the heads and shoulders of ten tired men would emerge.

Everyone worked like slaves on Saturday mornings, and after the ten-thirty tea-break we would be paid the first part of our wages. This was in the form of a chocolate ration – six bars in all – and since we had no regular money, chocolate became our currency. The value of each bar depended on its ingredients: milk chocolate having a higher rate of exchange than plain or 'basic' chocolate – except when we were dealing with two members of the base who actually preferred the 'basic' variety, and were therefore able to de-value our milk chocolate whenever they pleased. There was no other regular issue of perquisites except the beer ration – one tin a week for each man – but this was, by unanimous approval, set aside for parties – and some form of currency was essential among a group of men where arguing was a natural form of expression. Our society was an agreeable form of dictatorship, in which the base leader, Ron Worswick, had the right of veto on every suggestion put forward by the other eleven men. He also had the right to stop our chocolate ration if we displeased him, and although it was highly unlikely that he would ever have done such a thing, it was always something of a relief and a surprise to find the usual six bars of chocolate sitting on the bed after the Saturday morning tea break, after we had scrubbed out the hut and dried off the floor with blow-lamps, disinfected the lavatory, sledged the 'gash' down to the ice cliffs, re-filled the anthracite bunker, and re-stacked the kitchen shelves with hundreds of brightly-coloured tins.

Ron would sit at the head of the table at all meal times – the rest of us could sit where we pleased, and on cold days of course the seats nearest the fire were in the greatest demand. The meal was usually served by the cook's assistant – the 'gash hand' – who, like the cook, was an amateur, detailed under the roster system to toil for one week for the benefit of our well-being. The cook, unless he was an exceptionally good one, would have all his meals in the kitchen, with the excuse that he was too busy putting the finishing touches to the second or third course to sit with the rest of the men: but in truth the cooks were usually too embarrassed to sit at table and watch eleven men pulling faces as they picked up their cutlery and looked down at their plates.

It seemed to be a tradition at Hope Bay to criticize the cook: unless the meal were so horrible it could not be eaten. On those occasions no one said a word, but just looked around at each other with hurt expressions. It would have been just as easy to praise the good efforts of the cook and condemn his failures, but this never happened, and the ordeal of attempting to feed and please such a hungry and critical crowd of men was at first terrifying. Each cook was given the same basic ration of tins: there was no frozen food because the *John Biscoe* did not have sufficient refrigerator space to supply all the bases in Graham Land with carcasses and frozen vegetables, and in any case, at most of the bases the summer temperatures go above freezing-point, and without a refrigerator or at least an ice cave, the meat could not be kept in good condition. The standard ration included only three varieties of meat: Hunter's steak and kidney pudding, Crosse and Blackwell's stewed steak, and corned beef. To disguise these three basic meats, such great imagination and ability was needed that new recipes were jealously guarded; and even if a fellow stumbled by accident on another man's recipe, it was considered bad taste to serve it up and so rob its inventor of his speciality.

There were good cooks and bad cooks, and over the years we were served with a great deal of pathology that was hard to diagnose. It was no surprise to cut open a loaf and find in the middle a bandage stained yellow that had come off the cook's bad finger; or a button; or a butt-end or a piece of string. On occasions we were served with powdered potato that looked like white sauce, and cakes that burst into a fine spray of dust when accidentally knocked on to the floor; there are many ways of spoiling a meal, and they were all tried out over the course of two years. In summer-time the more ambitious cooks would supplement the tinned meats with penguin and seal. In the field, a big chunk of seal steak or seal liver fried in butter and well seasoned with pepper could not be surpassed, and fried penguin breast was also a most acceptable change; but back at base, men demanded that it be disguised and this often involved a great deal of extra work.

Take 'seal brains *au gratin*', for example. First kill a seal, and go to the grisly trouble of getting the main ingredients. Wash them in sea water – there is usually a seal blow-hole near by which gives access to an unlimited supply. Then when the brains are thoroughly cleaned, soak them in fresh water for an hour or two; and provided you have yourself gathered the snow and melted it into water, you may change the water in the seal brains pot on a number of occasions, to their advantage, and with the satisfaction of a clear conscience. After a good soaking, the brains should be placed in a lined saucepan, and after adding water flavoured with a little vinegar and salt, they should be brought slowly to the boil and allowed to simmer for about fifteen minutes, before being taken out and dried on a cloth. A white sauce is then made, and while it is simmering in the saucepan, grated cheese and chopped up chunks of brain are added, and stirred up with reconstituted onions and a man-sized pinch of salt and pepper. The mixture is then slopped into a casserole dish that has been well greased, and the bubbling mess is sprinkled with breadcrumbs, grated cheese, and knobs of butter, and cooked in a fast oven until nicely browned on top. Like most local dishes, it is eaten with relish by strangers until they find out what they have consumed; then they complain of indigestion or nausea, and spend the rest of their lives sickening their friends by telling them how much they enjoyed it!

It is impossible to disguise the colour of seal meat – it cannot look any paler than black; but it can always be covered with breadcrumbs, or poked below the surface of a casserole so that its discovery is delayed. With shag (*Phalacrocorax atriceps*), however, disguise is more difficult, and the meat needs washing thoroughly and hanging in the fresh air for about a couple of weeks, before being transformed into Shag Maryland, Jugged Shag, or Savoury Shag Hot Pot. But it is about as difficult to disguise a penguin egg as it is to disguise an Englishman, and the older they are the stronger they become. There are certain recipes that are strictly off when it comes to penguin eggs, for the 'white' of a penguin egg when cooked looks like a semi-transparent jelly and the yoke, which is a bright orange, can be seen in a green firmament like a setting sun. A couple of fried penguin eggs on a white dinner plate look like two bloodshot eyes. However, used in cakes, made into omelettes, or scrambled, they become quite acceptable.

Conversation at meal times narrowed steadily over the months, and Ron Worswick, who had heard it all before so many times, could seldom disguise his boredom. His enormous stature cast a shadow across all misguided enthusiasm. His physical strength was colossal, his manner was brusque north country, and his word was law. At the head of the table his power was supreme, for he was the focal point of the gathering, to which we automatically and often unconsciously looked for permission to prolong a theme of discussion. Meal-time conversation he very seldom entered, nor would he be drawn by skilful fishermen baiting a line with topics which interested him: he was aloof – and sat there with an invisible rein to each man; allowing his team its head and a bit of lively good humour, but his control was such that he needed only to glance over the top of his metal-rimmed spectacles to halt the conversation in its tracks. On those occasions, which were not infrequent, the motion would start again with painful slowness and deliberation, then gather momentum the farther it got from the last reproach.

Twice a day, at one o'clock and six o'clock, we sat at table and raced through the ritual of eating. Through the dessert course the pace of eating quickened, spoons moved faster, setting beards a'wagging like washing on the line. The first to finish obtained the best chairs by the fire, while the rest dreamed into the pools of black coffee spilt on the table.

During our time in the Antarctic we drifted with each other and with our aspirations into a funnel from which we eventually emerged so squeezed together by a narrow field of view and the pressures of our environment that almost every man was affected by the personality of the men with whom he came in contact. This was particularly so in the first year with Hugh Simpson and Ron Worswick. To a lesser degree the rest of the men contributed towards the structure of our community, but this brotherhood was like a stew of twelve separate ingredients, which we were obliged to accept because we had all spiced it, but in which each man thought he had more influence than he really did.

When that society was reduced to two men living and sledging together, sharing hardships, privations, and even thought space, there was no escape from the transmission of one's companion's personality. When two men set out together on a sledging journey, so too there sets out the creeping plague of resentment and intolerance, boredom and fatigue. It would overtake them as they weakened or as they fought their silent battles for supremacy of strength and will over one another. It would start to nag them when their stories were exhausted and their minds became occupied by the other's thoughts. Only if they were experienced polar men could they recognize the symptoms and hope to find the right antidote.

Experience was won hard in my first year South. Our aim had been to find a route to the Detroit Plateau, the only area within range of dog teams from Hope Bay that remained unexplored. Depots of food

and fuel had to be laid down the east coast and up to the plateau, so
that during the early summer months of October to December 1956
we could make our main journey along the spine of the Graham Land
peninsula and fill in the last blanks on the map. But it had been a year
of disappointment. Extensive pools of open water in the Prince
Gustav Channel frustrated our many attempts to lay depots, and
severe sea ice conditions on the peninsula side of the channel pre-
vented us from crossing to the mainland and investigating a route
up to the plateau. Time and again we set off down the channel to
move our depots a little farther south, and on each journey Ron took
a different sledging companion while Hugh and I drove the following
sledge. We travelled together well over a thousand miles that first
year.

Hugh's energy was boundless and very seldom wasted. He could
direct his concentration on any aspect of the sledging technique, and
bring to bear such enthusiasm, that he could rip through the toughest
fabric of personal comfort in his search for efficiency. He would
start preparing breakfast straight after the evening meal was over,
and bring it to the point of preparation where it needed only warming the following morning to make it palatable. Our ration of one
candle a day only just lasted out the evening meal and the following
morning's breakfast, so he could not read in the evening; he did not
smoke, so he could hardly pipe-dream, and his academic interests
found no scope in conversation with me, so as soon as he had pre-
cooked breakfast and written up his journal, he would crawl into his
sleeping-bag, wait until I had finished my journal, and then lean
towards me, like a cherub in the corner of an old sea chart with his
cheeks full of wind, and blow out the candle.

Every man has his idiosyncrasies, and one of mine at that time was
that I could not bear the smell of blown-out candles; but I was always
too timid to point this out to Hugh. I tried to draw his attention to it
by going into a fit of coughing, but it brought no response, and later,
when I challenged him directly, he expressed great surprise – apparently the smell was one of his favourites. The night after discussing
this problem with Hugh I expected him to put the candle out by
spitting on his fingers and pinching out the flame; but to my chagrin
he pursed his lips and blew it out just as before; he had simply forgotten. Malice had no part in his character, and I have never seen

him lose his temper. His alert mind had been trained to rationalize, and on scientific or mundane problems it worked with super-efficiency, but it would instinctively repress all thought about conflicts of personality. He did not sulk – that would have been foolish: instead, he just switched off and communication became virtually impossible. In those early days of sledging, my own reactions to clashes of personality were naïve and I would harbour such deep personal grudges that I would be unable to see the root of the problem. It was some weeks before Hugh and I found the solution and this goes to show how parochial inexperienced polar men can become in their thinking. One night I leaned across and blew out the candle so that the smoke clouded to his side of the tent!

Breakfast, to Hugh, was a physiological necessity, and during that meal his bodily energy visibly increased with each spoonful: to me, on the other hand, breakfast was a period between sleeping and waking in which food was eaten to fill in time. It was inevitable therefore that we would run into difficulties, and to make things worse we both had to eat our porridge out of the same pot. Porridge is a very drippy food, and to avoid waste, we would take it in turn to lean forward and put our heads over the pot to catch the drips. Taking it in turns would have been a fair solution if we had been equally matched eaters, but invariably one man would have to wait for the other, and sometimes the temptation was too great so he would get in another quick spoonful. But that was not the only source of friction, for Hugh, being a Scot, liked the milk to go into the porridge during cooking – if it had to go in at all – and large quantities of salt were essential to the brew before his stomach would accept it: whereas I, a sassenach, liked sugar on my porridge and the milk to swim around on top. It was difficult to find a compromise, but we ended up by having half the milk in the porridge and the rest on top; and we found an answer to the salt problem by putting half of it in the porridge during cooking and scratching a dividing line in the skin across the centre of the brew, on one side of which would go the rest of the salt, and on the other side the sugar; so that if either man complained, he was as good as admitting that he had poached on the other man's area. This was the closest we came to a real solution until we discovered that other polar campers used separate plates!

Our sledging journeys together were always either trials of

endurance or attempts at records. Sledging to Hugh was a test of prowess: man versus nature. If the weather was bad, it was called 'character building', which to his way of thinking was all the more reason why a man should go out and face it. If it was a raging blizzard he would lie in his sleeping-bag glowing with good humour and theories about endurance. If the weather was a 'white-out' and we were uncertain of our position he would be oppressed with the lack of action. You could ask him a question and get no reply: you could say 'to hell with you then' – and a quarter of an hour later he would give you a reply to the question as politely as if you had just asked it. During the day, while we were sledging, he would seldom say a word. He would be miles away in his thoughts: we would pitch camp, eat the pemmican, drink the cocoa, climb into our sleeping-bags – then he would suddenly open up and talk about his red deer and salmon-poaching days as an undergraduate and his death-marches over the Scottish Highlands, or he would read to me from a textbook of pathology. We went through a period of two weeks without speaking a word to each other, but the roots of a friendship which I respect and value deeply were planted somewhere in this apparently barren ground, although in retrospect I can only imagine it was planted by a determination to tolerate. Later this became far easier as we took away the mirror we had held up before us, and saw that the world was full of people different from ourselves.

Sledging with Ron Worswick was a totally different experience. His personal motives for spending five years in the Antarctic were less obvious. He was no enthusiast for dog-sledging and had long since built up a resistance to all the sights which enthralled the new-comers. It was hard to reconcile my effusive zeal with his dour attitude. I made only one sledging journey with him as a tent companion – towards the end of the sledging season of 1956.

Our hopes of making a plateau journey that year had gone. We had laid a depot of one and a half tons of food and fuel at Rink Point on James Ross Island; but it was not much use to us there. So in a last desperate bid to get past the pools of open water in the Prince Gustav Channel and to find an easy route to the Graham Land plateau in the vicinity of Cape Longing, Ron and I had set off with the crack team of dogs on 4 September.

It was a strange journey – an exciting, fruitless waste of energy which put the final seal on our season of frustrations. Ron had not encouraged poetic sentiment or any expression of delight in what to him was merely weather and ice, but he was not a flagellant – he preferred to make comfortable journeys, and so for the first time in my sledging experience I found time secretly to enjoy and revere the environment.

We had by-passed the pools of open water in the Prince Gustav Channel by taking a new route on to James Ross Island, getting back down to the sea ice to the south of the open water, and from there we had sledged down the channel close under the moaning-wind rampart cliffs of the island until we reached the huge tilted blocks of ice beset near the tongue of the Larsen Ice Shelf at Cape Obelisk. It was a blue-domed day, and the sun, lying low on the horizon, shot shafts of light arrows across our winding course through the deserted streets of an alabaster city. It was our tenth day out from base. Ahead of us, beyond the majestic castles and shanties of ice, lay the gently rolling desert, without wind-breaks or sharp shadows – nothing to relieve the eye but the cloud-capped spine of the Graham Land peninsula purple in the haze of distance.

The first excitement of our journey was a nightmare hurricane which beat our tent that night like the drums of a devil regiment. For five hours we had fought it in the darkness, feeling each press of the wind as we leaned against the back wall with every ounce of our strength draining from us, until, feather-light, we were vibrated into the dawn calm that followed. Every heartbeat then sounded like the muffled drum of a more sinister storm, and in the whimpering of the dogs I heard the pitiful cry of homeless children, cold and scared amongst the debris of war. But the mist descended and cuddled our camp, soothing the dogs and, as it squeezed the tent gently, we made preparations to move on across the ice shelf towards Cape Longing Col.

By mid-afternoon the mist had lifted to the jagged cliff-tops, while we, sledging over the barren plain, panted into our beards which froze in delicate crystals of down. The sounds of our movement were not broken with words – distance was on our minds that day. The rustle of windproofs and the creak of the sledge were the sole conversation of travel.

We had found at the col a small depot of food and fuel left there by

Ellery Anderson, enough to serve us as a reserve, so we decided to sledge a little farther south along the coast to fill in a very small blank on the map, before returning to the col and the main object of our journey – to look for a route to the plateau. We sledged down the southern slope of the col into gloom. A blanket of cloud merging with the horizon lay on the ice shelf and absorbed our shadows, but we travelled on until the sledge ploughed into the mucous of soft snow. There, six miles south-west of the col, we pitched our farthest south camp of 1956.

We were 120 miles from base, and to the south of us there was not a dog or a man on the eastern coast of the peninsula for over a thousand miles. I felt an overwhelming sensation of exposure, but if I had confided those feelings to Ron he would only have laughed in my face; so our conversation was as usual brief but polite, and at 9.30 p.m. the candle was extinguished.

A groan awakened us with a start. It came directly from beneath the tent; then a sharp pistol-crack. We had camped unsuspectingly on the bridge of a crevasse! Even as we frantically struggled into our windproofs and mocassins, part of the bridge fell in with the sound of falling ice crystals grazing the walls of the chamber, and the groundsheet sagged into the hole under the weight of the primus.

Through the sleeve door of the tent I bundled the sheepskins and sleeping-bags to Ron who threw them across to the sledge. The camp site was a warren of holes; each a puncture in the canopy of the crevasse. Never did I see a camp broken so quickly or a dog team awakened so rudely and driven so frantically into the night. I had wanted to probe the vicinity of the abandoned camp site and re-pitch the tent on the nearest safe ground, but Ron had insisted that we should sledge back to the Cape Longing Col, the nearest accessible solid land.

It was no night for travelling. The low ground drift hissed at our folly and torn clouds, like the black tresses of witches, cut loose and swept across the sky. Dizzily we plunged over silver snow and black lacquer glare ice, pitching and dipping and riding great rollers towards the faint silhouette of a distant col. Then into a black trough on our left we began our sickening slide.

The sledge grated sideways, screeching as it gathered speed and the horizon closed around us. We rode it stiffened with fear as the dogs' claws scratched the glass-like walls. It was like a nightmare nail-tearing slither over the edge of the world.

The rattling sledge skidded on to hard snow at the bottom of the trough along which the dogs galloped, whimpering and fouling the air until a crevasse swallowed the leading dogs and the remainder hauled back on their traces at the brink. The clouds parted and let the moon soak the trough in pale cobalt and liquid pools of silver light, casting long shadows from the dogs as they sat, legs splayed out against the weight of their companions hanging in the crevasse. I belayed Ron tightly as, one by one, he fished them out and set them amongst the others on the edge of the broken bridge. We then re-organized so that I was tied to the front of the dogs' trace; and stamping our crampons into the ice, we hauled the dogs off that fragile shell of snow up the slippery wave as a curtain of cloud was drawn across the moon. Its shadow flowed over the crest just as we reached it. We had found a safe place not a moment too soon.

I begged Ron to camp, but we were surrounded by the small-arms fire of cracking ice, and, like a battle hero, he wanted to charge through the night and reach the col whatever the cost; so I waited until the reaction gripped him, then taking advantage of his temporary weakness, I slipped the lash-line, tugged out the tent and made camp before he recovered. I got the primus roaring at full blast and the steam and warmth was like a soothing balm. I had snuggled once more into my sleeping-bag, but Ron could not relax. His knees were frostbitten and for hours he flogged them with frayed rope to restore the circulation and, after spending a sleepless night, he announced his intention the following morning of going straight back to base. The disappointment cut into me deeply, for it was our last chance to redeem a wasted season, and once more we had given in; but I had not realized at that time what a weight the burden of leadership could be. I was aching for the chance to lead my own party.

Our journey back to base took only five days and was relatively un-eventful, and there we lived and worked in great contentment for the next month. The weather was warming, the penguins were laying and we carefully stored thousands of eggs away in boxes of flour which would preserve them for the following year. We painted the ceiling, and varnished the timber walls of our dear old hut; we repaired the sledges, we patched the tents, and made plans for the summer. View Point had never been occupied during that season of the year, so I was delighted when Ron suggested that with three companions – Jim Madell, George Larmour, and Bill Nicholls – I should spend the summer there. We were to carry out a continuous meteorological record and were to make observations of the break-up of the sea ice in Duse Bay, but apart from that directive and helping Jim to complete his detailed map of the View Point peninsula, I was given a free hand to fill in the rest of the time in any profitable way that came to mind.

My party, accompanied by Laurie Catherall and Dick Walcott, reached View Point on 1 November after an exciting crossing of Duse Bay. It was mid-afternoon when we had driven our teams on to the ice and the glare ahead was so dazzling that it was impossible to judge the state of the surface. We had splashed through pools of melt water and many times had felt the ice bending under the weight of the sledge. Laurie and I on the leading sledge broke through the ice about six miles from View Point, ploughing a channel for twenty yards before the dogs hauled a tilting sledge and its dripping drivers back on to a firmer surface. But we had arrived at the hut in high spirits for the start of our sojourn, and were soon in warm clothes, drinking hot tea and chatting to John Noble and Hugh Simpson who had been occupying the hut for the past three weeks. We all agreed that there was no time to delay in view of the advanced state of the sea ice decay, so in less than an hour we had said our good-byes to Laurie, Dick, John, and Hugh, and watched them weave their teams out of sight back across the bay. Two hours later, through our powerful binoculars, we saw two dog teams climbing Last Hill, and we were all relieved to hear over the radio the following evening that they had got back to base without serious incident.

So started one of the most contented periods of my Antarctic experience. We became the centre of a dream-like world in which time had no meaning. Only what we saw was part of our world, for what lay beyond our visual horizon seemed more remote than the glaring sun. We were contented castaways, and life sustained itself on a simple diet.

CHAPTER FIVE

Contented castaways

For weeks the flag hung limply from the tent pole. The sun turned the snow to water, and the water ran in rivulets across the decaying ice down to the tide crack. The odour of blubber hung over our island of rock, set in a decaying sea of land ice near the wet and rotten sea ice. Skua gulls, bloated with decomposing seal, could only become airborne after spewing or by jumping off the ice cliff. Our dogs panted. We peeled off our pullovers. Winter was melting into summer and the rocks warmed in the sun.

We sounded the sea-bed through holes in the ice, and many a small wager was lost by a fathom. We plotted the break-up of the sea ice on charts drawn on each even page of an exercise book, and found naïve satisfaction in flipping the pages between thumb and forefinger to give animation to our record. We climbed the hills to observe the sea eating away the ice in the bay. Up in the hills where the snow lay clean and no smells polluted the air, we found solitude, so desperately needed, so precious to man confined by basic masculine thought.

Hours and hours in the hills; the sun warm on a prostrate form; snow sweating into beads of water, sparkling, shimmering on the jagged rocks; blue smoke curling from a cool pipe; a solitude full of unheard breezes caressing rock ridges and spurs; of hopes and dreams; of infinity. No other sound but the breathing snow sinking under the weight of summer warmth – melting; slipping; trickling. Down to the sea. Softly.

Our life was masculine in the extreme. We were men's men, so we thought – acting the part by living hard, and against our natural inclinations, limiting our self-expression to basic grunts, or competition. We were dedicated men: George Larmour, the softly spoken Irishman; cockney Bill Nicholls, or 'Nick', with his undiluted sense of humour; and Jim Madell, who always said just what he thought, then smiled in case we took offence. A quartet suspicious of poetry –

and yet it was on this we thrived. The safety-valve was solitude in the hills.

Over the hills and down to the coast, two miles from our hut was a refuge shack. 'Christ the Redeemer' it was called. The shack was dark and smelly, and so small it was almost filled by its occupants: Buonomo and Avilar. Those two friendly Argentinians would shuffle

The hut at View Point

out as we crunched down the hill, thump us on the back, and invite us inside where we would spin a yarn or two. They were the very salt of the earth – big and un-handsome sergeants they were. They had right-dressed their parade of dead seals on the beach, and could recite patriotic poems with real tears in their eyes. They were sentimental men, with whom we shared all of our provisions as well as many happy hours of deprivation just before the festive season.

Our store hut was almost bare by the middle of December – tins of plain flour, egg powder and salmon was all it had to offer. But each man had been guilty of slipping out, after his companions had fallen asleep, and padding in the twilight of early morning across rotten snow to the musty old shack. Caches had been laid all over the place during early December but none of those caches were brought to

light until Christmas Day when we and our guests had a marvellous
feast.

The day the sea ice finally broke up was dead calm. Overhead thick
rolls of cloud soaked up all sound and drained life from our familiar
world. The scene was one of leaden greyness, gloomy and yet with a
mysterious, imperceptible movement. A faint smell of the sea, a
muted groan, an eerie atmosphere which worked right through to the
pit of the stomach. We could sense these things as we moved about
restively, talking with bated breath. Slowly the ice began to heave a
fraction of an inch, no more. The faintest creaks and groans were
heard, then the gurgle of water between the cracks which opened
very slowly as the floes started to move. The strongest compulsion I
have ever experienced was to step on to the floe as it eased away from
the tide crack. I had to close my eyes and keep them shut until I
could tell by the sounds of ice movement that it was too late to jump
the gap. There on the floes that were moving away were our footprints made not a minute before.

The bay to us had always been the ice canopy above it: suddenly it
had come alive, splitting, creaking, moving past us. We stood
spellbound. Bergs that had been our winter neighbours, our familiar,
friendly land-based monsters, were sailing past us out to sea surrounded by fleets of jingling splinters and brash ice: the bay would
never be the same without them.

The summer thaw gouged channels out of the snow-fields and
down from the hills roared torrents of water which swept away our
timber bridges. Our island of rock grew bigger each day and we
marooned ourselves on it, occupying ourselves with tidal observations and synoptic record of the weather, while in between times we
lounged for hours on warm rocks smoking our pipes and sunbathing
a few feet from the sea.

There was a tacky smell about the place, an incense of burning seal
blubber, of decomposing heads and tails that had surfaced when the
snow receded. Bonfires crackled for days and spat out gobs of yellow
jelly as the black plume of smoke rose vertically. The sea gave off a
powerful odour. It is like a thin broth murky with marine organisms:
phytoplankton – the pasture of the sea, the food of the krill who in
their turn build the body of the blue whale, the largest mammal that
has ever lived. Krill is also the food of fish and penguins and the vast

population of sea birds and seals. The predation of penguins and seals is the work of the lithe Leopard Seal who in turn is the food of the Killer Whale, the most ferocious animal in the polar seas. Excreta and the debris of the kill sinks to the sea-bed and is broken down by bacterial decay: it is upwelled to the surface again as diatoms – the microscopic marine plants that utilize the energy of the sun to transform the nutrients in the water into living organisms – the phytoplankton on which the krill feeds. And so the cycle starts all over again.

The Arctic Terns arrived, pointing their red beaks threateningly at us as they circled and squawked overhead. They had migrated 13,000 miles, but arrived looking bloated on the krill they found when they reached the pack ice. The Greenland flocks migrate in late August across the Atlantic to southern Europe without rest, stops, or food; then after a short period of recuperation, continue their journey down the west coast of Africa, keeping well out to sea and flying seldom more than a hundred feet above the water. Some go south from the Cape into the pack ice and on farther to the Antarctic coastline; while others follow the equatorial currents across the Atlantic, then fly down the east coast of South America to the Graham Land peninsula. Very few flocks go south along the American coast, and they are rarely seen in the Pacific, which is strange considering their circumpolar distribution during the Arctic summer. These terns must fly a minimum of 26,000 miles a year.

The skua gull has an unpleasant habit of slowly circling a man who walks alone up in the hills. Perhaps the bird is just curious – but it always seemed sinister to me. I have always had a loathing of being watched by birds and a horror of being attacked by them. I tell myself not to look up, but as the bird's shadow slides over the snow, no force of will or rational argument can keep that skua 'ordinary'. They are not particularly ugly birds, like vultures – but they are fat and surly and arouse in a man the most animal kind of vindictiveness. Stones are thrown at skua gulls by men who suddenly smile tenderly at a Snow Petrel. If the skua would only make a noise, any noise other than the rush of wind, they would not be half so terrifying; but these great brown birds are as silent as death when they come into the attack. There were a few occasions when I stumbled alone into their nesting territory. They would circle slowly, flying low, then come in fast and straight for my head. I would yell and wave my arms, then duck, and the giant mute bird with vicious beak and talons extended would soar up, high, then start his circling once again. My progress in skua territory was never more undignified than when I was alone and without missiles. I would stumble and sprawl, get up and run, wave my arms and yell to try and scare them away, but they came on and on with a rush of air, missing my head by an inch or two – so close I could smell their dusty grey belly plumage and see the evil in their eyes.

The little Wilson's Storm-Petrels were far sweeter-natured birds, and the Snowy Petrels a pure delight. Even the Giant Petrels had attributes enough to offset their squirting a slimy brown fluid through their nostrils at men who were imprudent enough to get within range; for on the wing they are wonderful soaring creatures, circling and sweeping with a vibrating rush of wind. If only they would stay airborne, gliding on their six-foot wing span; but alas they have to feed, then they gorge on offal until their eyelids close and their bellies sink to the ground. Stinkers, Nellies, or G.P.s we called them for want of a more derogatory name.

Sometimes a slippery seal poked his head out of a lead, and glistening drips of water would slide along his whiskers as his big lugubrious eyes took a slow look around. His shining head would sink back into the water. His fleshy mouth gurgling a bubbled bark and, fizzing water through his nose, he would submerge and swim away. A thrash of water and he would re-appear, struggling to climb on to a floe, his flopping body slapping the ice and heaving repulsively. He would galumph a few feet, grunt, then languidly collapse and lie slug-like in the sun, occasionally scratching his tummy and smiling with an almost human expression curling the corners of his mouth.

We saw Leopard Seals scorching across tranquil pools of sea between the ice-floes in chase of a few stray penguins, who would pop out of the water on to a floe in a state of dignified alarm. We saw enormous icebergs roll over and boil the water with turbulence, then rise out of an apron of foam with water streaming off them: thousands of tons of blue-green ice heaving itself into the air in a slow-motion display, colossal and powerfully impressive. We saw schools of whales in the distant ice-free water: and watched a fight between a

Killer Whale and a Leopard Seal about a hundred yards out from the
ice cliffs, which thrashed the water into a stew of blood, meat, and
blubber; while fat skua gulls circled and hovered overhead watching
their meal carved up and killed. The floes and sea ice were alive with
interest. Sunsets and sunrises ran together and the weather always
changed its temper before it grew familiar.

The early hours of 22 January had started like any other day. Slowly
sunlight filtered through our sleepy eyelids. We moved like moths
towards the window and looked out towards the point. It was
glorious. Duse Bay was a patch-work of black sea and dazzling ice –
the sky was very blue. We were about to look away when, from
behind the point as if by magic, a ship sailed into view.

We were thrown into a frenzy of activity. Beds were made, the
windows opened, the floor swept and scrubbed. The serenity of our
life was shattered. 'She's almost here, man – hurry!' We got the blow-
lamp working at last and were drying the floor with it as the new
John Biscoe eased her way through the pack towards the ice cliff. At
last all was done and we ran out to meet her. What a beautiful ship
she was, and what seamanship Captain Johnston displayed in bringing her alongside the cliff, so gently that men could step on to the ice
even before the vessel had berthed.

During the unloading of stores for our hut I set off to walk over
the hills to our neighbours' shack. They had been snatched away a
few weeks before by a helicopter operating from the Argentine icebreaker, and had been obliged to leave behind three teams of dogs
for us to look after. Captain Johnston had offered to take the dogs
back to Hope Bay provided I could find a landing spot along the
rocky coast near the Argentinians' shack. I scrambled over the rocks
and peered into the water, which looked very shallow – a most
unsuitable spot so I thought, and was about to go off and look for
another, when to my horror the *John Biscoe* came round the point and
headed straight for me. On and on it came, pushing relentlessly
through the ice until it towered over the shore. It held its position by
pressing the bows aground in the sea-bed, and in less than a quarter
of an hour the dogs were aboard and the *John Biscoe* was moving
slowly astern.

Hanging over the forecastle rail were my three companions, grinning hard, and many strangers, a long line of bearded faces all looking down at me. I was alone on the shore. My friends were going off to join other bases for their second year in Antarctica, and three replacements had been left at our hut – a depressing thought.

The bows of the *John Biscoe* slid away, trailing a channel of swirling water which sucked small pieces of ice round in eddies. The engine-room telegraph rang and a white foam welled up under the stern. The fog horn echoed around the hills: then slowly the *John Biscoe* pushed forward into the pack ice, out of the bay. The chug of her engines died away until I was left with only the sound of the sea lapping the rocks on which I sat, and the soft tinkle of ice drifting into the channel left by the ship.

CHAPTER SIX

Hair-shirt and stone age

Plateau mania swept around the British bases in Graham Land during the summer of 1956–57. Perhaps the reason was the shift of personnel from one base to another during the summer relief operations: perhaps it was a sudden brainwave of the survey programmers at the Directorate of Overseas Surveys back in Britain who thought that more could be seen by climbing high: indirectly it might even have been because of the Commonwealth Trans-Antarctic Expedition, which had put fresh sparkle into the well-worn geographic term 'plateau' – for suddenly everyone seemed to be looking up at the massive buttresses and escarpments of Graham Land's magnificent flat-topped spine.

At the beginning of 1957, no fewer than four British bases had field parties out looking for routes to the plateau, and although no one admitted it openly at the time, the spirit of competition that developed drove them across the most frightful terrain in a bid to establish their priority. The four attempts were well spread out down a five-hundred-mile coastline; but I doubt if there was one man amongst all who did not in his heart long to bag the entire exploration for his own base.

There were known routes to the plateau at either end of the peninsula, and the bases nearest those known routes were in an enviable position. Operating from the original hut at Hope Bay in 1947, Captain V. I. Russell had discovered a route on to the plateau at the northern end, about ninety miles from base, but although we knew of the existence of his route, we had been unable to approach within thirty miles of it during 1956.

Hugh Simpson was determined to make an ascent of Russell's route as soon as possible after the change in leadership at Hope Bay, and he was strongly supported by Roger Tufft who had joined our base after spending a year at the meteorological station at Admiralty Bay. Dick Walcott was also keen to go on the reconnaissance of

Russell's route. Meanwhile other field parties from bases down the west coast were trying to snatch the priority.

On 7 December 1956 a party of seven men had been put ashore on the Reclus Peninsula in the Gerlache Strait, to investigate a route that had been seen from seaward through binoculars, and five days later they reported by radio that a possible way had been found. The *Shackleton* returned, off-loaded the stores and equipment for a small refuge hut, and by Christmas Day it was established. Shortly after New Year, a party of four men led by M. B. Bayly had set out and pioneered a route to the plateau and climbed Mount Johnston, which at 7,580 feet is the highest point on the mainland for many miles. The going was reported as being by no means straightforward for man-haulers, and for dog-sledgers it was considered severe; but it was the only route that had ever been found to the plateau along the five-hundred-mile stretch of west coast from Hope Bay to Darbel Bay on the Antarctic Circle.

Their reconnaissance had lasted a month, and as a result of their discoveries it was decided to let three men winter over at Portal Point on the Reclus Peninsula, so that they could lay depots of food and fuel in preparation for the field journeys of the following summer. The three men who were disembarked on 24 March 1957 – Dick Foster, Dennis Kershaw, and Ray McGowan – were destined to experience the plateau in its worst moods, and for nearly four months they floundered in deep snow to the limits of their endurance, up to and into that strange world of clinging clouds.

While I was still at View Point our new base leader at Hope Bay, Lee Rice, had arrived, and, so I am told, within a couple of weeks Hugh Simpson had thoroughly infused the plateau mania into his gentle nature and swept him off his feet in flights of fancy. The floor of the bunkhouse was covered with maps, photographs, and reports. Tea was spilt on them, cake crumbs were squashed into them, and faces beamed up from grown men who crawled over them like children in a nursery. His ideas were plagiarized, his pencils were snatched, his notebooks were scribbled on, and not until the festive season did he get any respite from talk of plateau journeys, or a chance to shake off the dizziness and settle into his new way of life.

It was Christmas Day 1956 when we at View Point heard his gentle

Irish brogue for the first time. We had just finished a hearty supper with our Argentine neighbours, Buonomo and Avilar, and were sitting around the hand generator helping to turn the handle when his voice filtered through the dusty cloth of the amplifier:

'Hellow View Point – this is Lee Rice speaking' it said with a crackle and a hum – then the generator seized up!

It was not until two and a half months later that I first met Lee. He was at the forecastle head of the *Shackleton* as it nosed towards the ice cliff at View Point to relieve us. There was a strong wind blowing and no pack ice in the bay to subdue the swell, so the risk was not taken of coming alongside the cliff; instead, a rope ladder swung limply down from the prow as outstretched arms reached down and plucked us off the ladder and heaved us aboard like carrion. The fog horn groaned as friends crowded around and shook us warmly by the hand, then we went below for a beer or two while the ship chugged slowly out of Duse Bay.

No ship has broken into Duse Bay since. The summer of 1956–57 was exceptionally kind to shipping in the Graham Land coastal waters. Even while we were singing under a hot shower, our vessel was moving at a steady eight knots down an almost ice-free Prince Gustav Channel that had never been entered by a ship before.

We sailed a course that we had sledged over so often the previous year. Every landmark was a reminder of lost battles with the ice or with the pools of open water that had stopped our progress south. Hugh pointed them out to Roger and to Lee, but never once did he mention the hardest struggles he and I had had – the struggles to find a harmony between two ambitious men. Lee listened politely, and his eyes smiled. I wondered why such a gentle man could ever have wanted to leave Ireland for the hardship and fierce competition amongst this rough and tumble world of men.

That evening a film show was held in the wardroom while the *Shackleton* lay gently rolling off Pitt Point, and early next morning a massive supply of stores was off-loaded on to the beach, from where Lee, Hugh, Dick, and Roger planned to start their depot-laying journey up Russell's route to the plateau. Our toil and frustrations of the previous year had resulted in a depot only half the size of the one left by the *Shackleton* at Pitt Point. It had been left on a raised beach at Rink Point over on the other side of the channel eight miles away. That eight miles had been the difference between us and success during 1956.*

I was taken back to Hope Bay on the *Shackleton*, and for the next seventy-three days, while I was enjoying the comforts of base life, Lee and his companions were suffering hardships away down the coast. The period they were in the field coincided with the worst weather conditions that can be experienced in the Graham Land area – the period between the end of a warm summer and the end of the equinoctial storms. For weeks the sea beat against the coast and sprayed their tents and dogs, until in desperation the party set off and tried to sledge around the head of the little bay to the south of Pitt Point. But on the piedmont ice the ground sloped towards the ice cliffs; it was badly crevassed and the only snow on the area lay in or over the crevasses.

Many times the sledges skidded on to the crevasse bridges, where the dogs delightfully gambolled, fought, or ran along until the crevasse petered out and the sledges ran once more on to a firmer surface. After laying a small depot, Lee and his companions decided to go back to Pitt Point for a rest, and instead of going around the head of the bay, they lowered the sledges and dogs on to the newly-formed sea ice and crossed the bay at a tearing speed just before it broke up and drifted out into the channel. Clouds developed, snow fell, winds blew and the sea ice slowly re-formed, rafted, then finally froze solid. The blizzards came and packed down a layer of snow, the bergs were imprisoned by the frozen sea and settled into their winter quarters, spreading their drifts around them.

The situation was ideal for Hugh's research. All through the previous winter he had wondered which aspect of cold acclimatization to study, and with a flash of inspiration he decided to study stress instead. During the summer at Hope Bay he had enticed human guinea pigs into his surgery with disarming frankness and had drawn blood off them like a vampire. He would draw it from a vein in the elbow and mix it with eosin stain, put a drop on a slide and look at it through a microscope. The eosinophil cells in the blood, which are made in the bone marrow, have a great affinity for eosin dye, and once they have migrated through the marrow vessel walls and into

* That depot at Rink Point was later washed away by the tremendous seas that thrashed the coasts during the autumn hurricanes of March 1957.

the bloodstream, the acceptance of dye is an easy way of telling them from the other white cells. When rats are under stress their eosinophil count is lowered and under severe stress might even fall to zero – at which point they probably die of fright. It occurred to Hugh that we might react similarly, and this prompted him to take his microscope into the field and draw off samples of blood from his companions when they were under stress to see if their eosinophil count would behave in a similar way. It did.

When the party set off a second time to investigate Russell's route and to lay a depot near the top of the plateau, a blanket of snow lay over most of the inland valleys that were in the windless shadows of the surrounding mountains. In many places they could see tiny holes where the fine crystalline snow had slipped into a crevasse, almost entirely bridged, but so delicately supported that a gust of wind would have collapsed it. Crossing such areas was nerve-shattering, but in spite of these ordeals they pressed on and up to the edge of the plateau. On the last nunatak below the escarpment, at a height of 3,250 feet, they found a depot that had been left by Russell ten years before, still in reasonable order; and there they left a load of food and fuel which was to be the basis of our supplies for the final journey along the plateau.*

By the time they got back to Pitt Point the equinoctial storms had started, at first sporadically, but each blizzard bearing the omen of worse to come. The channel was still unreliable as a sledging route, so they had to pioneer a route overland which took them through a most chaotic area of pressure. Both tents were flattened by a stupendous gust of wind, in which two tent poles of each tent were snapped, food boxes and personal gear blown over the horizon, and two fully-grown huskies lifted twenty feet through the air. Roger was outside at the time and fell to the ground just before the gust hit or he might have gone the way of the dogs. He and the others spent the rest of the night exposed to vicious winds and were very weak by the morning. They made one good tent out of the two broken ones and huddled together for days in cramped quarters and in constant fear of being blown away.

Hugh's physiological research programme had a gap in the records at that time, which even his tent mates in retrospect admit was a pity.

* This nunatak I later named after Dr Hugh Simpson.

They had all been under severe stress, and the fall in their graph of eosinophils up to the time their tents were crushed had in some cases been most dramatic. On arriving back at base a few weeks later, their eosinophil count soared way above their normal base level as if suddenly released from tremendous tension. We at base could clearly see this reaction in our companions because we knew them well and had not been under the same stress ourselves; but when a group of men come through an ordeal together, they cannot see the relief of tension in each other's faces; all they see is elation. They are like drunken men roaring their heads off and all swearing that they are sober.

The three men on the Reclus Peninsula meanwhile had set out to lay a depot at the top of Bayly's route to the plateau. For days they leaned into their harnesses and man-hauled the heavy sledges through the deep snow. In the evenings they crawled into their sleeping-bags exhausted, and fell asleep to the monotonous sound of snow falling on their tent. In cloud they relayed the loads forward, and followed with difficulty their tracks back along their route until they stumbled over the loads which had been left behind; then once again they would start their haul back to the tent. On and on it went – a trudging grind a few hundred feet at a time, a rest, a one-two-three-heave, and the sledge would jerk forward as they began the next gruelling stretch.

On the steeper slopes they packed the loads on their backs and, bent over with the weight, they climbed, rested awhile, and then staggered on, soaked with the snow which melted as it settled on their steaming clothes. They thought only of food and the next step forward, while somewhere ahead and way above them the plateau lay big and oppressive.

The wind would sometimes drive the drifting snow in a swirl around their shelter, sweeping the valance clean and piling a tail of drift downwind. After days it died away and the cloud slipped down the mountain side to a lower level, the sun shone, and they were rewarded with a rare view of the plateau and distant peaks of Brabant and Anvers Islands.

At an altitude of 4,000 feet there were no rock outcrops, so they built a snow cairn around the depot of three food boxes (enough food to sustain three men for twenty days), then they stuck a ten-foot marker flag into the cairn and set off down. Their hut lay only fifteen miles away and yet their journey had taken them thirty-four days; and although they had laid their depot not far short of the plateau, they were unable to find it when they took up their second load!

All these things had happened while I was living in the comfort of base, working on the field sheets for my survey, or doing observations of terrestrial refraction within hailing distance of the cook. It was a stimulating time to be at base, for the violence of the storms was very real and close. In the rattling, creaking security of my little survey office I could look out of the window at night and see the blizzard streaking across the beam of light which penetrated it like a torch beam in a fog. Sometimes there would be so much drifting snow in the air that it seemed as if the light from the window was being pushed back against the outer pane. These were the nights when the fire roared and we smiled cosily at the misfortunes of the men who were camping in it.

The day the plateau boys came home was a day of great rejoicing. We spoilt them, and they deserved it – they were our temporary heroes. We watched their every mouthful as they gorged themselves on grills. We handed them tomato sauce and great big chunks of bread; we marvelled at their weathered faces and gazed at their shaggy beards catching the dribbling grease; we saw the sparkle in their eyes as they talked about the stupendous descent from the plateau edge and the catastrophic winds; about flying dogs and chaotic icefalls – in relays, one man following the other. For two days they worked stories out of their systems and into ours. They lounged about, blissfully recuperating and smiling up at the ceiling, while we who had stayed at home began to feel caged by the walls that were protecting us, and gathered in groups to plan our great escape.

'You know, man – I'd like to do a man-hauling circumnavigation of James Ross Island,' said Hugh. One or two of us looked up from our sewing. It was a busy scene; a warm, congenial, bunkhouse time for planning exploratory journeys. With the big depot laid at Pitt Point by the *Shackleton*, and the depot laid just below the escarpment of the Graham Land plateau by Lee, Hugh, Dick and Roger, we found ourselves in the delightful situation of have two months to fill in before the start of our main journey.

'You can't just take off and go where you please – we're paid to spend our time profitably.' Sam Blake had taken the bait beautifully. He was our radio operator; a wandering romantic Irishman who had worked in Australia.

'Ah – you're too religious,' chimed in Pat Thompson.

'What the hell's that got to do with Hugh's man-hauling charlie around James Ross Island?' asked Sam, exasperated. We all grinned and carried on sewing dog-harnesses, and the banter flowed to and fro until Hugh, warming to his latest idea and anxious to defend his plan with a scientific motive, butted in:

'Of course it wouldn't be a charlie – I could do some very useful research into the physiology of stress during the journey,' and almost as an afterthought he added, 'and we could call in at Nordenskjöld's hut at Snow Hill Island.'

The idea was an immediate success. Mike Reuby glowed at the mere thought of it. Old huts had a strong appeal for him. The idea had caught Roger too, although far less dramatically; he just sprawled in his chair, splicing dog-traces and grinning comfortably.

It began to dawn on Lee that at any moment he was going to be put under pressure for his approval to yet another of Hugh's proposals, and in a hesitating voice he quietly asked:

'I don't think I've heard of him – who was he?'

'Who was Nordenskjöld!' a gasp of surprise came from the old hands. It seemed inconceivable to us that a Hope Bay man had not heard of Nordenskjöld. We had breathed the spirit of the heroic age in polar history through the fusty volumes that filled our library shelves. Adrien de Gerlache, Borchgrevink, Nordenskjöld, Scott, Charcot, Shackleton, Amundsen – those tough old explorers were our heroes. Their like would never be seen again in the Antarctic. We knew almost by heart every book they had written, and through months of travelling with them we had become familiar with their moods and every panting breath they uttered on their journeys.

'Lee – you can't be serious. Nordenskjöld discovered and named

Hope Bay on 15 January 1902. He sailed on down the east coast and
set up his winter quarters on Snow Hill Island, and his expedition
was only the second in Antarctic history to winter ashore. But
Gunnar Andersson is Hope Bay's real hero. You must have seen the
remains of that stone hut down by the Argies' floating jetty – that
was Gunnar Andersson's winter shelter in 1903.'

'What was he doing there?'

The old hands all started talking at once – each commencing from
a different point in Gunnar Andersson's story – as Dick Walcott
brought in from the kitchen some fresh bread rolls he had just made
and a steaming pot of tea.

'For goodness' sake let someone tell the story who can marshall his
facts properly,' he said, and we coaxed Roger, with a few promptings
to get him on his way.

'It was like this,' he began. 'Nordenskjöld's expedition had started
off-loading their supplies and building materials at Snow Hill Island
from the three-masted whaling ship the *Antarctic* some time in early
February 1902 – I can't remember the exact date, but I seem to think
it was a few days before Captain Scott's *Discovery* dropped anchor off
Hut Point in McMurdo Sound on the other side of the continent; but
whereas the *Discovery* wintered over in McMurdo Sound and provided
the expedition with a comfortable base from which to work, the
Antarctic had sailed north after Nordenskjöld had established his
expedition ashore, and the ship spent the winter in the South
Atlantic, visiting the Falkland Islands, South Georgia, and Tierra
Del Fuego.'

'Oh, get on with it Roger!' teased the men who were getting impatient. Others shouted them down. The wind was tearing at the
roof of the bunkhouse and creaking the timbers of the walls; the fire
was blasting out its heat and rattling the chimney.

'Dr Gunnar Andersson,' Roger continued, 'had taken a regular
"crumpet" passage out from Sweden to join the *Antarctic* in the
Falklands when it returned from its first southern cruise, and he did
some interesting trips ashore in South Georgia and Tierra Del
Fuego before sailing south on 5 November 1902. The Ona Indians
were living in Tierra Del Fuego at that time. Of course, they're just
about extinct now – as soon as they put on civilized clothes they
became soft. But Gunnar Andersson sailed down the west coast of

Graham Land and did a bit of survey before Christmas, hoping to give the pack ice in the Erebus and Terror Gulf time to shift. They tried once or twice to get in to Nordenskjöld's party, but there was not a chance of breaking through, so he and two companions – Lieutenant Duse and seaman Toralf Grunden – were landed at Hope Bay on 29 December 1902 with a small supply of food and some sledging equipment, and they set off to man-haul to Snow Hill Island one hundred and ten miles over what was then completely un-explored country. The idea was that they should contact Norden-skjöld and tell him that the ship was waiting for him and his party at Hope Bay, but Andersson's party only got as far as Vega Island before they met open water and were obliged to turn back. They reached Hope Bay safely and for the next few days pottered around collecting fossils from Mount Flora while waiting for the ship to come back and pick them up. But it never did come back, so they had to build themselves that stone hut down on the foreshore.

'Three days after landing the sledging party at Hope Bay, the *Antarctic* had been caught in the ice as Captain Larsen tried once more to get around Joinville Island, and for the next forty days the ship drifted with the pack ice until its back was broken by the pressure and she sank. The crew took to the ice and, dragging as much stuff as they could, they made for the nearest land, which was Paulet Island, thirty-seven miles away. The haul took them sixteen days, and on Paulet Island they built a stone hut in which they spent the winter. Paulet Island is about forty miles from here. So in 1903 there were three parties sitting out the winter – two groups in rough stone shelters, and the third in a wooden hut.

'At the beginning of March 1903, when the Hope Bay party realized that the *Antarctic* must have met disaster, they took stock of the remainder of their "civilized food" and started to build up a supply of penguins. Had there not been a large penguin rookery at Hope Bay they would probably not have survived. In all, they killed about 3,700 penguins, if I remember rightly. They shot about twenty seals, and caught a few fish with a hook made from a shoe buckle, using a line of seal skin. They supplemented this meat with a small daily ration of "civilized food", and by using seal oil as fuel they were able to survive.

'As for the hut itself, it originally had walls three feet thick built up with great slabs of rock that they collected and carried to the hut site on a hand-barrow. You really must go down there, Lee, and take a look at it. Of course, it's just a rough shell now and doesn't even look like an old hut, and the outer passage they built crumbled years ago. You won't find any roof timbers or slates either, because it had none. They erected their tent in the centre of the shelter and stretched a tarpaulin as a roof over the up-turned sledge which straddled the hut from wall to wall. The temperatures in that hut were often below zero Fahrenheit, and on the odd occasion when the temperature rose above freezing-point, showers of melting rime-frost falling from the ceiling turned the hut into a mire of sticky, semi-fluid dirt.

'Their stoves were made from preserves tins in which they put small lumps of blubber and a wick of rope; the chimney was made out of old tins which telescoped up through the tent and out through the walls of the hut, and that got rid of most of the smoke, except when the chimney was blocked with snow, but the soot in due course covered everything and worked its way so deeply into their skin and clothing that the only way they were able to wash it out was with urine – which they also used for washing their socks. Those were the romantic days of Antarctic exploration!'

A murmur of agreement passed from one man to another as someone threw a shovelful of anthracite on to the fire. Sparks rose crackling. Hugh kicked the doors of the stove shut to draw the flames amongst the new coals and an involuntary shiver passed around our company.

'How long did they live in that hut?' asked Lee.

'Six months wasn't it, Roger?'

'Yes. They spent the winter months making new pairs of mocassins from penguin and seal skins, and generally improvising items of gear that either they had never had or had long since worn out. On the whole, they came through the winter quite well, in spite of the hardships. Their wintering philosophy was interesting – probably the reason why they survived, come to think of it.

'They believed in the dignity of man, and respected each other as a duty. They shared all chores equally and put great store on simple courtesies: for instance – they would always end their breakfast or any other meal they might have during the day by saying "Thank you!" to which the cook would reply "Don't mention it!" Just picture them, Lee, three wild-looking men, blubber-stained and stinking, cramped in a squalid hovel: taking it in turns to entertain each other with anything that came into their heads, and sailor Grunden rendering a sea shanty through a matted beard.

'Anyway, they survived the winter and set off at the end of September 1903 on their second attempt to get to Snow Hill Island.

'They took the same route we always take on the way to View Point, but they were in poor shape. It took them seven days to cover the ten miles to the tide crack at what they called "The Bay of the Thousand Icebergs" which was later renamed Duse Bay. From there they headed out across the sea ice directly towards Vega Island, and by the time they reached it Grunden and Duse were frost-bitten and feeling pretty miserable, so Gunnar Andersson went up the hill to look for the depot of food they had left the previous January. By a stroke of luck he found it, turned his mittens inside-out and put a few titbits from the depot in them for his two companions then skied back to camp. He kept the secret for as long as he could, but finally held out his mittens to them and according to Gunnar Andersson: "their eyes began to light up with gladness, and the gravity of their wild, black visages, resolved itself into a happy smile."'

'Oh, come on, Roger!'

'It's true – read it for yourself. And you won't find any meetings in the history of Antarctic sledging more incredible than the meeting between two of the men from Snow Hill Island, with two of the party from Hope Bay.

'It happened on 12 October 1903, when the two men from Snow Hill Island were with a dog team on an exploratory journey which had taken them up the Prince Gustav Channel, and were rounding the northern end of Vega Island. Some distance from the coast, Jonassen thought he spotted a depot. But it was not until the object moved, and Jonassen had politely insisted that they should investigate, that Nordenskjöld got out his telescope and was astonished to see two men! He and Jonassen immediately turned the dogs and drove them towards the figures that were approaching on skis. They had never seen two more barbarous looking men in their lives, and Jonassen wanted Nordenskjöld to take out his revolver. But instead of being attacked by the two savage-looking men, one of them held out his filthy hand and said in the purest English "How do you do?"

to which Nordenskjöld, in the courteous manner of a Swedish gentleman, replied – "Thanks, how are you?"

'And in due course they introduced themselves. They went together to the shore where according to Nordenskjöld ". . . ere many moments had elapsed [they] were welcomed with unfeigned joy by the fifth man in the company thus unexpectedly brought together." Then the Southerners set up their camp alongside the Northerners' tent, near a cape they called "Well Met", and they talked, as we are doing, well into the night.'

'What a story!' cried Lee. A ripple of approval passed over the men. A foot reached out and flicked open the doors of the stove and the heat leapt out like a fierce animal. We threw ourselves into the backs of our chairs with shouts of alarm, and our shadows were pitched on to the walls and ceiling while the wind outside roared in fury and rattled the shell of our hut. In a wider circle we then sat and, shouting above the din of a hurricane, we made our plans for the winter journeys.

It soon became clear that Hugh, Roger, and Mike had set their minds on making the man-hauling circumnavigation of James Ross Island as part of Hugh's physiological research programme. So Lee and I decided to cross the Russell Glacier to the west coast of the peninsula where we would spend several weeks filling in some gaps in the map. Part of the route over the Russell Glacier was known to be heavily crevassed, so it seemed to me an ideal excuse to man-haul the sledges, for generally speaking this is a safer way of travelling across crevassed country. Lee was not quite as enthusiastic as I was, but he agreed to give the idea a try, and by the time we had made man-hauling harnesses and pruned all the weighty items of our standard sledging equipment we were already into August, so we decided to take a dog team as far as View Point, towing the man-haul sledge behind us, and go it alone from there.

On the day we set off the air sparkled with freshness. The sledge runners squeaked and the dogs loped over the hard-packed snow. We drove fast and smoothly towards the skyline of Last Hill, and as we sledged over the brow, an icescape of such splendour climbed into the sky that we were stopped in our tracks at the sight of it. We gasped and felt re-born into a new world.

We were standing on the exact spot from where Gunnar Andersson and his two companions Duse and Grunden had seen for the first time the 'sovereign dominion of ice'. Like them we stood silently gazing at a panorama of unbelievable grandeur. It stretched out before us in a vista of purple fields and pools of gleaming light. Fires of sapphire and emerald burned in the basements of castle bergs that dominated a plain scattered with the crystal villages of a petrified sea desert. Is it any wonder that those three intrepid explorers had gazed in rapture at the panorama that unrolled as they reached Last Hill?

In the perfect clarity of the atmosphere, we could easily see all the details of Cape Well Met, and the sea ice, for the first time in many years, was frozen so far out from the coast that, had we wanted to, we could have followed Gunnar Andersson's route directly to the spot where he had met Nordenskjöld. But we had our own rough trails to blaze, and no time to lose.

CHAPTER SEVEN

Self-imposed cruelty

I was impatient to climb into my smart new harness and to struggle across rough country. I wanted to feel my body aching while my mind ordered, 'This is your heritage. You must not give in and lower the standards set by Scott and Shackleton who blazed a trail for you across the white wilderness.' Who but a young man full of dreams would have had the temerity to assume that he was following in the footsteps of the great polar heroes; and that the blizzards beating his back like a whiplash were really prestige with a cheer in each sting? I will always be grateful to Lee for delaying my discovery that man-hauling is a self-imposed cruelty; that blizzards and snow-blindness and frost-bitten feet are miseries only masochists can enjoy; and that licking the wounds is a blissful delight compared with receiving them during the fight.

What a sensible fellow he was for insisting that we could accept without loss of dignity the offer of our two friends at View Point of a lift for the first thirteen miles with a dog team. So once more we set out from View Point leaving behind us mile after mile of silver tracks twisting out of sight, while ahead the soft drumming of nine dogs' pads beat the rhythm of running on hard-packed snow. Our bodies tingled with energy as we strode four paces and jog-trotted ten, and strode four paces more – on and on – into the plumes of breath that streamed from the dogs.

Thirteen miles south of View Point, as arranged, our two companions and their nine dogs cast us adrift and set off for home. It was one of those perfect moments: a crisp, cloudless day, with ten thousand diamonds sparkling on the surface in the full flood of sunlight. We got into our harnesses and lunged into motion, with deep draughts of pure air converted into energy, while our shadows slid over the smooth surface ahead like two giant bird-men. The anoraks rustled, the sledge rattled, and the tips of the ski sticks squeaked in the snow. We could scarcely feel the weight of the sledge, just an occasional press from the harness; and with no dogs ahead to curse or encourage, it was as strange a sensation as I have ever had – to feel such freedom of movement and mind. Neither of us spoke for a while, we just walked, and wondered if it could really be true that man-hauling was so enjoyable.

But fate soon led us into a belt of consolidated pack ice. We climbed an iceberg to look for a route. As far as the eye could see the channel was choked with hummock ice and angular brash. Great icebergs rose higher than the rest like dazzling cathedrals in a brilliant metropolis, with here and there a frozen pool, a plaza and many narrow streets. But size and distance are deceptive in the South: the streets we guessed would be bridle-paths, and the plaza only a frozen puddle; so we sat on our bottoms and slid off the berg and walked back to our sledge very depressed. We climbed into our harnesses and hauled and stumbled over the ice towards a small island.

The shifting shades of evening were moving over the icescape as we drove ourselves the last few yards towards a frozen pool; but all the misery and toil of the last few miles slipped away like a wraith from warm sunlight when we finally stopped and leaned on our ski sticks: for around us, the bergs and brash that a moment before had been the source of all our troubles, suddenly delighted us as they caught the last rays of the setting sun and turned pink while the rest shaded deeper to mauve. It all seemed so peaceful with the toil behind us, and tomorrow was too far away to be real. There were no dogs to feed, no pickets to hammer; no sound but our breathing and sighs of contentment.

We unlashed the sledge and pitched our tent, which went up just in time to catch a weak glow on the apex. Our pyramid seemed huge without the inner tent which we had left at base to cut down the weight; and the floor space looked naked without the thick sheep-skins, which we thought were too heavy and not really necessary. How rash, how naïve we were! So to cheer ourselves up we pounded the pump of the primus until it roared with such fury that it made us feel nervous, and reluctantly we let loose some of its pressure which hissed like a wild cat as we sat and shivered.

With only one lining of sun-bleached yellow material, the tent was suffused by a glow from the sky and we could see quite well without lighting a candle; but we lit one by way of celebration, for it was the birth of a sledging relationship which proved prone to many a minor disaster, to nagging discomforts, to days without food or weeks on short rations, and hour upon hour of supine prostration while hoar frost crept up the walls to the apex and hung like moss of a gossamer texture – threatening a cascade of glistening crystals if we so much as moved a muscle. Outside the temperature was minus 20° F, and the primus, which roared its heat up in a vortex, left the floor of our tent some degrees below freezing. We doubled the sleeping-bags under our bodies and rubbed our cold feet with hands warmed by the primus. With steam clouding around us we scoffed our stew, drank cocoa and chatted a minute or two; then we climbed into our bags and were asleep before the tent temperature fell and froze our breath – our snores of rime frost crusting on the down-filled sacks in which we lay shivering.

On one wall of the tent the following morning the shadows of ski sticks and man-hauling harnesses were cast like a mural symbolic of torture; but the tent was filled with the aroma of porridge, and through the thick pall of steam from the pot I could just make out Lee sitting like a big yogi, with spoon poised. We decided to have an easy day and to get fit comfortably. We were not in a hurry, and it was a glorious morning, so I lit my pipe and went for a walk. From the top of the nearest iceberg the going looked tortuous and this we confirmed when we started our haul. But some three miles on we began to feel sick with the uneven motion of the harness against our stomachs, so we stopped for a break and, before getting cold, made a reconnaissance. The nearest berg was a slippery one but from the top a heartening sight met our eyes: a smooth highway stretched away into the distance in precisely the direction we wanted to go. That long scar in the pack ice was probably the work of the very berg on which we were standing. It had probably drifted with the currents and, like an icebreaker, had left behind it a clear channel of water just before the sea had finally frozen over.

The temperature stayed steadily at minus 10° F, but the sun beat down on our backs and by 3.30 in the afternoon we had covered nine miles and reached the northern tip of James Ross Island. On top of the cape we hoped to set up our first survey station; so we pitched our tent on the sea ice at its foot and set off on our climb. But a strong wind on the summit made it impossible to use the theodolite, and the glare off the sea ice gave us no chance of picking out a route across the channel. So we returned to the tent and settled in for another cold night. Three times next day we climbed that hill and were blown off each time by a biting cold wind.

We set off across the Prince Gustav Channel, from the northern tip of James Ross Island towards the mainland, on the morning of the fourth day of our journey. There was something profoundly satisfying about the hard manual labour we were doing. I do not deny it was self-punishing, and our objectives were never reached; but until we were finally stopped by impassable ice, we held firmly to the belief that we were on our way to make a map, and that being a useful aim, we felt justified in suffering.

The next day we found ourselves in such a maze of icebergs that we dragged the sledge into the same cul-de-sac time and again. We climbed every iceberg hoping that from the top we should see a route, hidden from below by the scatter of splintered bergs which lay about in a confusion as awesome and stark as the debris of a blitz purified and turned to ice. But on the summits of those icebergs we would bathe for a while in the warmth of the sun, and the chaos of the ice-scape around us would melt into a wonderland of ice form and subtle shade.

On that particular journey the tent was always so cold that we preferred to do most of our chatting during the day-time when we were warm with exercise. But hauling through severely hummocked ice made it difficult to hold uninterrupted conversations. Even the shortest sentence was punctuated with heaves and grunts, stumbles and curses, while Lee puffed to me about oratory, spicing his views with anecdotes from his school-teaching experience. But mostly we talked about food and drink. Repetition did not matter – our conversations were mostly the vocal rumbles of the stomach. As we became weary, our conversations would narrow and settle on a steaming mug of coffee or a pint of beer, but by the time we finally camped, we were nearly always in agreement that the most wonderful drink in the world was a mug of thick cocoa with a knob of butter floating about on top.

The evening we met the impasse we also met a minor disaster. Our primus stove, which up to that time had performed very well, suddenly started to give trouble. The symptoms of its illness seemed to be the nipple, which was choked with grime and could not be cleared by the regular treatment; so we decided to perform the operation of taking the nipple right out and replacing it with a new one. This needs infinite patience and warm fingers. On that particular evening we had neither, as the trouble had occurred just when we most needed our cocoa and the heat of the primus to thaw out our bodies. We managed to get the nipple out quickly and cleanly, but when I put in the new one I stripped the thread in the burner. However, we felt smug, for we had taken the precaution of bringing a spare just in case of such an emergency. But to our disgust, it was the wrong size, and no amount of persuasion would make it screw into the body of the primus. The situation suddenly took on a serious aspect, for we had hauled our sledge six days' march from View Point, and without hot food and drink it seemed most unlikely that we would get back without discomfort.

The old burner was replaced but it was impossible to build up any pressure with a nipple that wobbled in the burner like a milk tooth in a young head, so we jammed it in with a piece of handkerchief. The handkerchief gradually charred and disintegrated, and after about three minutes it was blasted out of the burner, ricocheted with a ping off the bottom of the water pot, and the tent was filled with flames and choking smoke until the primus pressure was released. This process we repeated about ten times for half a cup of water each, but at the rate we were using the handkerchief, we estimated only three more half cups of water were left. When I had been with Hugh we had experimented with soup made from warm seal blood mixed with milk powder – which in food value was very rich, although the taste took some acquiring; and Lee and I seriously considered this as a sustenant beverage before realizing the difficulties of drawing a pint of blood off a seal without actually killing it. Dehydration is a problem in the polar regions. Unlike a hot desert, the cold deserts are for the most part covered with what is potentially water; all the polar traveller needs to quench his thirst is some form of heat over which he can melt a pot of snow; but without that heat his environment is waterless. He can pop a lump of snow in his mouth and melt it, but he will get very little water that way, far from enough to quench a raging thirst, and if he takes too much snow he will lower his body temperature and so weaken his resistance to the cold.

We nibbled the raw meat bar, which was an excellent replacement for pemmican – the traditional staple of the sledging diet up to that time – and then turned in for the night. The tent felt like a morgue as we climbed into our sleeping-bags, so I curled up in a ball to break the poignant resemblance between our stretched-out forms and the stiff forms on the slabs, and reluctantly shared my bag with my mukluks. I held close to my middle a mug full of snow which I hoped by the morning would have melted to water with the heat from my body, but it had spilt soon after I had fallen asleep, and by morning was squashed into pancakes of sludge.

We had a few biscuits for breakfast and pulled fifteen miles before crying for rest. But apart from our thirst there was no discomfort and we felt wonderfully warm while we were pulling. On a good camp site we set up our tent that evening and pushed into our sleeping-bags which were frozen quite solid. They resembled two green headless mummies and we crawled in after them and sat on their stomachs. Flames and fumes filled the tent and licked around the apex, and with every flare-up of the primus the soot rained down on us like a plague of locusts. It was nearly four hours before we succeeded in melting enough snow for a few gulps of sooty water; then we ate chocolate, biscuits, and great knobs of butter that were frozen so hard we could suck them like sweets. We had some raw porridge oats and nibbled a meat bar, then we shared out the sugar lumps one by one.

For the next two days a blizzard raged. The wind tore at the tent and shook off the hoar frost which fell lightly down like snow from the apex, while we lay with our faces turned upwards and talked to each other in plumes of vapour which shifted in jerks as they rose above us. There were no air currents in the tent to disperse them, for the pocket of air as a whole vacillated. The back wall of the tent held the wind like a sail, and the side walls were sucked in and out by the air flow which spilled out of the spinnaker face of the tent and was whipped down the sides in the full force of the wind. In the lea of the tent there built up a huge drift, chiselled by the turbulence and polished by wind. But the constant hiss of drifting snow became a soothing sound after a while.

We dreamed about sumptuous feasts with tables burdened with dishes; all of them, regardless of their appearance or ingredients, surmounted by butter and swilled down with cocoa. Our bags were sodden inside with condensation, but we only felt wet and cold when we moved; so we lay quite still. The hoar frost fell, and slowly our grimy soot-stained bags were covered by a fine sheet of pure white crystals.

It was actually pleasant in a strange kind of way, and, being a smoker, I felt the hunger less than Lee who was ravenous most of the time. But we kept persevering with the primus and managed to wet our parched throats with a dribble of water twice each day.

We dared not attempt to man-haul into the blizzard, dehydrated, hungry, and weak with fatigue, for flesh freezes in only one minute if the temperature is minus 22° F with the wind blowing steadily at twenty knots. Only our faces would have been exposed, but our bodies would soon have been chilled to the core, and the energy they converted into heat would have been disturbed and drawn off by the wind. We might have made two miles before having to camp. Even talking about our chances of surviving was wasting precious warmth which we should have been breathing into our bags; but the sound of our chatter was comforting.

The wind died away during the third night at that camp site and by the following morning it was calm and clear. But we both felt very dizzy as we dug out the tent and loaded the sledge. Even on a perfect surface we had to take frequent rests and our loads were lighter than they had ever been. Had we been fit it would have been the nicest day of the whole journey, but it developed into the most gruelling and desperate struggle to reach View Point, for, as the day drew on the weather deteriorated, and Lee's knee started giving trouble – he had dislocated it many years earlier while playing rugger. The thought of it jumping out again appalled me – so much so that I suggested putting up the tent for him, while I skied on alone to View Point where I could pick up a dog team. But he would not hear of my making a hero of myself on his behalf, so we struggled painfully on together.

It was dark long before we reached the Point and we were sledging way out to sea when we spotted a light from the Argentinians' refuge hut shining as a pin-prick from the coast. We adjusted our course by it, but as we reached the headland the blizzard started once more and visibility was cut down to only a few yards. Twenty miles we had hauled in just over eight hours: a nice climax, we thought, to an absurdly abortive attempt to sledge over the Russell Glacier to the west coast of the peninsula. But what luxury we wallowed in during our three days of recuperation. View Point had never seemed so warm, its walls never so friendly!

CHAPTER EIGHT

Vaguely like bodies

There was no hope of getting through the hummocked ice in the channel that had so recently turned us back, nor did we wish to man-haul again. We turned our thoughts, therefore, away from the west coast of the peninsula and planned a fast trip with a dog team down the eastern side of James Ross Island, to carry out observations of magnetic declination and refraction, and to investigate all possible routes on to the island. We also intended to visit the old winter quarters of Nordenskjöld's expedition, to see if his hut was in reasonable condition to justify stocking it out as a refuge.

Hugh Simpson was about to start out on his three-hundred-mile journey to circumnavigate James Ross Island as part of his physiological studies. The plateau depot-laying journey had given him valuable research data on men under mental stress, so he intended to man-haul all the way around James Ross Island in what is generally considered the best time of the year for weather, in the hope that he and his two companions, Roger and Mike, would suffer a severe but largely physical stress. The physiological data resulting from this would make an interesting comparison with his previous journey – or so he hoped. We knew when he was due to set out from Hope Bay, but could not get through by radio to tell him we had failed our man-hauling test and had changed our plans completely; so only the two occupants of View Point knew what we had suddenly decided to do.

Through the big binoculars we spotted the man-hauling party coming down Last Hill on the afternoon of 22 August and we set off the next day expecting to overtake them. We needed a copy of their route-map to save us a special journey back to base; but we were unable to pick up their spoor and decided to find our way to Nordenskjöld's hut by guesswork. Travelling without maps had its problems, but the delights of rounding a headland and not knowing exactly what to expect was almost as exciting as having the priority of discovery, and after the strains of man-hauling, dog-sledging seemed a blissful relaxation. On the very first day out from View Point we covered thirty-two miles with the greatest of ease, and we pitched our tent at the northern end of the Sound which lies between James Ross and Vega Island.

We were in an area which by repute has a heavy precipitation, but we camped on a surface of hard polished snow, which in places was practically ice. In that same area in 1945 a sledging party led by Major Andrew Taylor had ploughed knee-deep in snow and had to kill dogs to feed dogs as they struggled on their way back to Hope Bay after circumnavigating James Ross Island. We still had only one lining to the tent, and were without sheepskin mattresses; but our dogs were well fed and surprisingly peaceful, and the roar of the new primus was a comforting sound which filled us with snugness and loosened our tongues. We told stories for hours, and ate until we were obliged to lie down; well-being is a cosy blessing and we slept soundly until the following morning.

The day and the surface were really quite perfect – and riding my skis for the first time down south I covered sixteen miles with the greatest of ease, and wondered why I had only just discovered that it was easier to ski than to jog by the sledge. Lee was in his element. As we cruised into Croft Bay, he found a resemblance between sledging and sailing in the pace at which we moved past the coast landmarks, and the tendency of huskies to 'tack' their way forward; for running on a bearing they find very boring, and at the slightest excuse they will stagger off to one side to urinate on an ice knobble protruding through a pure surface of snow. Lee was a yachtsman with a trans-Atlantic crossing to his credit, but his 'flying fifteen' gave him greatest pleasure, and it was the pace of this craft he compared with dog-sledging.

As we closed on the land he wondered aloud what the place would look like covered with autumn-tinted heather and scattered forest glades; with rippling streams cutting into the hillside and the whole scene mirrored in the still water of Croft Bay. Certain parts of the Antarctic may have looked like that ages ago in geologic time, although more probably James Ross Island perspired under a luxuriant growth of sub-tropical plants. Fossil flora is proof enough to a scientific mind, and more than sixty different species of Jurassic plants have been identified from collections made at Hope Bay, where great plates of leaf prints lie about like stone weeds.

One hundred and fifty million years ago you would have seen the landscape choked with life: now you drive a dog team over frozen sea, past majestic rock ramparts. The downs, once wooded, are now capped with ice, and a shroud of cold air refrigerates the isolated heart of what once was Gondwanaland – the gigantic southern hemisphere continent which fitted like a jigsaw into South America, Africa, Australia, and India, all squeezing a warm-hearted Antarctica. But by the middle Mesozoic era their drift had started, and continental-sized rafts moved off to straddle warmer latitudes. Antarctica was left well stocked with flora – but of fauna it had none. A million years ago on other continents, a creature evolved and jumped down from his tree on to the plains in sub-human form, where he learned how to make fire and chop wood with a flint. While they grunted and battled for life, ill-equipped with intelligence or tools, the polar regions were gripped in the Pleistocene ice age; and it was not until the last warm interval some fifty-thousand years ago that man discovered that he could articulate and convert a cave into a dwelling place. But even in pre-history, man was man's greatest enemy, and at the end of the ice age the superior cultures invaded the sub-humans: and only five thousand years after Palaeolithic man had vanished from Europe Dr J. Gunnar Andersson at Hope Bay had grunted approval over plates of fossils of 'immense importance' – by which he concluded that Antarctica was green in the Jurassic era!

That evening, after bedding down the dogs and pitching our tents, we climbed the peninsula that protrudes towards the Naze and got our first glimpse of the Weddell Sea. As far as the horizon and no doubt many hundreds of miles beyond, the desolate vista of hummocked pack ice was unbroken by leads or even small pools of open water. We could imagine sledging from there directly across the Weddell Sea to visit Dr Fuchs and his party at Shackleton Base on the Filchner Ice Shelf; but to the south the weather looked foreboding – heavy and grey and very gloomy as it lay in the shadow of a thick bank of cloud. We rounded the Naze early next morning and started down the east coast of James Ross Island. The snow lay deep and soft, just as it had in 1903 when Nordenskjöld, Jonassen, and the

1. Blade Ridge and Mount Taylor, Hope Bay

2. Hope Bay

3a. Seal—'Come on in, it's lovely!'

3b. Penguins—at sixes and sevens on the pack ice

4. Antarctic explorer—a drawing by Wally Herbert

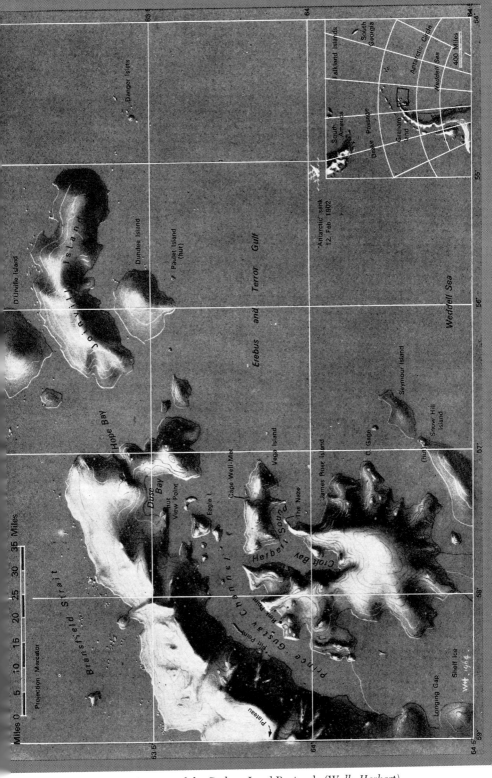

5. The northern tip of the Graham Land Peninsula (*Wally Herbert*)

South Shetland Islands

Hope Bay

Weddell Sea

James Ross Island

Snow Hill I.

Cape Longing

Sobral Peninsula

Larsen Shelf Ice

Bransfield Strait

The Catwalk

D r y s a l s k i   G!

The Waist

Trinity I.

Cape Sterneck

Hughes Bay

Cape Murray

Reclus Peninsula

Refuge Hut

C h a r l o t t e   B a y

'The Cwm'

The Traverse

The Big Drop

'Rendezvous Camp'

'The Cairn'

Two Hummock I.

ege I.

G e r l a c h e   S t r a i t

Nansen I.

Brabant I.

(a) Ron Worswick

(b) Lee Rice

7. THE BASE LEADERS

(c) Dick Foster

6. Perspective view of the
Graham Land Peninsula
north of latitude 64°50°S
(Wally Herbert)

8a. *Left:* Dr Hugh Simpson

8b. *Right:* Dennis Kershaw

8c. *Left:* Hosts
and guests at the
Reclus hut

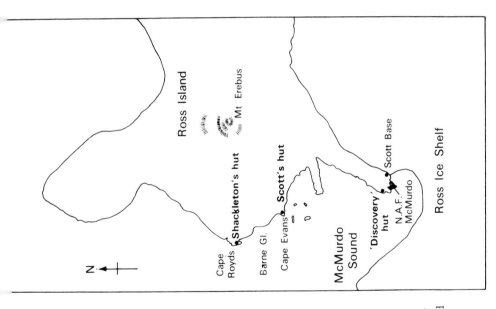

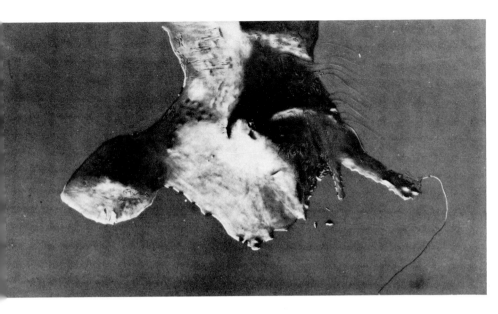

9. An aerial view of
the McMurdo Sound
and Scott Base area

10. A cup of boiling water exploding into ice at an air temperature of −80°F

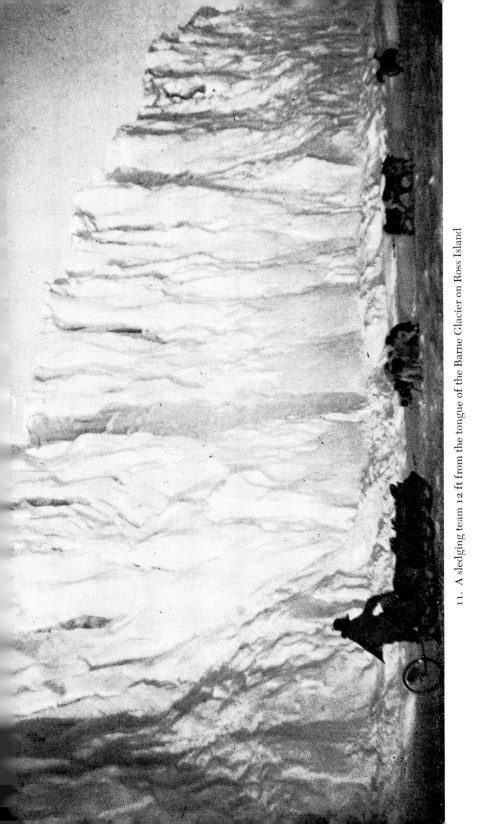

11. A sledging team 12 ft from the tongue of the Barne Glacier on Ross Island

12b. Shackleton's hut at Cape Royds

13. Captain Roald Amundsen

14. Camp near the
Polar Plateau

15. On the Axel Heiberg glacier during Wally Herbert's expedition on which he retraced, in reverse, Amundsen's route to the Pole

16a and b. Part of the Queen Maud Range and Axel Heiberg Glacier region

three 'wild men' they had met from Hope Bay, struggled through it on their way to Snow Hill Island.

Everything sank lower and lower, and ere long it grew heavy going on skis, even unburdened as we were. I had never seen the like in these regions. The sledge was turned into a snow plough; the dogs sank past their bellies and our party moved on at a snail's pace. . . . But since the increase of our party everybody worked with a light heart; we laugh at difficulties and joke at troubles, no one wishing to seem more fainthearted than the others.*

After about three miles of heaving and pushing, when our voices were becoming hoarse with shouting, we suddenly ran on to the track of a seal, a big fat one judging by his trail, and for the next two miles we raced along like a bob-sleigh in a compact course made by the seal's thumping great body. It was just wide enough for the spread of our sledge, and our dogs galloped along it with their noses to the spoor and their tails bobbing like plumes on a helmet. For two miles our seal's track lay in the right direction, and we began to wonder if he too was going to visit Nordenskjöld's hut; but then, for no apparent reason, he must have decided to go out to sea, for he turned a sharp right-angle which took us completely by surprise. I was smoking and looking around, enjoying the scenery and the wind of fast movement, while Lee was dreaming of facing his yacht before a stiff breeze, and he planed the slim craft until we were both jettisoned ungracefully. Our riderless team, still in the seal's tracks, galloped eastward towards the Weddell horizon. Our hearts pounded like muffled drums, and our lungs rasped hot with gasping breath as we chased and eventually caught the sledge. We gave ourselves a generous rest, then I set off ahead on skis, breaking a trail through the deep snow, and we made slow steady progress for a mile or two.

We ran into brash ice after two hours and the dogs found fresh interest (for with me they were bored), so I returned to the sledge and Lee drove by command until we found ourselves once again on the track of a seal. Whether it was the same one gave us a topic of lively discussion, but as the brash ice grew bigger our field of view was restricted, and it seemed more than likely that at any moment we

* Nordenskjöld, N.O.G. and Andersson, J. G., *Antarctica* (1905), p. 312, Kurst and Blackett, London.

would run right into the creature. We pitched camp and walked ahead for a while, but the tracks ended in a big black hole.

At seven-thirty the next morning the infectious sound of dogs stretching and yawning and talking softly to the rising sun worked slowly into our subconscious minds – then we too stretched, rolled on to our backs and murmured 'it's going to be a glorious day'. We had a lazy breakfast, a siesta and an easy start. We were going to visit Nordenskjöld, but there was no need to hurry; he was there in spirit only and was not expecting us.

Sledging was enchanting that morning. The snow was hard-packed and had a fine squeak in it. Polished ice knobbles protruded and tilted the creaking sledge, straining and rattling its boxes. Dogs panting and the patter of pads, and Lee's lilting calls of encouragement, were sounds softened by the sunshine. Through mocassined feet I felt a part of the ice, yet strangely detached, running in a cocoon of warmth held captive beneath an anorak, rustling and billowing. On my beard stuck frozen breath – on my scalp the itch of sweat; away in the distance the whale-back dome of Snow Hill Island, and somewhere there along the coast, Nordenskjöld's spirit resided.

We ran clear of the brash on to smooth flat ice and I joined Lee at the back of the sledge. For a few hours there was only the soothing hiss of the sledge runners gliding over a perfect surface as we closed on the shore of Snow Hill Island. But a string of bergs obscured our

Nordenskjöld's hut at Snow Hill Island as it appeared in 1957

view – white castles in a row. We drew close and weaved our way between them, up and down the pressure ridges. Suddenly they seemed to part – and directly ahead lay Nordenskjöld's hut.

Old huts have an atmosphere about them which extends as far as the eye can see. From the moment we spotted that old hut we were embarrassed to find ourselves talking in whispers. We said loud words to regain our dignity and profaned an intangible purity. We half expected old men to come out dressed in blubbery garments and big shaggy beards, and the leader to say: 'Come in young fellow, but mind you're polite. I'm Otto Nordenskjöld. What will you drink?'

We pegged out our dog team and pitched our tent, not wishing to impose on their hospitality; then we climbed the moraine to pay our respects and could feel them all round us but saw no one there. The windows were barred up and the door was jammed solid, but on the north side of the building the window shutters were broken. We peeped in, glanced over our shoulders, then shinned over the window sill into the hut. Two feet of ice engulfed the hut like a rising flood, so that only the tops of the chairs stood above the slippery surface. On top of that lay piles of snow which had blown in fine streams through the cracks in the boarding, but it was fluffy and easily shifted, and we shovelled it out of the broken-down window. The place smelt musty and up in the loft we found boxes of chemicals, stuffed penguins and skuas, and old rags and nick-nacks all covered with grime; while downstairs on the bunks lay blankets in untidy heaps, looking vaguely like bodies. Perhaps Nordenskjöld had left in such a hurry he had not had time to waken everybody! We knew that to be untrue, of course, for he had taken a last stroll through the rooms before carefully barring the door and walking down to the shore.

His last two days at Snow Hill Island were so full of wonders that even the musty smell of his old hut still seemed to be charged with excitement. I could almost sense the rush of air as the men ran out of the hut on 8 November 1903 to see who it was that walked towards them across the ice; and their feverish haste was mixed with sorrow as they busied themselves with the packing of their precious records and instruments, ready for shipping out to the relief ship *Uruguay*. The ship was in command of Captain Julian Irizar and the entire relief expedition had been commissioned and equipped by the Argentine Government. With her arrival it had become clear to

Nordenskjöld's party that the *Antarctic* and perhaps her entire crew had been lost: but even while Nordenskjöld was writing a note to leave at Snow Hill for the commander of the Swedish relief expedition, which was expected to carry out a search for the missing *Antarctic*, the dogs started howling as they always do at the arrival of strangers; and out on the ice Captain Larsen and five of his companions were seen approaching.

With the exception of one man who had died during the winter on Paulet Island, Larsen's party had survived their ordeal well, and on 31 October he and five companions had set off on a perilous journey through pack ice in an open boat to Hope Bay, where they had found Gunnar Andersson's winter hut and the note he had left; they had then rowed all but the last few miles to Snow Hill Island. Nordenskjöld says of that day and the meeting: 'No pen can describe the boundless joy of this first moment. It was plain that both misfortune and suffering were hidden in the period, so long concealed in the mists of uncertainty, that lay between this hour and the departure of the *Antarctic* from Hope Bay. I learned at once that our dear old ship was no more in existence, but for the instant I could feel nothing but joy when I saw amongst us these men, on whom I had only a few minutes before been thinking with feelings of the greatest despondency, and when I recollected that now we could all leave these tracts in company.'* As I stood towering above the top ten inches of the plain wooden chairs which protruded above the level of ice in the living-room, it was easy to visualize the feast of food and stories they must have had that night.

Early on the morning of 10 November 1903, they all climbed into the ship's long-boat and were rowed out to the *Uruguay*, whose officers and crew lined the deck and gave Nordenskjöld and his party a thundering cheer as they went aboard; then after sailing to neighbouring Seymour Island to collect the geological specimens they had left there, they set sail for Paulet Island to rescue the remainder of Larsen's party.

I know well the feeling Nordenskjöld must have had as he sailed away from his old Antarctic base; they are the sentiments of most men who have wintered in the 'South', and although each man expresses them differently, in their hearts they all feel the same. 'But

* Nordenskjöld and Andersson, op. cit., 1905, pp. 510–11.

in the joy we feel in the certainty of now being on our way home, and in the knowledge that we are henceforth free from the cares which have so long burdened our minds, there mingles not a little melancholy. A phase of our lives has ended, never more to return. How many memories are there not attached to every rock the eye falls upon! Never, never can I forget these two naked sandstone islands which have been our home for two long years!'*

Lee and I stayed one full day at Snow Hill Island doing our observations, and it was about lunch-time on that day, when both of us were about a mile down the coast, that we heard voices. But we needed binoculars before we could make out Hugh and his two companions man-hauling towards the hut. We took a bearing on them with the theodolite – which was set up at the end of a measured base-line from which we had been making our observations – then Lee set off back to the tent to put on a brew for the new arrivals; and from the bearing he took on their line of march towards the hut we later calculated that they had been just over three miles away when we had first heard their voices. This distance was confirmed by the time it took them to reach the hut. The clarity of a polar atmosphere surprises few people, but the distance that sound travels on a perfectly calm day never fails to amaze even veteran explorers.

Three days later, on our return journey up the east coast of James Ross Island, we had occasion to test these calm day accoustics again; Lee stayed at the camp site with the theodolite – the position of which we had fixed – while I skied off to an isolated rock to make a check on a magnetic bearing. The distance of this rock from our camp site was almost exactly three miles, and on reaching it I shouted at the top of my voice. Lee heard the shout quite clearly, although I could hear no reply, which he gave much to the alarm of the dogs who were all sleeping. There are of course some sounds which travel much farther than others, and on one occasion three of us at View Point were watching through the big binoculars a dog team descending Last Hill. When they got on to the sea ice eight miles away we distinctly heard dogs howling. We checked up on this with the drivers later when they arrived at View Point, who confirmed that their dogs had howled just before they had set off across the bay!

The Antarctic offers many strange experiences to the traveller and

* Nordenskjöld and Andersson, op. cit., 1905, pp. 516–17.

the stay-at-home alike, but there are few trials of humour more dis-
concerting than walking round in circles in a blizzard, or walking
straight into an iceberg in a white-out. When Lee and I got back to
View Point after our delightful and profitable journey to Snow Hill
Island we decided, against our better judgement, to leave the dog
team with our comrades where they would be well looked after,
frequently exercised, and well fed on seal meat (of which there was a
scarcity at base). Meanwhile, we would for the last time put on the
man-hauling harnesses and make the journey back to base the hard
way. Within an hour of setting off the visibility had decreased to fifty
yards and then it started to blow. We had no compass and even while
we were making up our minds what to do, the visibility closed in to
less than ten feet; so thinking that the blizzard might last for a week
and knowing that we only had two days' food with us, we swung
around and set off back in the general direction of View Point. We
estimated that we were about three miles from the hut at the time of
turning back, and after two hours terrible hauling through the most
turbulent blizzard we had ever experienced, we decided to camp and
wait for a slight clearance before continuing the struggle. What
puzzled us most was the way the wind kept changing direction – for
there was no question in our minds about the course we had been
keeping; and we sat miserably in our tent all day cursing the impatience that had driven us out on our journey and in such a hurry
that we had forgotten the sugar and cocoa!

By seven o'clock that evening the blizzard had weakened to an
occasional violent gust, and we untied the sleeve entrance and peeped
out to find that the visibility in the lulls was about three miles, and
the View Point headland was just visible in the opposite direction to
our course at the time of pitching camp. For the next three days we
lay about on the bunks in the View Point hut while the weather
worked off its wild mood, and between huge feeds discussed our
most recent and most abortive journey. By carefully comparing
notes on how many times the wind had appeared to change and in
which direction it had swung, we concluded that we had made no
less than four circles, and yet even had we realized that the wind was
blowing from a constant direction, setting a course by it would have
given us an almost physical ache that we were going the wrong way.

That blizzard was the first of the spring equinoctial storms, and wiser men than we would have taken ten days' food for a man-hauling journey of eighteen miles back to base, but with the offer of a tow across the bay with dogs to give us a good start, and with the prospect of only ten miles of man-hauling before us, we again set off with two days' rations – but this time carefully made up and checked. We were cast adrift from the dog team at the tide crack on the opposite side of the bay on the morning of 9 September. Ahead of us by half a mile, man-hauling up Last Hill and into the cloud, we could see Hugh and his party, who were also on the final leg of their journey back to base, and decided to try and catch them up as they had a compass and a set of bearings, and we of course had not.

The party ahead were soon lost in cloud, and drifting snow almost obliterated their tracks, so we decided to pull straight up the hill in the hope that we would catch them up by luck – which we almost did for, as we neared the summit, the visibility lifted for an instant, and we could just make them out not more than a hundred yards ahead. But a blizzard started. We got off course, slipped down a steep hill, pulled away from the bottom of it and camped – completely lost.

We took great precautions with the tent that night and pitched it very securely with an enormous amount of snow piled on the valance to weigh it down in case of violent gusts; then, feeling very cold, and rather miserable at not getting back to base, we crawled into the tent and sorted out the pots and pans. Everything seemed to be in order – nothing was missing; but to give ourselves a good start to the evening, we filled up the primus (which was half full of paraffin), primed it with methylated spirits – of which we had very little – and lit it. At the appropriate moment the primus was pumped hard, but absolutely nothing happened; so we pricked it and tried again without success. We substituted practically every part of the primus with spares – which we had carried in great quantity since our first man-hauling journey! – but it was impossible to raise even a yellow flame from it. At long last we suspected the only thing we had not tested – the fuel we had picked up at View Point. It was diesel oil.

For the next four days the temperature in the tent did not rise above zero degrees Fahrenheit, and the wind screamed continually at a constant pitch. For four days we lay weakening, and the only water we had was on the first night when a little snow was melted down with the remainder of the methylated spirits. Our two days' ration of food was easily enough under the circumstances, for most items were so dry that they could not be eaten without creating a raging thirst.

We lay for hours numbed with the cold, in a flapping tomb with hoar frost spreading up the walls like a white fungus. It would grow into a million fleecy beards, growing while we lay watching without really seeing or caring. Day and night were fused together by the incessant hiss of drifting snow. Raw coldness crept through the sleeping-bags and lay on our flesh with the touch of dead fish. Shivering convulsed our stiff bodies, until sleep seduced us, smothering our minds and sapping our resistance to the cold. But sleep could not hold us long. It would pale into shuddering wakefulness, and without turning our heads we would pass muffled words to each other, while the word-vapour drifted up to the apex and moved in slow swirls amongst the trembling beards of frost. Every few minutes a fleecy patch would peel off, burst in a cascade of delicate crystals and float towards us as we grimaced and shut our eyes. The crystals felt like spiders' webs on our faces and we would instinctively splutter to rid ourselves of them; but they would melt and trickle down our cheeks. We dreamed only of drink and warmth and food. We lost the will to move.

Late on the fourth day of the blizzard the wind eased, and through a hole we made in the tent wall a faint outline of the nunatak at the top of Last Hill was occasionally visible. At that nunatak we knew there was a well-stocked emergency depot and it seemed to be only two hundred yards away. We had to make an attempt to reach it in case the blizzard grew stronger. We were too weak to break camp and haul our sledge nearer the depot, which would have been the sensible thing for a fit party to do. Cold, starvation, and weakness make the simplest task one of abject misery.

All our clothes had been kept inside the sleeping-bags but even there they had frozen, and most of the garments were so old and tattered that the wind bit through them as soon as we got outside the tent. We loaded the sledge with light items of gear with which we could mark the route, then I hauled it until I collapsed – a mere forty yards from the tent, which was already lost in the swirling snow. Lee had stuck two markers in up to that time and when my dizziness had worn off he took over the hauling while I stumbled along behind until all the markers had been used up. We abandoned the sledge and went on together, climbing the hill we had come down four days before, and plodded along the escarpment towards the summit where vague rocky shapes loomed out of the blizzard. There were many small crevasses along that escarpment, and I managed to fall into one of them, but eventually we found the depot.

In a wind which tore at our clothing and drove snow like grains of sand hard at us, we re-filled our two-gallon can and staggered under the weight of a new food box back along our tracks, which were almost covered. The markers were hard to find, and on a couple of occasions Lee had to go ahead to the point where I almost lost sight of him before he could see the next stick. Inside the tent, with the last reserves of our energy, we got the primus going at full blast, and dragged off our mukluks. Our socks were frozen solid and our feet had lost their feeling; but slowly we were warmed back to life, and the temperature inside the tent rose to 38° F – higher than it had been during the whole month we had been away from base. We had a steaming mug of cocoa each with knobs of yellow butter, then we lay on our sleeping-bags and fell asleep. We did not wake up until the primus had lost some of its pressure and the tent temperature had fallen twenty degrees.

We still felt very weak the next morning, but the blizzard had eased and the visibility had increased to about three miles. We could just make out the next landmark and broke camp as quickly as possible, in case the cloud came down again; but as we moved forward the cloud closed in on us, so that by the time we had hauled two miles we could see no farther than a few feet. It was a most gruelling haul, and with our heads tucked well into the hoods of the anoraks to find shelter from the wind, we kept bumping into each other, for all we could see as we staggered forward was the sastrugi underfoot and the ground drift which snaked and softly hissed over it. Then we became oppressed by a feeling of something enormous to our left – we looked up and gave quite a start. Out of the mist rose a huge sombre form which seemed to swallow us. The Pyramid! Half an hour later we fumbled from one boulder to another along a line of moraine which led to the edge of the escarpment – then over the crest, and, riding the sledge, we went downhill in a rush of wind. We were home!

CHAPTER NINE

A grey, desolate world

We had only two weeks to prepare for our main journey, and it had become obvious to Lee and myself that we harboured a jinx in our organization, which had to be exorcised not only for our sakes but in deference to the other half of our party. Hugh and Roger for a long time had been regarded as a very strong partnership for the plateau journey, but our plans had been changed when Hugh was appointed to lead a man-hauling party to Livingston Island, of which Roger and I were also to be members – hence the craze for all that heaving and straining! We were practising – getting our muscles in trim – while redundant dogs were seen to grin and ease themselves into a slumber which lasted until Lee and I had become exhausted. Shipping dates finally settled the matter, for Hugh and his party were scheduled to leave Hope Bay before the plateau party returned, and the base was split by its allegiance to traditional or conventional travel. So Ken Brown, Pat Thompson, Lee and I set off with two dog teams on 9 October in our attempt to sledge as far down the plateau as food, time, and conditions allowed, hoping that we would meet the three men from the Reclus Peninsula, who could guide us down to the coast to be picked up by the *John Biscoe* and shipped back to base.

We had planned to set off on 1 October, but nine days of blizzards had pinned us down. We made every provision in choice of equipment to meet all contingencies morbidly thought of – these came through the medium of nightmares, when blue mouths would open wide and swallow us whole.

There were nightmares of driving the dogs through brash ice, weaving the team around tortured icebergs that leaned over threatening to topple upon us, or reflecting our image like a hall of mirrors, so that hundreds of dog teams would mêlée around us – a rush-hour in a canine metropolis. My recurring nightmare was the worst, for repetition never mellowed the fear that stirred in me every time Lee and I drove our team into that cul-de-sac surrounded by towering warped walls of ice; that small arena in which there was not enough room to move the dog team around and make an escape; and in which there would always materialize a dozen or more Leopard Seals with huge ugly heads split in half by a mouth that opened and shut with a snap of sharp teeth and a slap of saliva, while their lithe streamlined bodies slithered snake-like towards us. The fearless dogs would rush in to attack them, and one by one the Leopard Seals maimed them – a horrible sight! But with only two dogs left and the seals closing in, I would always wake up in a sweat wondering if such a situation could ever occur in the world of reality where man is master.

But all these bad dreams ceased from the moment we left base, and even the most persistent ones did not recur. No matter what situation we had met during a sledging day, our sleep was always free from incubus, although we often had amusing dreams, and sometimes even coloured ones, which were delightfully refreshing both first- and second-hand, for we had run short of stories long before 'the point of no return'. The subconscious anxieties which had shown themselves in ominous nightmares before leaving base also showed themselves in each man's eosinophil count, which made a significant drop (usually about ten days before a start of a long sledging journey) and did not regain their normal 'base level' until a day or two after a man had been in the field (when presumably his subconscious mind thought – 'it's not so bad after all!').

The Reclus party, as we were later to learn, had set off three days before us, and back-packed the first heavy loads up the cwm-shaped icefall which was their first obstacle; but on 9 October they were lying in their tent with the mists clinging closely and the snow falling steady while we were on the first stage of our journey. Then for two days while we were at View Point waiting for travelling weather, they were back-packing their stores in relays across the crux of their route – a very steep traverse. On the morning of 12 October we set off in earnest, and after carefully checking all our equipment, made a very comfortable twenty-two miles (the farthest we sledged with dogs in one day during the rest of that journey). We pitched our first camp near the northern tip of James Ross Island, and Lee and I crawled into a double-lined tent with new sheepskin mattresses, plenty of candles, and a primus that worked! For dinner we ate great juicy seal steaks.

Our second day dawned windy and, sledging along the coast of James Ross Island, we were buffeted by turbulent gusts and drifting snow; but passing the two embayments north of Rink Point, the cross-winds were so powerful that we could not hold our course and were bodily skidded sideways. Dogs were blown over and pieces of ice the size of a fist were dislodged and hurled like pucks along the smooth surface. But they were obviously local föhn winds we encountered, for the temperature, which was 30° F as we drove across them, dropped twenty-five degrees as soon as we found shelter from the main blast and turned off across the channel from Rink Point. We camped that night a few miles off the coast and experienced the following day the first really big blow of our journey. On that same day 110 miles away the Reclus men were perched precariously, while the surface all around them eroded away and the wind pounded their tent.

On 15 October we both reached our depots: the Reclus men trudged up a long, steep escarpment to 4,000 feet and were more than relieved to see a small flag protruding through a blanket of snow marking the depot they had laid on their second journey; while we sledged across the Prince Gustav Channel and camped at our main coastal depot laid the previous summer by R.R.S. *Shackleton*. It was a short but most unpleasant trip; we drove into a cold headwind which billowed our anoraks, while the ground drift snaked and swept up around the dogs as they ploughed their way through it whimpering. We had left Pat and Ken some way behind by the time we reached the grounded bergs beset near Pitt Point, and as we steered through the maze of white monsters the chill wind was broken up and deflected. The sun filtered through a fine haze and warmed us; the dogs found fresh life and raced along at full gallop.

Suddenly, on rounding a particularly big berg, we ran right into a school of dozing Crabeater Seals. It was too late to stop the team so we yelled like maniacs and drove them straight through. Bedlam broke loose in a moment and every seal awoke from its deep sleep. They reared and joined in the chorus, with a sound you could see starting down in their stomachs and pressing a bulge as it moved up their necks, till the anger and fear it contained burst their pink mouths open and let out a belch. Dogs were bowled over with the flick of seals' tails, and, as we roared through the ranks of thrashing, terrified seals, our sledge jumped and bumped and slid to dodge the most unusual obstacle we ever met.

The first step of our climb to the plateau was an ice cliff about a mile from our coastal depot. Next morning, with ice-axes and shovels, we hacked out a furrow, built a ramp, and fashioned steps; then we drove the dogs up – an extraordinary sight! But the whole operation had taken two hours and we had only succeeded in climbing twelve feet above sea-level. The loads were too heavy to move off in one haul, so we relayed stores for the rest of the day and camped among crevasses at 300 feet. We had all been in crevasses up to the waist at one time or another during the day, and twice had been obliged to unload sledges that had broken a crevasse bridge and hung dangerously poised; so we slept very well that night and felt refreshed to tackle the crux of the route, which according to Lee should have been the next few miles of the climb: but there we found perfectly good going with all the crevasses well bridged, and the most hair-raising part of the journey turned out to be a short, but very steep fall of blue ice which had been well covered with snow the previous April.

It was only a drop of 300 feet, but the ice was so polished that even the thick rope brakes we tied round the runners were no more than a token attempt to create friction, and it was obvious that the sledges would be fairly screeching by the time they reached the bottom of the run, where the surface was coated with hard-packed snow chiselled by gusting winds into knife-edged sastrugi. Unless the sledges hit the snow with perfect alignment they would be dashed to pieces and the journey would have to be completely abandoned. We let off all the dogs at the top of the slope and took one sledge at a time over the blue fall. The tension of the ride would have stopped a weak heart, for the speed it developed was close on forty miles an hour. Both sledges hit the snow with a sickening crunch and rattled to a halt after scattering the dogs, but we all breathed a sigh of relief when we found no major fractures in the sledge timbers.

The route from there took us over bad country, with many minor crevasses which nagged at our nerves and bad light in which the rise and fall of the ground and even the mountain side became melted into a watered milk-whiteness – a shadowless firmament in which we could feel firm snow beneath our feet but could see nothing of it. That white-out settled on us quieter than mist and had we not been stumbling over unseen sastrugi it would have resembled gliding in thick cloud, for even the dogs a trace length away were drained of colour and looked no more real than a shadow. When the dogs ran up an invisible stairway we knew we were about to climb a steep hump, and even crevasses looked as harmless as a streak of pale blue drawn across a white floor.

I had taken off my goggles at the top of the slope and had forgotten to put them back on again when we picked ourselves up at the bottom, so I suffered snow-blindness all that night and much more so the following day. But the weather was vile so I had a clear con-science about staying tent-bound, and lay most of the time blind-folded with a black bandage with my head in the sleeping-bag. It was an interesting experience being temporarily deprived of my sight even though the discomfort at times was harrowing. The sounds of tent life were so familiar to me that I could guess exactly what was going on, and I enjoyed the attention that I was being given (it would not have been so friendly had the day been fine). I heard Lee opening a new box of dog pemmican in which the packers at Bovril's had put magazines – a refreshing gesture of good-will from the girls at the factory to the boys in the field. Opening these boxes was always a delight, and Lee with a gesture of unselfishness read aloud some short stories from *Woman's Own* – but with my eyes flooding tears and my chuckles suffocated by the close atmosphere of the sleeping-bag, I did not derive my usual pleasure from the letters written to Evelyn Home. When darkness came at last that evening I emerged for dinner and the spoon found my mouth by trial and error, then after cocoa as usual I longed for a pipe but could not light it because the light from the burning match hurt my eyes, so Lee, who had never smoked in his life, did it for me.

One eye felt much better the following morning and although it kept crying all through the day I managed the climb of 2,000 feet up to the Simpson nunatak on which our last depot was laid. But ski-ing ahead of the dogs on a safety line, with a bandage over one eye and goggles over both, with my 'good' eye crying and steaming the glass, while we tugged and pushed and zigzagged through crevasses seemed endless, and I grew very angry when I selected a camp site and Lee quietly insisted that it was no good. I cursed him roundly, and his patience and tolerance I will never forget, for the camp site I had chosen was a sixty-foot windscoop. Lee certainly had a deep understanding of human nature. An apology seemed inadequate for the first time. Had we apologised for every transgression of courtesy during the many hard days we spent together we would have grown sick with the monotony of it; so there evolved a system of behaviour in which no apology was ever given voice; but through a set pattern of action we would demonstrate un-emotionally the good-will which existed between us, in spite of each gruelling day which put a heavy strain on our sense of humour.

If I was the 'inside man' I would lay out neatly the interior of the tent while Lee was busy with the outside duties of bedding down the dogs and shovelling snow on the valance, so that by the time he was ready to come inside the tent for the night it would already be warm; and from the outside he would hear the roar of the primus, and see steam rising from the chimney near the apex. He would then ask politely if he might come in, to demonstrate that he took nothing for granted, and I would welcome him no matter how disgruntled I might have been feeling up to that moment. Inside the tent he would find his daily ration of chocolate on his rolled-up sleeping-bag, and by the time he had hung up his outer clothing in the apex, a steaming mug of cocoa would be ready. This simple routine was responsible for the harmony that existed between us in the tent during the entire journey. Even the most compatible travelling partners need an exact time daily at which they spontaneously forget all ill feelings and start afresh.

20 October was a superb day, and while Lee and I were fixing our position by sun shots, Pat and Ken were relaying loads to the top of the plateau escarpment. They reported a magnificent run down but it was not until the following afternoon that I had completed all the observations and computations and was able to take my share of the store hauling. From the top of the escarpment the view was grand, and the Prince Gustav Channel, covered by a thick grey blanket of cloud which lay low over the sea ice, looked like an enormous river in spate with dirty glacial melt water surging between James Ross Island and the mainland.

We had high hopes that by 23 October we would be on the plateau, for all we had left to carry to the top were the tents and our personal gear, and it seemed almost certain that we would be there by my birthday on 24 October; but it was not to be. For the next three days the cloud clung around us and snow fell continually so that my twenty-third birthday was spent reading *Woman's Own* during the day, and enjoying a social evening, of which the highlight for all of us was the opening of a tin of pineapple. We made contact with base by radio, and they played some gramophone music for us which sounded so tinny that it was a torture to listen to, but with only one pair of earphones between us we were spared all but a quarter of the concert. There was still no news about the Reclus party (in fact they had free-skied up to the plateau on 20 October when they got their first view of the Weddell Sea), and without knowing anything of the coincidence both parties camped for the first time on the plateau on 25 October.

Our climb up the escarpment was a gruelling performance, the slope lying under a foot of soft snow, through which we waded and yelled at the suffering animals and collapsed for a rest every few feet. We had thrown off all but two sleeping-bags and a box at the bottom of the hill so that our first trip up would be just a trailblazer, and I had shuffled along ahead of the dogs up and down the route three times to gouge out a roadway. It was a very slow climb of 1,500 feet which went up through a layer of cloud from which we emerged just before reaching the top. There Pat and Ken set up their tent, while Lee and I prepared for our run back down.

Few things stand out clearer in my memory than riding the brake of that empty sledge on that glorious descent. Lee sat up front to keep the sledge in balance, the dogs galloped flat out along the deeply-gouged trail, their breath vapour mixing with the loose snow they kicked up which streamed towards us like steam from an engine, and we raced into the cloud and tilted downhill. In only a few seconds we tore through the cloud. The sensation of falling was felt in the stomach but the eyes could see nothing except grey swirling fog; then, with breathtaking suddenness, we burst clear of our blindfold and the earth fell away from us 4,000 feet, down to the sea ice far, far below. For a split second the ceiling of cloud was no more than an arm's length above us, and the compelling sensation to reach out and grab it welled up inside us; but we plunged from safety and

2. Mt Erebus—the end of winter

gasped with fright as the dogs went for their lives with the sledge in bounding pursuit. For almost a minute we lived through a thrill which petrified screams as they roared up our throats, and flooded veins with so much life that they stood out like cords of blue wire, until the pace slackened and we glided more gently along the trail down to a small pile of boxes.

We could hardly move for a minute or two after we had stopped. Then slowly, as the excitement drained out of our systems, our voices came back with a strange-sounding note – but in a while we made sense, and looked around at a trail which climbed into the cloud like a thin pencil line drawn on a white wall. The atmosphere was full of minute ice crystals – glittering diamond dust picked up by the sunlight and transformed into a gorgeous display of haloes and pillars, tinted with the colours of the rainbow spectrum, and intersected by a weak thin tracer of white light which shot out from the sun and circled our horizon. Mock suns illuminated us from the sides and the real sun beamed full on our faces, as we stood bathed in a diffused light with our long-legged shadows pale and tripled. With each deep draught of air we breathed, a million sparkling crystals were sucked into the stream. The parhelia dissipated after a while, and in minus 5°F we stripped to shirt sleeves and struggled once again up the escarpment, through the cloud to the plateau, with a sense of foreboding.

It was a desolate world of deep snow and mists which lifted a little then fell back lazily on the soft cushion of a gently undulating desert. Sometimes the mists darkened into sombre forms which swirled around and through each other and lifted the snow into quietly hissing drift. Sometimes the wind became a living thing which would scream in rage and fill the air with choking snow that poured past the tents like a flood. For days on end it would hiss and howl, tear at our tents and spit snow at us, as it tried to blow us off the back of the plateau. We would lie and wait for the harmony between wind, and cloud, and drifting snow; and when it came, if only for an hour or two, we would break our camp and stagger forward a mile or two – sometimes more. We would shuffle forward as far as we could see, leaving one man in a tent at the last camp site, and sticking marker flags every 300 yards along the route: then as the first few blasts of cold air blew across our track, or when the clouds slowly smothered us, we would pitch the forward tent and leave a man in occupation, then travel back along the route to find the man we left behind. One more gruelling journey forward and the entire party would be re-united.

It was strange to be left alone. Alone and no sound. It was weird with no wind, only mute mist for company. It would move like a sinister stain. It squeezed the tent gently. If you left the door open it would creep in after you and flicker the primus flame. Sometimes the wind moaned with melancholy, and the drift hissed softly as though to say 'I'm covering their tracks – they'll never find you.' Hours would go by – hours filled with activity which beat back the oppression and distracted attention from the moods of the weather, and from the wrist-watch which told you that the return of your companions was long overdue. Or you would stop work for a moment at the bottom of a deep pit dug to measure the compression of snow on the plateau and into the pit fine crystals would fall on your upturned face as you listened intently for the panting of dogs and the creak of a sledge. No sound would be heard but the flap of the tent and the faint rustle of drift weaving over the ground surface above your head. Then suddenly three men and two dog teams would appear out of the mist – what a relief it was!

'Were you worried?'

'Of course not – I enjoy being alone!'

'Sorry we're late.'

'It doesn't matter at all!'

The return journeys seemed not nearly so long as the wait in the forward camp or at the previous camp site, for we then were the active ones about whom the other two worried; we were the life-line on whom they depended. We never thought of it in any other way, even though all we carried was a spare primus stove with one day's fill, some reserve pots and pans, a handful of food, and a shovel for digging a grave-like shelter in case we got lost. We would tear away from the forward camp in a flurry of snow, back along our tracks and into the mist; and when the two teams had settled down to a steady fast trot, the drivers would climb over the handlebars and sit on the light sledges and time with their wrist-watches the passing of markers but no word was said. The ground drift would have covered the out-going track by the time we had travelled a few hundred yards, and sometimes the mists would close in and bleach even the faintest of shadows below the dogs' bellies. They would seem to be running on nothing more solid than the heavy stagnant mists we disturbed in our passage. The motion of sledging on those occasions gave the illusion that the dogs were a ghost team that ran without moving, and the sledge sliding and squeaking over a soft cushion of snow was but part of a dream through which we were living. Only the marker flags had any movement. They loomed out of the mist and glided gracefully by. Migrating beacons they were, and all on their way to the same destination, with the same sense of urgency. Then suddenly a pyramid tent would appear and come rushing towards us. Jumping up we would scramble around for the brake to save a collision. Our senses restored, our progress halted, and from out of the tent door a grinning face would appear and invite us inside for a quick brew of tea. Our relay journey would be a long steady plod; there were no more illusions to float along with – all was a cold reality. Marker flags were gathered up as we went by and at the sight of the tent we breathed a sigh. The journey had taken longer than we had estimated.

'Sorry we're late, Lee.'

'Oh! That's all right.'

Day after day our progress was recorded as a traverse line drawn on an almost blank map. An occasional contour crossed our path and gracefully meandered parallel for a while, then it would sweep away under our feet as we moved more easily down a slight drop. We climbed sometimes, ran level, and fell, though seldom more than a few feet in a mile. The monotony of the terrain was felt, not seen – the experience at times was deeply impressive. You could feel it while ski-ing well ahead of the dogs, into a world of no colour but for the tips of two skis that swished through the loose snow and marked a man's path – a trail very soon to be covered again. Only when I looked back could I see men and dogs; two teams moving towards me over a desolate white plain; but the mind did not search for reasons – we were there, that was enough for us and our questions were simple. Which way do we go? How far have we done? How much longer will this surface go on? We kept on a bearing by lining the sledges behind the ski-runner who went well ahead and looked over his shoulder now and again and adjusted his course if the teams were off line. Sometimes on windless overcast days I would aim at a smudge of shadow on the cloud base, and become so mesmerized by the empty horizon that I would doze off and wake up to find that I had stopped, fallen over, or skied way off course. But those days all came early on in the journey, when the plateau was wide and the blizzards were few – when we averaged as much as four miles a day.

By the time we had eaten enough food to lighten the sledges and make relaying unnecessary, the plateau had become an inferno of swirling mists and strong winds which lifted the snow into choking blizzards. Sometimes the winds teased us by letting the sun's rays shine through blue patches of a wild sky of scurrying cloud which transformed the scene into one of great beauty. We would break camp in a hurry and set off on a bearing along the hump of a constantly narrowing plateau, in some places less than a mile between gigantic escarpments falling 3,000 feet. At each survey stop my companions grew agitated by the delay while the weather was fair for travelling, and even as we scribbled quick notes and took compass bearings on the meandering course of the plateau edge, long fingers of cloud would creep up and over as if feeling for a grip or for men that might be there. With hardly a warning the wind would start blowing, and within minutes the plateau would be swept by a blizzard, and four men would struggle to erect two tiny shelters.

By the time we had travelled forty miles on the plateau, our average daily mileage had fallen to three miles, which had to be increased if we were to reach the head of the Reclus men's route without cutting down on our consumption of food. But for days we were pinned to the tent by blizzards, or by bad visibility which made it impossible to estimate the nearness of the escarpment. We had noticed on days when we could see a few miles that the edge was either bitten cleanly away by the avalanches, or it sloped suddenly down, splitting open in enormous crevasses. We should not have risked travelling in visibility less than a quarter of a mile – but on many occasions risks were taken just for the exercise. We would drive forward in a snow-storm, so close to each other that I could feel the dogs slipping when they stood on my skis; and looking over my shoulder I could just make out Lee and the lead dog of the following team, but no sign of Pat and Ken. Goggles would steam up and clog with snow, heads would be turned out of the wind for protection, fingers and feet would numb with the cold, and anxiety about the edge of the plateau would grip us – then our camp would be pitched with enormous relief. We made our shortest day's march in appalling conditions – a mere five hundred yards.

Our theoretical point of no return was the half-way mark in our supplies, which we treated as a social evening extraordinary, for we normally had a social gathering only on a Saturday. We decided unanimously to go forward and hope that the Reclus men would be on the plateau to meet us and guide us down to the coast; but to give ourselves a margin in food – in case they were not there and we had to return – we agreed to cut down on our rations. It was just as well that we did: four days of blizzards raged and brought our average daily mileage down to 2·8. We went outside only to feed the dogs, and to make it easier to find the team we always tied the rear guy of the tent to the sledge, and spanned out the dogs still fastened to the sledge by the long centre trace. Lee had been outside man on the last day of that particular blizzard, and had worked his way around the side of the tent to the back guy and followed it down to the sledge, where he had collected nine blocks of pemmican and felt his way along the sledge to the centre trace. He had found each dog after some difficulty and when he had fed the last block to the leader, he had estimated his course from the direction of the dog trace and tried to take a short cut back to the tent. It was no more than ten yards in a direct line, but he got off course and decided to scoop out a hole in the snow and wait for a clearance; meanwhile I was getting worried about his delay and was fully-dressed by the time he got back to the tent feeling shaken by the experience. When the lull had finally come he was only three feet from the corner of the tent, but during the fifteen minutes he had been lying outside, he had seen only a screen of blinding snow.

23 November was a great day for the Reclus party. On that day they got off the plateau and down to their last depot at 4,500 feet, after eighteen days confinement to their tent by bad weather since 1 November. For us too it was a day blest with good fortune from midday onwards when I was able to get a series of shots at the sun for a latitude fix; and discovered a way of recovering some of the precious pemmican that had been eaten in huge quantities by three dogs that had got off the traces during the previous night. With their mouths still bleeding from the cuts they received on the tin box they had ripped open, we ran them in the front three places of the team –

driving them so fast that the sudden exercise aggravated their bowels, and the following dogs fed on the excreted pemmican – paper included – which had passed right through them still only partially digested. This novel feed-time proved such a great incentive to the forward motion of our team that we made splendid progress over the first few miles through the lifting mists, and soon came in sight of a remarkable geographic feature.

We had been sledging around the south side of the plateau dome following the contour of the slope at 7,000 feet, through inclement weather which had made it difficult to judge the lie of the land ahead. The contour started to sweep away in a north-westerly direction and we grew anxious lest we crossed the centre line of the plateau and started circling back in the direction we had come. But there was something odd about the terrain; for through the mists which were slowly dissipating, we could see the plateau stretching away to the south-west, but could see no connecting link between the plateau we were sledging over and the plateau we could see in the distance. We began seriously to believe that we had discovered a break in the great spine of high ground thought to run the full length of the Graham Land peninsula, and eventually right on to the polar plateau. We drove faster and faster, but at each change of direction I had to return to the sledge to take a reading on the sledge wheel and make notes on the new country which opened up before us, and the delay became as much a test of patience for me as it did for my companions. The distant plateau projected towards us in a tongue which slipped in great waves of pressure down towards the tip which we knew held the answer to the mystery. The snow we were working through was about six inches deep, but it was powdered and lightly pressed by the recent winds and gave a fast surface. Only the faintest trace of mist hung around us as the skyline which was obscuring the tip of that tongue sank lower, and we shot forward at the best speed that our skis and dogs would permit.

The plateau we were standing on, and the plateau opposite us, fell away to a catwalk which joined them together. The plateau edge at that point dropped a sheer 1,500 feet to an ice ramp on both sides, which slipped a further 1,000 feet down to the small glaciers which flowed away from them at the bottom. Without the snow coverage the feature would have been no more than a sharp ridge linking two massive highland regions which extended for a hundred miles along the Graham Land peninsula to the north-east and many hundreds of miles to the south-west. The discovery of The Catwalk (as we decided to name it) was so deeply personal for each man, that the sight of it alone was reward enough for all our toil. As if by magic the mist disappeared, and the sun, shining out of a great blue dome for the first time in the month we had been on the plateau, bathed us in warmth.

The Catwalk was just over a hundred yards long and domed quite steeply between the two precipices. The safety margin for travel was no more than twenty feet on either side of the summit line. If the dogs were permitted to run only slightly off course, the sledges would slide down the slope and over the edge. Huskies are notoriously fickle in temper and are also at times oblivious to danger; so to be quite sure that we kept them in control, we stopped the teams short of the steep drop down on to it and put rope brakes under the sledges. I fastened a line to the front of the dog trace, and wearing crampons to get a good grip on the surface, I led the first team down on to the route while Lee stood on the brake and controlled the descent. Even the wisps of cloud that had blown over The Catwalk continuously during our approach, ceased from the moment we set foot on the crossing, where we found an incredible surface of ice knobbles, fist size and glazed as hard as iron. They could be chipped loose only with hefty blows of an ice-axe, and the ferocity of the wind that had chiselled them could hardly be imagined.

Why we were privileged with so much good fortune, not only to see that remarkable feature, but to be allowed to proceed safely across it in flat calm, was beyond our comprehension; for even as we struggled with double teams to haul the first sledge up the steep pressure waves on the south-west side of the col, cloud started pouring over it once more: The Catwalk had closed the route behind us. We took the leading sledge up 300 feet above the col with a double team of dogs before letting them off and returning for the second sledge, which had been left just clear of the wind funnel (the limits of which could be judged quite accurately by the nature of the surface). I have seldom been so sharply aware of the narrow margin between safety and disaster as we stood there for a moment watching the cloud surging over the col, and listening to the whine of the wind which increased to a scream and chilled us with fear, so close were we still to the edge of the wind stream. We drove the dogs frantically up that steep slope and the cloud level followed us – creeping up like a flood. We reached the other sledge, reorganized the teams, and as if the dogs sensed the urgency of our escape, they pulled their hearts out for the higher ground. As long as I live I will never forget the feeling of relief as we camped that night safe and high up on the big broad back of a friendly plateau that was soft to the touch.

It was hard to believe that our good fortune would revert to what we had almost come to accept as normal. We had been on the plateau for thirty days; behind us lay eighty-eight hard-won miles and what surely was the crux of the route. Our average daily mileage was still below three, and only one topic of discussion found favour – 'how much farther, and do we have enough food?' That night Lee took my turn as cook which gave me more time to compute the last fix and plot up the day's march across the field sheet. We had travelled twelve miles, but on a twisting course which seemed like poor progress when plotted. From the dead-reckoning position of our camp site that night to the head of the Reclus men's route to the plateau was about thirty miles of unknown country – a blank on the map – where the destination was almost as uncertain as the nature of the terrain which lay in between. We hoped the Reclus men had been on the plateau, and that they had left a cairn for us somewhere near the head of their route with a message telling us how to get down to their refuge hut at the coast. But there was a chance that any cairn built on the plateau would be blown down or buried before we reached it, and without the guidance of the Reclus party we would probably not find their route off the plateau, and would have to return to Hope Bay along the plateau by the way we had come, killing dogs to feed dogs and men.

Thirty miles is an easy day's distance for fit dogs pulling light loads over a fairly good surface but the plateau had taught us that by its favours we would sometimes make twelve miles on a travelling day, then for a trio of days blizzards would reduce our miserable average to three. So when the next day dawned with the tent flapping madly, we just shrugged our shoulders and ate our porridge; snoozed a while, then told a few stories.

They were stories we had told many times before, but it was not for the telling we told them again; for where is the fun in telling a

story where the minor details slip the memory? We told them because
the listener delighted in building up the suspense within himself, so
that when the amusing bit came at last, he could burst with a laugh
which had filled his inside from the moment the familiar tale had
begun. If the story-teller made a slight slip with the facts – so much
the better – it added spice to a delicious tale, that could be rehashed a
hundred times without going stale. The story-telling and listening
became an essay of our sense of values and compatibility. 'Tell me
how you gave that bad boy a fright – that's always been my favourite!'
– or – 'Let's hear that patio story again – when you were picked up by
a Turk and taken to his home.' Where is the need for a fleshpot
existence among men who with practice can find entertainment from
the mere repetition of very old stories, told on half-empty stomachs
in a cold polar tent? If his sense of values is right he cannot get bored,
for his intellect is certain to keep him awake. In a world of men, a
man is alone unless he can make harmony with his fellow men and
the wild ice-covered country they live in.

There was, however, an undercurrent of anxiety which swept
through the latter days of that journey, and occasionally it boiled to
the surface. Action deflects an in-growing fear out on to the surface
where hard physical toil shakes most of it off in sweat and heat loss –
but sunshine works the same miracle without sapping a man's energy,
and so it did the next morning when it flooded our plateau world
with warmth and hope. We ate in a hurry, packed up in haste, and
moved off smoothly across a firm surface. From the dome of the
plateau we could see all around. Anvers and Brabant Islands we saw
for the first time – dazzling diamonds in a jet black sea: but on the
Weddell side of the peninsula a thick layer of cloud tumbled in grey
rolls like a nightmare ocean welling up in a flood from which we had
no escape. We made fast progress towards another 'waist' of the
plateau, and beyond it Mount Johnston rose like a small mound and
marked the head of the Reclus men's route up from the coast. But
before we had left six miles behind us the cloud of the east coast had
risen to the brink of our plateau, and the faintest breeze breathed
wisps of it over us as a hunger for distance drove us faster and
faster. We sledged through a white-out for almost two miles until the
nervous strain grew intolerable, and in fear of the edge we pitched
camp to wait for the cloud to clear.

Never once in our experience on the Graham Land plateau did the
cloud lift in less than twelve hours from the moment it first settled
upon us. Many were the times early on in the journey when we would
set up one tent – even that only temporarily then sit in misery and
discomfort for four hours or more before despairing of hope and
pitching camp properly. We grew wise with time, and, when be-
clouded, pitched our tents and bedded down, taking a roster system
of night-watching to keep all moods of the weather under observation. This policy paid its reward at five-o'clock on the morning of
26 November. The cloud sank away like a receding tide, leaving
everything coated with fluffy hoar frost and a snow surface scattered
in specks of light which twinkled like stars in a spectrum of colours.
Our camp had been pitched on the east side of the dome, which
obscured our view of the western coast; but overhead not a cloud
smeared the sky, and the cold still air cleared our minds for a moment
of all anxiety.

We moved off at eight o'clock that morning, after I had taken a
series of sun shots for longitude, and climbed slowly back up to the
dome of the plateau from where the view of the west coast was
breathtaking. We could see the Reclus Peninsula west of Charlotte
Bay, with Portal Point at the seaward tip nearly 7,000 feet below us
and fourteen miles away. We even thought we could see the hut
through the big binoculars, and the longing to be safely down there
gave us almost a physical ache. With the naked eye the view seemed
unreal. The clear atmosphere brought distant islands and ranges and
laid them before us – an arm's reach away. It was like a huge mirror
on to which projected headlands and capes with deep bays in between. Islands sat on it reflecting themselves, and enormous icebergs
were minute pricks of white sand scattered by a careless hand. It was
a magnificent white model, precisely correct: there was Anvers, there
was Brabant, there was the Gerlache Strait. The place where we stood
was apart from it: there was no middle distance to give us perspective – to associate us with the scene below. But even as we gazed
at a panorama with too much grandeur, too much compass to be
taken in at a glance – a Snow Petrel flew over us, and we craned our
necks to watch it circle. There is no white whiter than the Snowy
Petrel's against a clear Antarctic sky, it deepens the blue of infinity;
and when the bird rests on the dazzling snow, its whiteness bleaches

its own shadow. It was a creature with so much grace and beauty bestowed on such a delicate frame, that the only word for it is 'heavenly'. If only we had had wings too we could have flown down to Charlotte Bay – we could have been there in about an hour, and all our hardships would have been over; but as we watched it fly away across the plateau towards the Weddell Sea, we came sharply back from our fantasy; for already cloud was forming fast, and fingers of it crept across a narrow waist in the plateau ahead of us.

The waist was about a quarter of a mile between escarpments, and we were travelling on a compass bearing directly towards it at the time we stopped to gaze over the edge. Beyond the waist the plateau rose gleaming white above the cloud, while behind us rearing up like a monstrous wave, a great grey cloud tilted us forward at full speed and drove us along like surf riders. If it caught us up the run would be over, so we ran down into the finger of cloud which covered the waist, and felt our way through it to emerge triumphant above and beyond in glorious sunshine. The surface improved and for almost an hour we travelled with light hearts across a very broad dome, but the ground fell away into a basin as the high ground went away to the east; and going down into it we found deep snow. Wisps of mist shifted lightly around us tumbling gently over their shadows, while above them the wind lashed the sky with white cords of hooked cirrus; and all the time over the edge of the plateau crawled the thick cloud. It crept after us as we climbed each skyline and slid into another depression towards yet another long miserable climb. Suddenly Mount Johnston was directly ahead: we had no more than six miles farther to go before knowing if the Reclus men were waiting to help us; but between the high ground on which we stood and the summit of the plateau near the base of Mount Johnston lay a 1,000-foot drop to another narrow 'waist' which was partially covered by a pocket of cloud. With the binoculars we scanned the horizon for a tent, but we saw nothing and our hopes sank. Then, on sweeping the glasses over the ground just in front of Mount Johnston at an altitude of about 7,000 feet, there came into view a tiny speck of a cairn.

We took a compass bearing on it and tore down the hill – a magnificent run with a cushion of cloud at the bottom of the slope into which we sank – then gathered ourselves and started the long steady climb up the far side. But the cloud climbed too, so we took extra care and kept the sledges and ski-runner dead in line. An hour went by and we were still struggling, and all that time the cloud nestled close – each bump of sastrugi was a cairn in the mist. We grew so tired of being certain we could see it ahead only to be dis-illusioned, that we plodded on, our minds quite blank, out of the cloud – and there it was! The dogs sensed immediately that the cairn was man-made. They leaned into their harnesses at a full gallop, and wrapped themselves around it in a tangle of traces as we beat in the sledge pickets.

A marker flag stuck out of the cairn and to it was tied a plastic bag with some papers inside. Were the Reclus men waiting near by, or had they left us to find our own way? There we stood in a huddle – four men to whom the cairn was a symbol of life in a hostile world. Lee handed the notes around for each man to read, but no one said a word until we had all had a turn; then we beamed with delight and relief, for the notes told us the bearing and distance to their camp, which was not half an hour's ride down their route. We laughed until tears came to our eyes.

The message directed us to travel on a bearing of 320°, and after about two miles we were to go down a steep drop and find their tent pitched at 4,500 feet. The puzzle we could not resolve was why the ski tracks from the cairn went off in a different direction, but we wisely ran on the bearing given. We left the cloud behind us sitting upon the plateau, and in glorious sunshine we swept towards the edge of the escarpment. Near the crest of a mighty drop we stopped and fastened rope brakes under the runners, and when both teams were ready we moved over the edge.

The ground fell away 1,500 feet to a neck of high land which ran out from the plateau along the Reclus Peninsula. On either side the ice plunged in massive ice falls down to the sea, and beyond, the magnificent mountains of Brabant Island rose out of the Gerlache Strait. On the neck of land far below us a minute speck sat in the solitude of a brilliant white field. Their tent! Many were the times Lee and I had discussed how this meeting should be. We both visualized something dignified, where back-slapping would follow an incongruous speech, and had carefully planned accordingly. Hanging from the handlebars of the sledge were both cameras, loaded and set, ready to immortalize the stretching of hands an instant before the leaders' hands met. Lee would run out ahead of the dogs, while I held back the team with the sledge foot brake and took photographs of the men approaching each other.

Our descent of that slope was fast and straight, with the dogs at stretch-gallop and the snow peeling into a plume of fine crystals which lifted from the footbrake and trailed out behind us. We were about half-way down when from out of the tent came a tiny speck that obviously spotted us for it went quickly inside again and in no time at all three specks were there; and we abandoned ourselves in shouts of joy. One speck went back inside and the other two started walking towards us up the hill. We sobered into a dignified mood, and when we were about a hundred yards from the approaching men, I jumped hard on the brake as Lee ran past the dogs to take up his position for the great meeting. But the dogs suddenly realized that the men who approached were strangers to them and went wild with delight. They gained on Lee against all my efforts to hold the team back; but desperate to get a picture at all costs I reached for a camera and took a quick snap.

The dogs tripped Lee up and surrounded the two men, who were clearly alarmed by all the commotion, as dogs tumbled in a seething mass of fur and fight, and the Reclus men scrambled clear in fear for their lives. We beat in a picket at the back of the sledge and laid into the dogs with marker flags, and as the fight broke up the sledge pulled loose and the team set off at a canter towards the tent. We all four scrambled and caught the sledge – there was no time for 'Hello's!' – and our vocabulary blossomed in husky abuse. My feet were hard on the brake and the team slowed down a little, but we could not avoid tripping the mast of the radio aerial which came crashing down as the dogs ran to both sides of it, then into the guy ropes they ran with a twang which shook the tent so violently that it shot out the third man like a cork from a bottle. We threw ourselves in amongst the dogs again as they bowled over in a blood-thirsty fight which threatened to capsize the tent, and dragged them away to a safe distance, beat in the pickets, then turned to shake hands.

We saw each other through the glazed eyes of relief. We laughed at nothing and everything. We sat down, and stood up and sat down again. Our faces ached with splitting grins. We could see no farther than the nearest man.

CHAPTER TEN

Sea sounds and liquid ribbons

It was sixteen miles down to the refuge. The men who were to guide us talked of obstacles on the route – the big drop and the dreaded traverse, the ice fall called the 'deadly cwm' – with an undramatic reverence. They briefed us casually about a route engraved on their memories. Of the last fifty days they had been in the field, thirty they had spent tent-bound, be-clouded, or pinned down by blizzards, existing on depleted rations, their patience stretched to the limit – waiting and waiting while there was the slightest chance that we would reach the plateau cairn and need their guidance to get safely down.

The trio were tall by Hope Bay standards. For eight months they had been together, influencing each other – but traits smoothed of their sharp edges had remained hard-cored in spite of pressure. Dennis was a Lancastrian with unshakeable resolution, and there was no delicacy or voluble diplomacy in Dick's approach to men and problems in his way – all were fair game, and on the field his opponents were there just to be floored. These were two energetic tigers, sparsely bearded, lean and tough. Ray was far less angular – and philosophically inclined against unnecessary grind. With his weighty beard and glasses, he looked like a witty priest who had just enjoyed an enormous feast, which he hoped would be allowed to settle.

We set off the day after our meeting shortly after the noon sun shot had been taken, and sledged two miles over an easy surface until the ground fell away in its first big fall. The 1,500 foot drop looked so steep that we let off all but three of the dogs and put thick rope brakes under the runners before risking the descent. We entered the cloud at the base of the drop and sledged into it on a compass course for about a mile before pitching camp – and another fine party was had that night. Seven men sat Buddha-fashion, conversation flowing freely, laughter spilling like a fountain in a sparkling pool of brand new stories. Some were stories we had heard related many times, but the new tales and the yarns of the Reclus men came in a language all their own, for each group of men make their own slang.

We awoke at 6.30 the next morning, and after breakfast started our trudge up a steeply-traversed slope, one sledge at a time. Thirteen dogs and six men made the first climb, but the cloud had settled on us once more, and loose dogs and their masters all walked single file down the sledge tracks to the glacier below, where we had a short break, then resumed the toil.

Our camp that night was at the start of the dreaded traverse, in cloud that squeezed like a clammy hand, and with the temperature just above freezing-point everything was wet and warm. We wrung out of our socks the fluid grime which had matted the fibres for so long, and mukluks hanging up to dry dripped into the stew. Cloud swirled around all the next day, and since the traverse would not be attempted in poor visibility, we squelched from tent to tent in turn, smoked, talked, drank tea and fed from different plates on different food.

There was an atmosphere quite distinct about another tent; somehow it had a different smell, although the things that lay about were the same as lay in our own. In winter cold air snuffs out a smell before the nose detects it, but cold air does not stop the smell from accumulating, it simply gives the smell a prolonged smell-less hibernation. When the air temperature creeps above freezing-point the dormant smells all come awake. Summer was obviously approaching! With the summer comes smells, and ships. We would soon be leaving the Antarctic: all of us, that is, except Lee and Ray who both had one more year to do. We could hear them in another tent making music of the spoken word in tales of their home town and boyhood memories of wanderings in Northern Ireland.

The following morning at seven o'clock we were out and away on the first stage of the traverse, back-packing great loads for one and a half miles across the steep slope, below a wave crest cornice that hung dangerously poised. It was a day of stress as hard as any we experienced on the plateau journey for there were no obstructions on that slope for a sliding man to check his shoot straight down to the sea 2,500 feet below.

All day we trudged to and fro on that traverse. The only loss was an empty fuel can which had not been pressed firmly enough into the snow and slipped out of sight in a matter of seconds. We originally planned to take each dog across separately, but by the time we had back-packed all the gear over, a pathway had been stamped out across the face of the traverse just wide enough to take the sledge; so a few dogs were used by tying them on the up-hill side of it where they instinctively pulled up the slope against the drag of the sledge down-hill, while the forward motion was provided by man-hauling. In very cramped quarters we camped that night, and with only one day's food left we set off the next morning at eight o'clock, with a swoosh and a cry, down a steep drop, chasing the man-haulers who were sweeping away towards the top of the cwm-shaped ice fall.

On that day the mist hung in small pockets around the top half of the bowl and gave it a formidable aspect. The drop was about a thousand feet, and it was said to be a most exhilarating experience to set the sledge in the right direction, sit on it, push off, and leave the outcome entirely in the hands of fate. There was a run-off at the bottom of the cwm over which a plummetting sledge could expend its speed, and the only crevasses were on the inside course, which was virtually impossible to sledge over as the momentum of the descent would throw the sledge to the far wall where the surface and angle of the slope were superb for the down-hill run.

Dick took the man-haul sledge down the cwm single-handed in a demonstration of ski-ing which was wonderful to watch. He used no ski-sticks, only a line in each hand – one to the front of the sledge and the other to the stern; with these lines he controlled the direction and speed of the sledge by moving down the side or sweeping around the back: it was like watching a gull gliding and swooping behind the sledge, which banked in a fast run into the bowl. Dennis free-skied in pursuit of Dick, while the dog-sledgers helped by Ray entered the cwm riding brakes, dragging the dogs like sea anchors and churning the smooth slope into a wake. From the bottom of the cwm our gouged trail scarred a purple-grey wall which rose into the clouds. We were safely down the worst of the route so we were told, and about a thousand feet above sea-level. Before us lay six miles of gently undulating snow-fields with the peninsula narrowing all the time.

It was a delightful run from then on: the end of a long journey nearly always is. The Reclus men, ski-ing alongside us with their sledge in tow by the dogs, pointed out landmarks as each came into view, and the blissful feeling crept over us that the journey was almost done. At the end of the peninsula we started the last fall: gradually at first, with Dick and Dennis out ahead man-hauling their sledge for the final run in. We sledged down a steep drop and on to a narrow ridge with a drop either side down to the sea. Gulls circled and dived and were lifted by up-draughts, and their calls and the sea sounds rose up to greet us. So long, it seemed, we had been on the plateau where the wind and ground drift were the only sounds, and the horizon gave no relief to the eyes, that the coastline had become a new world – a world of life and sounds, of sea and strange smells. It was an encounter so sensual we had to stop, until the elation subsided and we could again concentrate on the final steep fall.

For some strange reason all perspective was lost when we approached the crest of the fall and looked down at the sea. We had the impression that an enormous drop lay just ahead; then suddenly the roof of the refuge was directly below us – had there been a chimney we should have seen right down it! It seemed so near, so suddenly, that one mighty leap was all that was needed to land us right there.

The high sea-level temperature had rotted the snow, which lay deep and decaying. In it we floundered and sank to our thighs, our feet slopping in melt streams and puddles of sludge; but nothing could detract from the delight we all felt as we staggered towards the hut.

The hut was no more than a big box steeply roofed, with two windows, a door, and three primus stoves. For an oven they had a battered old tin with an asbestos door which flapped in the breeze and permitted a glimpse of the bread while it baked in the 'oven' balanced neatly on two primus stoves. There were three bunks, a small table, a bench, and two chairs. There was a loft and a glory hole and a bit of a kitchen; socks and tea cloths hung on a line; the gramophone sat with its mouth open wide, blaring out melodies like *The Nun's Chorus* that everyone knew by heart, while the man whose turn it was to keep the spring taut, sat winding the handle like a barrel-organist.

In years to come, young men will enter that refuge on tiptoe and

The Reclus hut

whisper – 'how eerie, what a strange atmosphere' – and they will
half expect the apparition of a big bearded Irishman to lean out of
his bunk and say – 'I heard no knock on the door young fellow; have
the men of today no manners at all?' Like all other huts built in the
Antarctic, it will be worn by the blizzards, its timber will shrink, and
through cracks in the walls or a broken glass pane the snow will
drift in fine plumes and pack into ice. But it will never be an eyesore
on the Antarctic coastline, for an old hut moulds in the course of
time into the scenery, as if man and nature find their harmony only
when man has long since passed on, and his spirit alone with the
musty smell stays behind.

For one month after we got down to the coast we happily shared
the cramped space of that shack, despite the dwindling supplies of
food for ourselves, and the daily search for seals to feed the dogs. The
last of the pemmican was fed to the dogs on the evening that we got
down to the coast, but we had no anxieties then, for the *Shackleton*
was to have picked us up very soon. Had the *Shackleton* not hit a
bergy bit, and sent out a distress signal as her forward hold flooded;
had the crew not been obliged to make immediate repairs so that the
ship could limp back to South Georgia – we would not have been
faced with the food shortage, but we would also have missed the most
relaxed and enjoyable month of our lives.

There had not been enough room in the hut to sleep seven men, so Lee and I had set our tent a few yards away on the very first evening we spent at sea-level. We lay that night no more than ten feet from the gentle lapping of the sea around the rocks at the edge of the promontory. The sound was so soothing, so enchanting that we lay awake for hours listening to it. Not a word was spoken. We breathed as quietly as men can breathe for fear of discording with so perfect a sound.

Wakefulness came slowly the following morning. The sun, warming the tent and diffusing soft light on us as we dozed, awoke our senses of smell and hearing. The sea, so near it filled our tent with its aroma, ran amongst the rocks. Every day started in the same pleasant pattern. Only the weather made a day different from any other we spent while awaiting our rescue.

Breakfast we took all together in the hut. It was always the best meal of the day. After breakfast we would go off in different directions, some out to sea in search of seals on a raft made of sledges and empty oil drums and paddled with shovels; while others would go for a stroll around the coastal rocks with a dog or two for company. If a seal was found somewhere near the point, he was chased to within a few feet of the sea before being killed and gutted; then, strung to a line and towed around the coast like a pet seal obediently following its master, it would be beached and butchered and fed to the dogs after the best cuts had been put aside for the men. Each man had his favourite haunts where he would go on a sunny day after the chores had been done. There he would smoke his pipe in the tranquillity so hard to find and so treasured by a man that you would say 'sorry' if you stumbled upon him, and make some excuse to be soon on your way – perhaps to find a new hideout where you too could sit and watch the ice moving lazily in the swell and the birds fluttering above a small shoal of krill.

The evenings were when we would meet and spin yarns, gather around the radio from which news of all kinds was gladly accepted, torn apart, sifted and finally re-sorted. Our topics of discussion widened their range as we settled down together and plumbed each other's past and our hazy future. Civilization loomed before us as a seductive monster, like something we had known years ago that now threatened to devour us body and soul. There were high-lights to our simple life: Lee's thirtieth birthday was one such occasion, when a cake was made in the tiny tin oven. It was an ingenious piece of culinary art, for the oven would glow red hot underneath while the sides and the top would be no more than warm. The solution was found by burning the cake's bottom then turning it over and burning the top: the charred top and bottom was then cut away, and what was left was cleverly decorated with a model yacht sailing over a sea of improvised icing and a candletop lighthouse standing sentinel over some jagged rocks made with chunks of lump sugar. The birth of some pups was another occasion of great rejoicing, and the day Dennis and I swam out to an iceberg caused quite a commotion – particularly to our nervous system, for the sea temperature was 29° F.

There was one evening in particular that stands in my memory. We had finished supper and lit our pipes for the final smoke before turning in, when we became aware how silent the night was, almost as if nature itself had stopped breathing – a snatch of breath which she held for a moment in her year-long cycle of roaring and screeching – a gasp and a pause as she looked with amazement at her own sublime beauty. It was late and the air temperature had fallen below freezing, and had knit the snow surface to take our full weight as Dick, Dennis and I plodded up the hill to get a good view of the country around us. The sun was just below the horizon and not the smallest of wavelets rippled the bay. The sky to the west and north was evenly overcast with a deep wash of blue-green, mirrored so exactly that no horizon came between sky and sea; while icebergs, so numerous and widely scattered, were soaked in the most delicate tone of pink, and hung weightless, without common plane in a firmament suffused by a deep hue of moist colour. Away in the distance a smudge of alpenglow lit the rugged peaks of Brabant Island, while in the opposite quadrant the sky was ablaze with colours, which ran together and doubled themselves in the still water of the bay.

I have seldom felt as contented as I did that night. We could see the plateau rising majestically – still and clear, with a sharp silver skyline which lit each small rise and fall in the surface over which we had crawled a month before making an average of less than three miles a day.

We looked down at the promontory on which sat the hut, the tent, our sledges and dogs. The water was so calm and clear in the small bay to the east that we could see every rock that lay on the sea-bed. To the north and far distant whales were blowing – their great backs breaking the mirror-like surface of the sea, awash with water which released pricks of light. Their fountains rose. Steamy sounds echoed off the nearby slopes; very muffled sighs, hardly audible. Cape Pigeons were scrambling over small pieces of ice which rocked and capsized as the birds paddled away in jerky movements. They hustled each other, sending out ripples across the water which took reflected colours from the clouds and shimmered them into liquid ribbons. Wilson's Petrels flittered past like enormous butterflies, while on the point in all their pomposity stood two Gentoo Penguins, little knowing the scarcity of food for our dogs which threatened their lives; but on such a night slaughter would have been sacrilege!

On 28 December the *John Biscoe* was spotted weaving her way towards us, and our lazy, happy life with the residents of that refuge hut came to an end in a flurry of excitement. The launch and scow were soon approaching, while a hundred and one things were still to be collected. There was little time to savour that wonderful moment; all was haste and hustle. The boats came alongside and the first man to jump out had a voice as familiar as any I know, but the fellow was beardless and spotlessly clean. Hugh Simpson shook us all by the hand, and Roger Tufft followed him, then with characteristic enthusiasm they picked up the first boxes. In a matter of minutes it was all done.

Dogs were hoisted aboard and secured to the rail and soon the Reclus Peninsula was lying astern. It had slipped away as we read our mail and was gone by the time we ran on deck to bid it a long farewell. It was with sadness that we eventually went below for a beer or two.

CHAPTER ELEVEN

Walls of sliding water
People, people everywhere

Hugh and Roger were on their way to Livingston Island for the summer, but the rest of us were back at Hope Bay in time for the New Year, and my last three months passed by quickly. It was a time for adjustment to new men and their habits. Only my bunk and a few well-known faces, my favourite walks and the survey office could take me back to the times I had known.

We had lived for two and a half years in a womanless world. A gorgeous sunset, or a towering iceberg, in spite of its beauty of colour and line which cried out for response, had raised no more than a grunt of approval. The howl of the dogs, the moan of the wind, the groan of the sea ice pressed by a strong tide, the squeak of hard snow under mocassined feet, those were the sounds that had shaken us alive. But our delight had always been strongly repressed and our need for self-expression turned into energy, which was then burned up by running all day to the point of collapse.

Each man's bunk-space had been his personal domain, and whatever was pinned to the wall of his bunk was studied with interest by all his companions as soon as he had gone out of the room. But in three months a significant change had occurred: pin-ups of bathing beauties went out of fashion, and had not re-appeared until the new boys had arrived. There had been no question of resurrecting our original pin-ups to supplement those of our new companions, for they had either been burned or used as dartboards when we had tired of their impersonality. Pictures of girl friends had seldom been displayed. Although the 'opposite sex' had been a topic of conversation every day, it became buried finally beneath talk of dogs, the weather, or the South. Full-blooded arguments had raged frequently. There had been pull-ups and press-ups before going to bed, and the most mundane chores had been done with great fervour – each man trying to do more than his share. Filling the coal bucket or emptying the 'gash' had become a duel of efficiency between one man and the next. Everything had been regarded as a test of a man's prowess: putting teacups on hooks was a race against time and a stop-watch was taken to each man in turn. Men had shuffled in blubbery clothes through a base that had never been an untidy sight; but twice a year we had dressed up in the finery of suits after a hair-cutting, beard-trimming, shoe-cleaning day, just for an evening of elegant drinking and to repair the torn fabric of our social decorum.

We had created a way of life unnecessarily tough – a world of men ascetically disciplined, where physical hardship was the safety valve for the pressures a man's will could not control. But those hardships had often exposed a man's temper, a sadistic impulse or an uncanny calm: they had sometimes ravaged a man cruelly and cut him open for his companions to see how much courage he had under his cloak of strength. Scared men singing loudly to drive away fear had suddenly sunk into repressive silence, and as the limits of tolerance in each man became clear we had learned to accept them for whatever they were.

With our sledging companions, thought had become a communion in which each possessed the other's mind, and nothing one could do or say surprised the other. In the course of time, when words had run dry, the sympathy between two minds had found a soothing comfort in unspoken conversations.

Our sense of values had changed as we became enriched by the life we led. Yet we had reached the end of that road still needing desperately to express how much we loved that desolate place where we had lived and strived together.

There had been so much bustle down on the beach, everyone shouting and joking and scrambling in and out of the launch, that we missed our chance of saying good-bye. Small figures on the shore were waving and their voices carried over the choppy water. Spray beaten in sheets from the bows of our launch was caught by the wind and whipped over the sea. Only then, in the cold solitude of memories, did the full impact of leaving grip us.

The men ashore were still climbing the hill up the base as the *John Biscoe* moved slowly out of Hope Bay. I stood at the stern gazing back on the scene. Blue-grey clouds were spilling over the high ground and sinking with the weight of heavy shadows down the escarpment towards the base. Ground drift furred the sharp lines of the rocks, spinning out over the ice cliffs and settling into the sea by the time those tiny figures had reached the hut and stood where I so often had stood.

The wind was blowing harder. The flag above the base was stiff. Drifting snow curled around the hut until that long low building seemed to be floating. I watched the tiny figures through my binoculars as one by one they all went in – a new world of men.

As I write, that hut is locked up and dead. It has served its time as an oasis from where men have made their long sledge journeys; it is now just another shrine on the 20,000-mile Antarctic coastline, marking the passage of time and men, and filled with ice and memories.

The *John Biscoe* wallowed in enormous seas. Walls of sliding water rose around her from the troughs. Once more the *John Biscoe* would ride clear just in time; past the teeth of flying spray on the crest – a mountain top in a barrier range of watery hills which heaved and fell under a sky of snarling black clouds, their edges torn by hurricanes. Our ship would heel right over, and the screech of wind in the rigging would rise in pitch until our ears seemed to be splitting. Again we overhung a precipice of sea. There seemed no end to that nightmare voyage, and when grey-green seas broke over our ship it felt as if the vessel was stunned; then she would yaw and lurch until the creaking sounded like a plea, and just an extra push from the wind would have sent her to the ocean bed.

We lay low in the slough of misery listening to the crash of crockery and the sea chests sliding across the deck thumping the bulkhead like an irregular heart-throb. Was a return to civilization worth so much malaise? Had we not found contentment in the life we had led? On and on the voyage went until the heaving waters calmed and the ship ceased its rolling – and there was Port Stanley climbing a hill, with each house like a kindly face flushed by a shaft of late summer sun which had pierced the grey-soaked clouds above. Was ever a small port more pretty! We hurriedly washed and put on our clean clothes, opened the portholes to let in fresh air, and staggered up on deck.

That night a dance was held in the barn of Port Stanley's town hall, and what an occasion! The townsfolk turned out to make us feel welcome, and men we thought we knew got up and pranced around the dance floor. We who were left standing shyly to one side deplored the way some men melted so easily. Men's men they had been not a moment before, transformed in an instant into quick-stepping gigolos who called over their shoulders 'grab a woman, and don't be so daft!' Three ladies' excuse-me's they had that night and some of us ran down the street as if devils were chasing, and into the pub where we sank a few drinks to give us the courage to return once again.

I suddenly realized that I knew none of those men as completely as I had believed. Without a woman, a man is incomplete; part of his personality lies dormant in a society of men. His reactions to the Antarctic environment were but a small part of his total complexity. The nature of conflicts he faced in the South dug into the fundamental stuff of the man and showed him for what he basically was; but re-set in a civilized community he is immediately cloaked by social custom.

A waitress glided across to our table with a tray of tumblers slopping water and jingling their cubes of ice. We ordered coffee and sipped it slowly. How cruel yet exciting civilization seemed to us on that first afternoon in Montevideo. How uncomplicated, by comparison, was the world of men we had left behind, where the only sensual feeling we could ever have was the warmth of the sun, and where white roads still untrodden by man stretched out to the horizon.

We left the café and were jostled by crowds as we walked back to the ship, timid and confused. Overawed, we were no longer the boisterous sailor-like figures who had strided out of the dock gates a few hours before. We had been South too long just to need a sailor-like spree to readjust ourselves to civilization – we needed time and tolerance. But alas, most polar men never quite find it and spend the rest of their lives being 'different'.

> There are some who hear a different drummer,
> and who march a different pace.

They are escapists. Restless people, wanting peace of a kind; wanting a cure for their disease.

If escapists had courage enough to face the treadmill of big city life there would be fewer compulsive wanderers. It is the men who deny themselves the delight of doing what they choose who make the world go round. It is they who have courage.

We had a stag party on that first night ashore which started with an enormous feast. Our talk was all about the South – what else could we talk about: we were familiar and comfortable with that subject; we could not climb back to a strange way of life as easily as we had changed into our musty suits. In a bunch we played the casino next, then we started our tour of the smart nightclubs, working our way slowly down the list from the best to the roughest dock-side bars; but always together in a group. We observed those haunts and their clientèle over the shoulders of our solid comrades who drank beer, and blushed when a woman pushed by, and we staggered back to the ship early next day. She sailed for England just before noon, leaving a few of us on the quay who had elected to make our own way home.

For me ahead lay a 15,000-mile journey – a solo hitch-hiking trip all the way back to Britain. Like Dennis, Roger, and Hugh I possessed that feeling that makes a man want to put distance behind him. We felt goaded on to leave a trail that we would see through ageing eyes.

But the wake of our ship had been a more poignant trail – is it not always just that way? We had left behind us what we had loved.

I journeyed 15,000 miles alone, and solitude made more receptive a mind which often pined for company. I was scared by things that I would have laughed at with a friend, but the closeness I felt to everything I saw and my personal involvement with each adventure went far deeper than it might have done if I had not been alone. I lived and travelled with Indians, drawing portraits for my board and lodging.

I had made a similar journey three years before when I hitch-hiked from Egypt back to England; but similar only in the loneliness of travelling dumb through countries where the peasant talk bubbled with chuckles and friendly banter I could not understand. My memory of South America is now mere impression – hazy months of broad-bosomed mountains, thin atmosphere and bursting lungs, rasping breath and peeling lips. I can feel the sticky breath of Indians bursting in laughter in my face. I can taste choking dust, hear market bustle. I can feel burning sun and smell squalid shade. I can go back amongst the River Indians on the Magdalena banks and feel the closeness of the nights, but I cannot see the details clearly. My loneliness intensified the atmosphere I felt, and the sensual richness of the experience after two years on ice moulded my memories into this impression.

I reached Britain exhausted, and collapsed at home. Nothing would induce me to talk about my travels. I harboured an almost inexplicable dread of stagnation, but was too tired and too short of money to set off on another journey. I felt for the first time that I was growing old.

CHAPTER TWELVE

A different polar scene

For several months the other surveyors and I worked on our maps at the Directorate of Overseas Surveys at Tolworth in Surrey. For eight hours a day we would re-plot the traverses we had made, re-living each stage of each journey, each camp site and cairn we had set up in the Antarctic; then we would go back to our flats, fry a bachelor's dinner, and head for the nearest pub to drink to our future. I shared a flat with Dennis and Dick to prolong the moment we knew had to come – the moment when our maps would be completed, our reports all written, and we would drift apprehensively in search of our niche in the civilized world.

It was not until after my friends had all gone that the idea of lecturing around the schools of Britain caught my imagination. I had hoped it would be a therapy through which I would work the Antarctic out of my system, so I committed myself to an agency and stood before an audience as often as twenty-five times a week and just talked about Antarctica.

It did not matter what kind of school or where it was. The boys' growing interest in the world around them through literature and television had expanded their scope of potential heroes so rapidly that their choice had become influenced by the national vogue rather than simple preference. Yet there was still an insatiable interest in robust adventure, and the Antarctic with its timeless magic was the flint with which I tried to strike sparks from my audiences. But sadly I was no orator, and there was no regret when my lecture tour came to an end for I had burned myself out. My message had been full of new horizons, but I could not prove that they existed. Looking back on my three hundred lectures was like looking along a beach strewn with mounds, all alike, each a fading memory of a talk I had given. Once those mounds had been fine castles, built by the imagination of children; but their relentless flow of interests, like the ebb and flow of tides, had worn away each castle as soon as I moved on. My message had been quite sincere, but towards the end the words nagged at me continually to practise what I preached; so when Hugh Simpson approached me with his plan for a physiological research expedition to the Arctic island of Spitzbergen, I agreed to join. This was on 1 May 1960.

Our Arctic adventure took us through the magnificent mountain country of southern Norway, along roads that twisted up through fir forests and out on to mountain passes in the crisp air and the dazzling glare of sun and snow; then down again, falling steeply, gears grinding, the gorges below us cleaved through interlacing curtains of mauve mountains fading with distance to steel-grey – and in the valleys far below, silver fjords, threads of water laid across the russet carpets. We were early in the season – ahead of the tourists.

In the market square of Trondheim, stalls under their gaily coloured awnings were laden with fruit and vegetables and business was conducted with quiet dignity. The vendors did not shout for customers but stood neatly smocked, while the housewives buzzed like bumble-bees from one stall to another. It was a tidy, charming city, warm with contentment and early summer sunshine. It was one mile farther north of the equator than Hope Bay was south, and in the days that followed Hugh and I could not resist comparing the latitude of each village we passed with the sledging territory south of our old Antarctic base.

We crossed the Arctic Circle at a stretch of country bleak and windswept where the snow lay rotting and small streams dribbled into rivers congealed with ice and slush. Left behind were the great roaring waterfalls and boiling rapids. Ahead lay less spectacular gorges, less towering snow-capped mountains: but ahead lay north – we were drawn towards it.

Down we drove once again to sea-level and the fertile valleys dotted with pretty Norwegian villages. Mist swirled around the rugged hills and clung to us as we crawled along the cliff road. Tromso should have been in view but we could see nothing of it until we lost altitude, and there it was under a layer of cloud – a township of coloured houses peppered around the sea-shore of a small island and creeping up the side of a hill. It was the township from which Amundsen had set off on many of his voyages; and it was there that I received a cable from New Zealand asking me to go to Greenland to buy twelve huskies for the New Zealand Antarctic Expedition.

I had to be in Greenland by the beginning of September in order to allow myself at least two clear months in which to select the huskies and transport them down the coast to Søndre Strømfjord, the American Air Force Base. The U.S. Military Air Transport Service had agreed to fly me and the dogs from Greenland to New Zealand and on to the Antarctic, where I was to join the New Zealand Antarctic Expedition for two summers and a winter at Scott Base in McMurdo Sound.

McMurdo Sound – that magic name, the heart of Scott and Shackleton country. I would be seeing their old huts no doubt and treading where they had trod; perhaps even seeing the great Beardmore Glacier, perhaps even sledging to the South Pole on the fiftieth anniversary of the historic race between Amundsen and Scott. There were no limits to my joy; but it was short notice for Hugh to find a replacement and in any case I was set on the idea of visiting Spitzbergen, so I decided to go north, and take passage on the S.S. *Lyngen*, sailing south from Spitzbergen on 19 July. That would leave me only three weeks back in England to prepare for my trip to Greenland. However, in spite of having time only for a fleeting glance at the Lapps and a month on the island of Spitzbergen it was worth all the anxiety I later experienced.

We penetrated the vast moorland country of rolling fells, ever more and more of them rising in a purple haze towards a sombre horizon; past lakes and rivers bordered by stunted birch and willow trees, right into the heart of Lapp territory. Kautokeino, the capital of Finnmark, we half expected to be a 'Katmandu' of the tundra, but we found only an air of cynical hopelessness hanging over an agglomeration of huts occupied by sad, puzzled people. Their brightest aspect was their dress. Their facial skin was parchment crinkled, swarthy, and blushed by driving sleet, and seldom traversed by a smile.

Nor did the sun shine on Spitzbergen, that rugged, snow-capped archipelago set on the edge of the Arctic Ocean. Savage, icy seas pound the eastern seaboard, while on Spitzbergen's northern shore the great white desert of polar pack ice presses, cracking and groaning, high on to the beaches and well into the fjords. But up the west coast drifts the warm sea current that has mellowed the climate of the British Isles and the long coastline of Norway, and, although diluted and cooled considerably by the time it reaches Spitzbergen, it eats away the polar ice as far north as Latitude 81° during the summer months before sinking below the cold waters of the Arctic Ocean.

We disembarked at Longyearbyen, the largest mining settlement in Spitzbergen, but what a nether-world atmosphere that place had! The roads were inches deep in coal dust. 'Ghost' trucks roared along the road trailing tornado vortices of dust, which settled like a dark grey mist on the countryside and rattled in our nostrils. Streams of melt water flowed like soup between banks wet black and gouged away, while near by, Snow Buntings, like sooty sparrows, shuffled in their dust baths vainly hoping to get clean. Overhead the gently swaying aerial coal tubs, like wingless buzzards, moved silently in slow procession. It was a dismal scene of dereliction. Men occasionally emerged from shacks and scampered quickly out of sight as if afraid of daylight.

We sailed up Ice Fjord to our base camp at Brucebyen in the beautiful launch belonging to the Governor of Spitzbergen. But our vigil on deck was shortened by the buffeting wind which drove us below into a cabin bursting with seamen – burly and hairy-pullovered men, who wriggled their buttocks along the bench seats to make room for us at their table. The tinkle of ice against the wooden hull had awoken in us a nostalgia for the South, but it was a different polar scene that drifted by those portholes.

On Spitzbergen our routine of research was simple. There was no isolation; there was no long duration of great stress and hardship; there was no time for discontent to mar our relationships, but time enough lazily to watch the urgency of life around us. Birds flew to and fro all day or sat and strained to lay their eggs while the late June sun baked their backs and the tundra steamed around them. The eggs hatched out and the symphony of bird song rose in pitch and volume. The snow-bed plants burst into bloom, and melt pools that had teemed with larvae became dance floors of gnats, black midges and mosquitoes. Warmth drew the vegetable matter and the odour set the insects humming. Warmth melted the surface of the glaciers and water perspired down the smooth green creases. It trickled in little streams, and the streams joined up in torrents which boiled and cascaded with a roar into crevasses which in time filled up and flowed over. Great chunks of overhanging ice, eaten loose by the flow of melt water and the ambient pressures in the glacier, broke off and slithered or crashed into the sea.

But my month in Spitzbergen was soon over, and I had to leave while the tundra still hummed and steamed with summer – long before the chill autumn breezes paralysed the plants and froze the unborn flowers in bud. I had to paddle a canoe eighty miles along the fjord to catch the S.S. *Lyngen* sailing south, a three-day struggle through breaking seas, along a coastline aproned in scree or scarred by rushing melt streams; under towering, fluted cliffs of rock, past shimmering curtains of nesting birds, and through the ice-choked water in front of a glacier. I was cramped, wet, and very weary. On the second evening I capsized and steam curled off my sodden clothing as I lay beside a driftwood fire sinking into the spongy tundra which oozed moisture like brown beads of sweat.

That last morning I awoke to find a blue-grey fog smoking lazily off the swell and tumbling softly around a dead camp-fire. My body was stiff and cold, my clothing clammy with morning dew. I could see no more than twenty yards when I resumed my journey along the coast, so I hugged the cliffs which rose sheer from a froth of white water. The mist put a mute on sound that morning; even the plunging canoe only made a soft thud. The sea was like a pool of oil – the waves were smooth and slippery, and the seals that followed me for miles breathed quietly through dribbling nostrils. The cliffs had loomed, then drifted away, and my eyes had strained to find them as a cold dread chilled my aching body. Mist clung to the sea all that day, but by the evening I had reached a derelict cluster of mining shacks on the opposite side of a small tributary fjord from my destination. It was two miles from there across to Longyearbyen. the *Lyngen* was due to sail early the next morning.

A wiry, strained-faced man strode down to the water's edge, and together we lifted the canoe high on to the beach, then picked our way through the debris of broken-down buildings and abandoned mine workings towards a warped three-storeyed house. Most of its windows were shuttered and the door flapped gently, groaning in a steady breeze. Inside it was dark. Pit props held up the ceiling. The whole building leaned and the crumbling staircase creaked as we climbed to the attic.

My host was a recluse who had spent two previous winters in Spitzbergen hunting polar bears, and who was gathering together his stores and equipment for another winter. The squalid attic was his temporary retreat, until the time was right to occupy his tiny hut on the north shore of the island, where he would bait his traps, set his fixed guns, and wait for the bear to come. He was a man with a stare in his eye; a man who wintered alone by choice, a man with poetry in his soul – a hunter. Not for him the expedition with its snug comforts brewing friction. He was a truly polar man, a man who wintered without boast or praise; a nocturnal man who awakens at sundown and prowls around in polar darkness. We came from different worlds he and I – yet we spoke a common language, and while the wind moaned past the window we talked away the hours of sleep.

We talked about the Siberian driftwood that litters the shores of that Arctic island. Three years at least it had taken those timbers to drift across the Arctic Ocean. What a tale they could tell of their trans-Arctic journey had the knots in their grain been human eyes and the slits in their sides been mouths! It is hardly surprising that on the edge of that Ocean we contemplated the northern horizon.

A warm sun blazed in the eastern sky when we shook hands and parted the following day and I paddled the canoe the last two miles across the fjord to catch the *Lyngen*. Two hours later I was sailing south.

CHAPTER THIRTEEN

Sons, daughters and dogs

'Scandinavian Airlines announce the departure of their flight SK 935 to Søndre Strømfjord, Greenland. Will passengers for this flight please board the bus at gate number four. Thank you!'

Six days before I had left home. I knew the feeling well: a dragging in the pit of the stomach which lightens as the train starts rolling and lifts into a yell of joy as soon as I am on my way. I spent a few hectic days in London, which came dramatically to an end as I caught the flight to Copenhagen, with barely a minute or a breath to spare, and spent two days there making final preparations for my flight to Greenland. I had just over £400 left and a long directive on what had become known as 'Operation Husky'. My assignment was to purchase twelve huskies in Greenland and transport them to the Antarctic.

The aircraft roared down the runway at five minutes past midnight.

It was dark and raw, and about ten minutes to one, when we stepped out of the aircraft on to a blustery tarmac and ran for shelter towards a covered way which led directly into the hotel. It had taken only forty-five minutes by local time to fly 2,200 miles from Copenhagen to west Greenland!

Dawn crept over the rolling hills. A steel-grey runway, like a frozen lake, lay in shadow while the low sun washed the cliffs and fells and seeped down the hillside until it flooded the airstrip. But when it brightened into the glare of daylight it drained all beauty from the landscape, which became a desolate, seared scene of parched grasses and dust-devils swirling, cold tarmac and grey naked hills.

Away in the distance the American base sat purring with activity: it was from there I would fly with my twelve dogs if I could shake clear of that depressing prison and get into the villages to find them. For three days I paced the dusty roads counting minutes wasted, or listlessly flipped through magazines like my fellow men waiting for the fogs to lift along the coast. At last we were bundling aboard an amphibious plane and lurching in our harnesses as it trundled towards the start of the runway. An hour and a half of turbulent flight over rock-strewn fells and tongues of ice, along fjords gleaming in the sun, out to the sea and circling as the water rushed up to meet the floats and we thudded across the choppy bay to settle gently rocking beside a small launch spluttering, full of stocky Greenlanders, their faces wreathed in smiles. It was a different world!

The houses of Egedesminde were small and steeply roofed – maroon boxes scattered around the rocky outcrops, each sitting squatly on its nest looking blankly at its neighbour through white window eyes. On the quay Greenlanders stood sinking into rumpled trousers – bow-legs like pillars arched to support a paunch draped in scruffy sweaters – shoulders drooping, hands in pockets, their faces never far from smiling. Dogs scavenging around the sea-shore, loped from one rock to another, snarling, growling, gambolling; under-nourished dogs they were, galloping everywhere, or lying curled up in the dust. Little girls in long dresses carrying cans of water, picked up stones when dogs came near. Many children had been mauled by packs of dogs ravaged with hunger and a child had been eaten only three days before. They were not the dogs I needed. I wanted healthy, well-fed creatures from a village where the fishing was good and where the Greenlanders fed and were proud of their dogs.

There were four settlements on the west coast that had huskies with legendary strength, but these settlements were widely spaced. There was Quanak to the north of the new Thule, that enormous prefabricated American strategic air base. The Eskimos of Quanak had been re-settled there (ousted from their ancestral home) when the noise of a modern air base dispersed the hunting for miles around. Quanak was near good hunting territory; the dogs were well-worked and very strong. That would have been an ideal place had not so many died of rabies in the previous two years. But there was Upernivik, south of Melville Bay, and Umanak tucked away in a pocket of good hunting territory a little farther south, and finally there was Disto Bay where the settlement of Jakobshavn had a dog population of just over 3,000 – two dogs to every human and all well fed, for the fishing was good. Jakobshavn had supplied the dogs for many polar

expeditions in the past and was the nearest of the three to Egedesminde. South of Egedesminde there were no dogs, for the economy
was largely agricultural. So Jakobshavn it was to be, and by a stroke
of luck I found a berth that night on a supply ship sailing the next day.

They were a hard-bitten but a friendly crew, and in great demand as
lovers along the coast of Greenland. It is no wonder that the ethnic
features of the Greenlanders are changing fast. In the crew's quarters
through half the night we drank black coffee from chipped, dirty
cups, while the bo's'n and his sailors instructed me in the art of buying huskies, until I gently protested that they had never bought any.
They shrugged this off by insisting that it was the same as seducing
women – 'all you need is determination' – and so they talked on until
their latest girl friends dragged them protesting off to bed.

Jakobshavn was a tiny land-locked harbour surrounded by low
craggy hills under a dusting of summer snow. Cold, rough-hewn
hills they were, like a giant bird bath, its water sprinkled with brash
ice and sludge and tide marked with pale ochre stain. At the head of
the little harbour, windowless warehouses stood with their founda-
tions in the water, as if the hills had pushed them to the very edge.
They were in the shadow of the hill behind them, a shadow which lay
across the ice-choked harbour and stained the brash and sludge pale
blue; while in the sunlight the brash ice glistened and doubled each
piece in a reflection. Away from the water's edge, on each bald rock,
small box-like huts and houses stood – but there was not a soul in
sight save for two men in a launch which pushed through the ice
towards us.

The launch came alongside and we clambered in as it thumped
against the towering red hull of the coastal freighter. Last words of
advice rained down on me from the boatswain and his men as we
moved away, and into the tinkling ice we glided, poling our way
carefully between the green growlers and fending off the smaller
bergs that dazzled white in the warm sunlight. Alongside the quay a
row of huskies were standing, watching with interest as we climbed
the steps. They looked enormous from that angle, but once on the
quay I had a shock. The place was a seething *mass* of dogs, a human
settlement plagued with dogs! I saw no people about except the
passengers who had just come ashore, and they were as alarmed as
me. Past the warehouses and up the steep cinder hill to the road we

walked in a tight group, while around us the lean, wolf-like animals loped and galloped. We ploughed our way towards the Governor's office and burst through the door with a sigh of relief. 'You'll get used to it,' we were told by the laughing Danes who jumped up from their typewriters to come and shake us by the hand.

Three thousand dogs in one small village! But the main road I soon discovered was the only route a dog could take who had a mind to wander from the safety of his home. It was the precious right of all huskies in Jakobshavn to walk up and down the main roads without being attacked: over the rest of the district every square foot of ground is the territory of one pack or another. The boundaries of these territories are imaginary lines drawn on the tundra encircling the house from which the owner throws them food, and they end (in theory) at the near side of the road. Even so, dogs on the main road are harassed by the packs on each side – they are only relatively safe. A dog attempting a cross-country route from one side of the village to the other, would be torn to pieces and devoured if the kill occurred in the territory of a pack who had not been fed for a week. Boundary disputes between neighbouring packs are bloody affairs, and packs that are weak in number or courage are sometimes driven right under their owner's house. There is no bigger disgrace for a Greenlander than to own such a team.

The Greenlander's dogs are his pride and joy – even in a modern society where money has a value. The transition from hunting to a fishing economy robbed the Eskimo of his true dignity, for in the old culture only the finest hunter had real stature. He was a proud man who could entertain his neighbours with the best cuts from the game he had caught, and the feast would be conducted with great play of etiquette. He would welcome his guests and after casual chat about the ways of their world he would suddenly remember to offer them food. His guests would insist they had not come to eat, even though the host was renowned as a hunter, but they would accept his offer nevertheless. The host, after making much apology for the inadequate treat he was about to bring in, would drag in the largest carcass from his kill and chop it up with a show of embarrassment, while his guests would salivate audibly, then grab and eat the delicious meat raw. Praise was heaped on the hunter who fed them. But now that money buys most of their food and there are few great hunters left to admire, honour has shifted to the Greenlander who owns the finest dogs.

Many of the Danish administrators run excellent teams of dogs. The select group of men who changed the course of life in Greenland were all great travellers and hunters. The ironic thing is that many of the Danes' dog teams and driving techniques are equal to or better than the present-day Greenlanders', but the truth would never be admitted by the Greenlanders. For generations the Polar Eskimos were supreme in the technique of survival in the severe, implacable Arctic winters. The coming of the white men proved it to them: 'They are like children in our country,' the Eskimos would say with a shrug of resignation, '. . . and it is undignified to contradict a senseless child.'

But those days have passed. The Greenlanders now have large mortgages on small fishing boats. Many have nest-eggs in the bank. The comfort of a wooden house, with all the trappings their neighbours have, is too novel to be ignored, so they ignore instead their traditional skills, while the sporting Danes train up their teams and compete with the Greenlanders in the annual dog-races. The reason the Danes never win, according to hearsay, is because the Greenlanders cheat when they are out of sight of the settlements, rather than be beaten by a white man. When national pride comes up on trial the judges stand on very thin ice!

I did not intend to buy any dogs until I had seen as many as possible and had selected without committing myself. There were good reasons for being cautious: I had to have the best twelve dogs and time to prime the owners with favours, but I did not want to buy the dogs until two weeks before I sailed so that I would be saved the expense of feeding them during my first five weeks in Greenland. As house guest of the Governor I soon made social contacts and had a notebook full of dog-owners' names: Hans Kristiansen, Usias Falarine, Ellias and Isaiah: few of them had Eskimo names – they had changed their names when they became Christians. Indeed, they had changed their whole mode of living.

Gone were the turf and stone huts of the past where a visitor would enter through a long low tunnel crawling on his hands and knees – a hut almost circular, dingy inside, where the only light came from the tunnel and a window-pane made from the split intestines of a bearded seal, dried, sewn and stretched across a hole in the wall above the entrance. The hut would be bare of furniture of the conventional type, with only a platform of stone a few feet off the floor reaching from one side of the hut to the other, a communal bed, covered in skins, and a perch in the daytime for the women who sat making clothes for their family from bird skins, seal skins, and polar bear fur. A winter hut was lit by a blubber lamp and tended with care by the wife of the hunter, but it would be abandoned in the spring after its roof of flat stones had been stripped off to let in the crisp, pure air to drive out the odour of wintering – the odour of blubber, putrid meat, and stale urine.

Their houses are now built of wood brought from Denmark and erected under Danish supervision. I visited hundreds of houses during my short stay in Greenland. There were some so 'ripe' the smell stuck in my throat; others so clean I had to take off my boots and pad stocking-footed across parquet floors, but they all had a Greenland atmosphere about them.

Greenland has a charm all its own. This charm is a fusion of people and scenery warmed together into an impression that cannot be split up and studied closely. Sailing up the coast, you feel it. Sitting alone on the tundra, you feel it. High above a deep fjord watching the icebergs drift out to sea, you feel this same stirring of 'the soul. It is experienced by all men who live in Greenland for a while, although no man could ever fully express it. You become strangely conscious of direction: facing the sea you can feel the ice dome behind you – turn around and there is nothing in sight. And yet, you can sense that 'way up there' a great dome of inland ice is slipping towards you, fracturing, splitting, melting away, draining into morasses of slush and spilling into deeply gouged streams of melt water which roar down to the sea. You can feel the ice front of the glaciers calving. You can sense the struggle for survival, and the spiritual reserve that strengthened the Eskimos. It is profoundly moving.

The villagers seem lethargic now. They are in the twilight between the old and the new way of life. The villages still have atmosphere, but it is not felt when the Greenlander is singing hymns, nor is it felt in the fish market, or in the store or bakery: it is felt in the homes that smell of blubber, and down at the sea-shore where the kayaks are racked; it is felt in the old folks' sanatorium where I sat for hours drawing faces scarred with sharp winds and many hard winters; it is felt in the meeting houses and in the schools when there is talk of dog sledging and hunting. Only then does the soul of the Greenlander sing with the spirit of his forefathers.

I visited many villages from Jakobshavn to Upernivik searching for suitable dogs and giving slide shows about the Antarctic in the meeting houses and schools. At every show the huts were crammed with Greenlanders, and at one village they took down the back wall so that those who could not get into the hut could sit on the tundra and watch. The atmosphere at those lectures was unlike anything I had experienced before. It was a concentrated enthusiasm. A delightful rowdyism. Shrieking women and belly-laughing men drowned my translated commentary, and yet every picture that was flashed on the screen was studied for its minutest detail. The faces of the audience were masks of emotion, so engrossed in pictures of 'the other world of ice' that they were no longer conscious that I was present. They became once again the sons and daughters of Eskimos, living in each picture in which there were no white men, gasping in wonder at the strange snow scenes, ecstatic at the close-up shots of seals, and more and more puzzled as the pictures kept coming without sign or hint of any white women. The more curious they became the more subdued their response. Discretion forbade them to ask the burning question, and the first slide show had ended under a polite

Husky

but oppressive cloud of disappointment. At each slide show there-after I asked the interpreters before we went to the meeting house to add to their commentary the full but sad reasons why there are no women in 'the other world of ice'; but the truth upset the audiences even more than their own misinterpretations.

They were delightful old rogues to deal with when it came to buying dogs, and some of my happiest recollections of Greenland are of the wranglings that were conducted between the dog-owners and myself through my two interpreters. I often received the most incongruous answers to questions that were presumably lost in the translation somewhere between the four of us, but by drawing portraits of the dog-owners and priming them just before the final purchase with a crate of beer I eventually got the dogs I wanted.

The night was dark and still. The lights of the village were behind us – pricks of yellow, like a strange constellation hanging in the sky. Their reflections in the harbour shimmered and danced over the ripples, and blacked out when a berg glided by. It seemed as though our launch was motionless, and the gentle breeze which caressed our faces was bringing a ship through the night towards us. It loomed above us suddenly; the lights on the mast head silhouetting the sailors who leaned over the rail to welcome me.

'I hope you've got some good dogs there' – the bo's'n's voice, I recognized it.

'Twelve of the best that flattery could buy,' I grunted back as I heaved the first dog up towards a grapple of hands that reached down to take him. One by one the dogs were hauled aboard into the pool of light which flooded the well-deck and at last I scrambled up the ladder and over the rail to join them. The engine-room telegraph rang, the searchlights flashed on, and the Captain's voice shouted down from the bridge:

'Herbert! Dine with me when we're clear of the ice.'

'Thank you!' I shouted above the noise of the howling animals. And I stood there amongst them, a heart full of pride.

The lights in the well-deck had been switched off. All forward-facing portholes had been covered. Only the dim lights on the instruments suffused the bridge, framing the windows in a greenish glow. There was an occasional spurt of a lighted match: a canopy of stars above: no other light but the powerful beams that pierced the darkness from the stern and bow. The gentle throbbing of the engines soothed the dogs to just a whimper, and I moved among them talking softly while the ice slid by with ghostly grace. We were sailing south past the Jakobshavn Ice Fjord, which had been storing its bergs for many weeks. They were now pushing out into Disco Bay and we were weaving our way across their path. I have no memory of Greenland more powerful than the memory of that evening. Icebergs twenty times the size of our ship appeared as wraith-like forms on the port bow, growing, brightening; monsters swelling, fine aprons of foam around their base. Spotlights from the bridge and stern, range-finding the distance between ship and icebergs, looked like white eyes moving over their monstrous faces. They loomed and swallowed us with their size, slipped silently past or chased us a while, then faded less dramatically than they had appeared into the tenebrous depths of the night. More appeared and even more, while smaller pieces chattered and crunched down the ship's sides, and all the time those shafts of light, like sensitive feelers, caressed the bergs and seemed to push them gently out of the way.

Great friends we were, the Captain and I. He took the dogs and me 160 miles off his course, up the narrow Søndre Strømfjord, to save me chartering a fishing boat in the height of the season which would have cost me over £200 to compensate the fishermen for their loss of time. Three days the whole sea voyage took. Three happy days with a happy crew, while the dogs cried with sea-sickness and the other passengers grumbled. A big sea was running at the head of the fjord when the time came to ferry the dogs across to the shore, and the launch alongside was rising and falling six feet in the swell. There was not the finesse of winches and cradles to lower the animals into the launch, so we had to time its rise precisely and pitch the dogs on to its deck, which was slippery with their excreta by the time I made the leap myself. Only the safety line around my waist saved me from skidding over the side.

We rocked and leaped across to the jetty and made the landing without mishap, and then the ship blasted farewell and sailed away back down the fjord. I had sent a cable to the Transport Officer at the American air base two days before asking to be met, but there was no one in sight. The deserted harbour camp was scattered over a glacier-gouged valley, dusty and dry. It was an utterly desolate place, eight miles from the American base. All the huts were locked and shuttered, there was no fresh water for the dogs, and the dismal thought crossed my mind that if my cable had not reached the air base, only the ship's captain and crew would know where I was, so I tied the dogs up and started walking along the dusty track. I was met by a truck two miles up the valley and a colonel got out to welcome me, but because of the camp regulations that dogs were not allowed on base I had no choice but to leave my twelve huskies where they were. I had vaccinated the dogs against rabies and three other common dog diseases but the commandant of the base would not waive his regulations in the case of my dogs, nor would he permit me to live at the harbour to keep the dogs company. I was to be the guest of the Officers' Club and have transport to and from the harbour once a day to feed and water the huskies – there was absolutely no alternative.

For the next three days I was demented with worry, but at last my flight was confirmed and I took a truck and twelve aluminium dog-crates out to the harbour to collect my huskies. They were wild and scared and I was bitten three times before I had them safely crated and delivered to the airstrip. At dusk they were hoisted into the belly of an enormous Globemaster of the U.S. Military Air Transport Service, and it roared into the night on the first stage of my flight to the Antarctic.

We landed at Dover Air Force Base in Delaware at 3.30 a.m. local time and I was met by Wing Commander John Claydon, the New Zealand Air Attaché. He had been in charge of flying operations with the New Zealand section of the Commonwealth Trans-Antarctic Expedition, and his company was a pure delight. For the next five days the dogs were kennelled in quarantine, while as house guest of the Claydon family in Washington I enjoyed a round of private and Embassy cocktail parties, car rides and picnics in the country. I flew on with the dogs to California, and across the Pacific to Hawaii, Canton Island, and Fiji. At each landing, special quarantine regulations had to be honoured, and the dogs were rattled around in their crates as they were shifted from one place to another. It was an exhausting flight, confused with problems, arduous and swelteringly hot. The 'dog flight' as the Americans called it seemed to take weeks, and drained the energy out of the animals with each pant of breath as they softly whined in their oven-like crates. The Press at each landing crowded around expecting to see ferocious animals come bounding stiff-haired and snarling from their crates. They were disappointed. But leis of flowers were placed about the dogs' necks in Honolulu and they were patted by a nervous Miss Fiji who did not really need such publicity, so by the time we reached Christchurch we were hardened V.I.P.s who could put on a polished performance.

Dick Walcott met me at Christchurch airport. It was a delightful reunion with an old friend of Hope Bay days; but we had little time to reminisce for he was to take the dogs on to Scott Base in Antarctica and return to New Zealand on the first flight back, while I made my reports and presented records of my expenses to the Government accountant. Mr Markham flew in from the Antarctic even while Dick and I were chatting. He had been on a quick tour of inspection, and looked drawn and very ill. I had somehow expected the Superintendent of Antarctic Division to look differently, for my only contact with him up till then had been at the receiving end of lengthy directives, finished off with a flurried, mural-type signature. I had got the impression of a meticulous mind controlling a small but efficient organization. What I saw was a man dressed in 'scruff order', coughing with rage because his suit had not been sent to the airport, his face ashen, his hair dishevelled – not a rugged, dynamic explorer, for that he would never be: he was a Civil Servant, an administrator, with a flair at phone calling, a raucous laugh and usually a twinkle in his eye. He welcomed me with apologies for his sour demeanour and we boarded the domestic flight for Wellington.

The following day I proudly made my way with an account of my expenditure on 'Operation Husky' to the Government department that dealt with such things. By my modest estimate I had saved over £300 by using portraits as currency, and building with them a pile of goodwill from the top of which I could see routes through a maze of expensive problems. The office was in a wooden building and I was shown into a room full of desks and clerks, and introduced to an officious little man who went through my entries one by one demanding receipts to check against my figures. He became sarcastic as the interview dragged on, and the underlings in the office pricked their ears with interest. He challenged me on the beer I had bought for the Greenlanders to anaesthetize them while we came to an agreement and before I took their dogs from them. He challenged me on the cigars I had put in their mouths and behind their ears. But where I had saved on living expenses by living rough or staying as the guest of kindly folk, he scoffed at my honesty in admitting it and added tens of pounds on the basis of a daily living allowance. To my horror I felt myself fluttering in the web of officialdom, and in tearing myself away I left behind my statement of accounts.

Two days later the report came through. By my honest reckoning the assignment had cost £600 18s. 2d. This was 18s. 2d. more than I had been given in London with which to buy twelve dogs in Greenland and to keep myself and the dogs in a state of good health until we reached the Antarctic. In fact I had brought thirteen dogs with me from Greenland, for the day before I had sailed from Jakobshavn an old Greenland woman had made a present of a three-month-old husky pup which I had slipped into the crate with the bitch. The dog crates had cost £188 but that bill had been paid in Washington by the New Zealand Embassy, and the prohibitive cost of the airlift from Greenland to the Antarctic was the generous gift of the American taxpayer.

My grand total expenditure on 'Operation Husky' according to the Civil Servants was £613 15s. 4d. and a note enclosed informed me – with the compliments of the accountant – that they had paid into my bank account the 'over-expenditure'. I had made a profit of £12 17s. 2d.!

CHAPTER FOURTEEN

Scarcely a moment to shudder

My mind had been so preoccupied with problems of my Greenland mission that I had spared little thought to my forthcoming sojourn in the Antarctic. I could not hope to recapture the same feeling of elation that I had had on first entering that world of ice; but what nagged me more than nostalgia for Hope Bay was the realization that the Antarctic was under assault. I had grown accustomed to the size, the power, and the isolation of that continent. The time we had spent in Graham Land had left its mark on us. Ours were not transient memories, we had felt the solemnity too deeply. We had heard, of course, of 'Operation Deep Freeze' – the colossal American onslaught on Antarctica, but we could scarcely credit it. The Antarctic, we felt, would not permit its face to be scarred by thunderous machinery – it would not suffer the presence of men who did not pull their own sledges or drive their own teams of dogs. The Antarctic, in short, had been and always would be for explorers only.

Around A.D. 650, according to Rarotongan legend, the Polynesian voyager Hui-te-rangiora, had sailed his canoe so far south that he had seen 'things like rocks' amongst the frozen sea. The Dutchman, Abel Tasman discovered the west coast of New Zealand in 1642 and believed that his discovery was part of 'Terra Australis' – a hypothetical continent existing in the minds of the geographers of that time, and occupying a large expanse of the southern hemisphere on their globes of the world. Ever since the Portuguese sailor Ferdinand Magellan had sailed through the straits that bear his name, 'Terra Australis' had been an attractive idea; but between 1772 and 1774, when Captain Cook made voyages into Antarctic waters without sighting land, the geographers began to lose faith in their hypothesis.

Captain Cook had no successors for nearly fifty years, for it was not until the Russian, Thadderus von Bellingshausen, circumnavigated the Antarctic in 1820 that any ships entered the pack ice for the sole purpose of discovery. There was a very active sealing industry in the Southern Ocean during that period – the British and Americans vigorously competing – but most of the sealing skippers were too busy to go in search of new land. There were, however, some exceptions: Edward Bransfield and Nathaniel Palmer both reported discovering the northern part of the Antarctic Peninsula in 1820; James Weddell two years later made a deep penetration into the sea that bears his name; and of course, there was John Biscoe, the most renowned of all sealer/explorers, who circumnavigated the continent, discovered Enderby Land, and annexed Graham Land for the British Crown in 1832.

With the Antarctic found at last, the temptation to send expeditions south was irresistible, and early in 1840, within a few days of each other, the Frenchman Dumont d'Urville and the American, Charles Wilkes, both discovered continental ice south of Australia. But it was James Clark Ross, with the *Erebus* and *Terror*, who made the most momentous discovery. Ross sailed south from Tasmania in 1840, and his two ships fought their way through a belt of pack ice into what is now known as the Ross Sea and, sailing in almost ice-free waters, traced the spectacular coastline of Victoria Land for nearly 500 miles, finding at the southern limit of their cruise two massive conical mountains, one of which was an active volcano. He named them Erebus and Terror after his ships, while the bay to the west he called McMurdo. He charted the sea front of the Ross Ice Shelf for 200 miles and came within fortune's breath of using McMurdo Sound as wintering quarters for his ships. Ross was knighted for his discoveries, but almost sixty years went by before the balance of geographic interest once more tipped towards the Antarctic.

The stage was set for the epic adventures – heroism, patriotism, the race for the Pole, the saga of Ernest Shackleton – the setting was ideal, the time was right.

The overture was the work of Adrien de Gerlache and the Belgian Expedition at the end of the nineteenth century. Their vessel *Belgica* was beset in the ice of the Bellingshausen Sea and drifted through the first winter in the Antarctic. The sufferings of the crew were terrible. Many of them might have died from scurvy had it not been for the skill and courage of the ship's surgeon Dr Frederick Cook and the first mate of the *Belgica*, Lieutenant Roald Amundsen. In 1908 Dr

Cook attained the North Pole (although attainment is controversial), and in 1911 Captain Roald Amundsen reached the South Pole, beating Captain R. F. Scott by thirty-five days.

The Norwegian, C. E. Borchgrevink, on 1 March 1899, planted the Union Jack near Cape Adare. There his party spent the first winter ashore on the mainland of Antarctica. Nordenskjöld and Scott followed two years later. The decade of Pole-seeking had begun. From the *Discovery*, wintering in Hut Cove, McMurdo Sound, Scott set out with Dr Edward Wilson and Lieutenant Ernest Shackleton and sledged to Lat. 82° 17′ S, setting up a record farthest south. But they were only beginners in the technique of polar travel.

Shackleton, sent home as unfit from Scott's first Expedition, returned with his own expedition in 1908, which was an outstanding success, a triumph marred only slightly by the misfortune which robbed him of being the first man to reach the South Pole. Shackleton had been obliged to winter at McMurdo Sound – much to the displeasure of Scott who considered it his preserve. McMurdo Sound was ideally situated as a base for explorations in Victoria Land – and, by following the coast southward, across the Ross Ice Shelf, the party could gain access to the polar plateau and the Pole up the Beardmore Glacier. That route, discovered and pioneered by Shackleton, was used by Scott in 1911 during his gallant trudge to the South Pole, while Amundsen, blazing a new trail to the east, forced a route through the Queen Maud Range up the Axel Heiberg Glacier and on across the polar plateau to the Pole. McMurdo Sound was also used as a wintering location by the Ross Sea support party of Shackleton's Imperial Trans-Antarctic Expedition 1914–17. That expedition was without a doubt the most abortive and yet the greatest saga in the history of the exploration of the continent.

Those were the true heroes, the true explorers of the Antarctic. Their stories were the raw material of my feelings for the South and, mixed with my own memories, they had branded me an incurable romantic. So it was with their spirit in my heart that I stood before a desk at Christchurch Airport, under a sign marked 'Antarctic Flight'.

There were two New Zealanders waiting for the same flight as myself and we were soon in conversation, sharing as much information as we each had to offer about Scott Base and the U.S. Naval Air Facility at McMurdo. The question that had been puzzling me was why the Americans were prepared to give so much assistance to the New Zealanders in the Antarctic – assistance which clearly went far beyond ordinary good-neighbourliness. I was told that apparently there was an agreement between the two governments, under which facilities were made available to the United States Antarctic Expeditions in New Zealand, in return for the provision of air-transport for New Zealand personnel and equipment to and from the Antarctic, and the logistic support of New Zealand field parties. What 'logistic support' meant I was not too sure. I had heard those words mentioned frequently over the past few days in Wellington at the office of the Antarctic Division and at the Department of Lands and Survey, where the Surveyor General had cross-examined me on my surveying experience. He had also pointed out a map of the Ross Dependency, the area in which I would be working during the coming season, so I was able to pass this information on to my companions – but they did not seem particularly interested.

Even less excited at the prospect of going South were the American servicemen who stood about in groups beside their bulky flight bags. I could not overhear their conversations but they all seemed considerably relieved when we were given our flight numbers and told to report back to the flight desk the following morning.

The flight was postponed until 5 p.m. The weather-ship on station half-way to the Antarctic had reported strong head winds at the flying altitude, but these slackened during the day and we boarded the Globemaster as the shadows lengthened. Inside that overheated whale of an aircraft we sat like so many little Jonahs, our safety-belts tied to the ribs of the monster whose innards were an odd collection of crates and miscellaneous equipment. The other Jonahs were almost all soon sleeping off a good last night in Christchurch. Of those that were awake there were none who wanted to go South – for them, so they told me in no uncertain terms, it was just a bad posting, and their knowledge of the Antarctic was elementary.

When the announcement came from the 'bridge' that the Captain was going to 'cool the aircraft' to acclimatize the passengers to the Antarctic, the men changed into their polar clothing without a flicker of excitement, then curled up in balls and fell asleep.

There is only one way to go to the Antarctic, I had told my two

New Zealand companions, and that is to go by sea. Only by plunging through hurricanes in a tiny ship groaning with the wind screaming in the rigging, and only when the weight of life seems heavier than death can you appreciate fully those sea lanes through the dazzling pack ice, and the tranquil pools where nature rests and mirrors her beauty in the surface. Only after days of crashing and groaning through narrowing leads and after the ship has been beset in the vice of pack ice can you appreciate the joy of the final breakthrough – the release, and the first sight of ramparts of ice along the coastline. Only after all this can you feel the immensity and the isolation of the white continent. But from the small steamy windows of that giant aircraft flying in the slit between sea ice and the cloud ceiling I had a new aspect of the Antarctic, and saw what I could never have imagined.

The splendour of the ice world below had an ethereal quality. On the port side, the Ross Sea stretched to the horizon carpeted with ice. Green-greys ran into mauves and lighter purples under clouds moist with strokes of shadow. It was about 3.30 a.m. The diffused light of the sun on the port quarter soaked the clouds in a glow which bathed the carpet of ice. Shreds of brilliance in the leads caught the sun for an instant and shot out beams of blinding light. The waterways were still, but as our aircraft droned above them, sunlight brushed them into animated lanes and lakes which sank into indigo and were left behind as jet-black scars across a deep mauve field of ice. On the starboard side the scene was a spectrum of texture and colour. The mountains of Victoria Land were banked in clouds warmed into pastel browns by the low sun, their tops touched with pink against the pale blue patches of sky. The snow slopes blushed in alpenglow, and the rock cliffs, dark grey in the shadows, warmed in the pools of sunlight. The carpet of ice on the starboard side was softened with purple-grey and caressed by the delicate pink of sunlight which seemed to breathe over the surface as our aircraft droned south. In just over an hour we had flown down the coast of Victoria Land and were cruising over McMurdo Sound. Ships would not break through that barrier of pack ice for another three weeks, and the first aircraft of the new Antarctic season had landed at McMurdo Sound on 3 October, two months ahead of the icebreakers.

Mount Erebus rose as we lost altitude and the small bays and capes on Ross Island stood clear-cut against the indigo sea, ice-free in a small stretch along the coast. We were flying past the old huts of Shackleton and Scott, but I could not see them against the rash of dark rocks that spread up the slopes. Mount Erebus moved across the path of the sun and lay in deep shadow on her western side. From her volcanic cone a puff of vapour caught the sun and turned to gold. We sank lower until we could see sastrugi on the white surface below. Tracks over it led our gaze from an airstrip cross gouged out of the thick bay ice, towards two capes of light-brown rock, encroached on by a flow of black basalt which did not quite reach the cluster of minute buildings nestling between them. Beyond the southernmost cape stretched the Ross Ice Shelf – the great white desert.

Our aircraft circled above the airstrip as the baggage master ordered everyone to fasten their seat belts. The reluctant passengers looked out at the dazzling white world which rose up to meet the great wheels of the aircraft, and cursed. There was a lurch and a roar of engines, then a long whine and a bumpy ride off the runway. I was once again in Antarctica; but five years older than I had been when I leapt from the motor-boat to slippery rocks of Duse Bay on the other side of the Antarctic mainland in Graham Land.

The wings of the Globemaster were still flapping as we clambered down the ladder on to the ice, and the cold hit us like the first sea breaker over a sunbather's body. The sky was without a single cloud, the air was crystal clear and sharp. There was not a breath of wind. It was quite unlike Graham Land. There was grandeur – space for mountains to grow to great heights and yet look small under the dome of cold blue sky. Mount Erebus, 12,450 feet, was dwarfed by the immensity of the scene, but in the clarity of the atmosphere every detail was finely chiselled and tricked the eye into believing that the volcano was only a few miles away. We, the New Zealanders and myself, stood engrossed while our fellow passengers were boarding the 'taxi'. We did not hear them calling to us; but we were quite content to walk the three miles from the airstrip to the camp and to indulge in a long draught of that pure atmosphere.

Low ground drift was snaking across the ice by the time we staggered into the American base, a mere cluster of huts when it was established in 1955 as a staging-post for long range-flights, but now affectionately known as McMurdo City and housing in the summer as many as six hundred men. We walked down the draughty streets past sailors muffled in parkas striding hastily from one hut to another, and entered the mess hall in time for breakfast. It was a cafeteria-style service and the food was excellent. An enormous Negro, sweating and smiling, served us with ham and eggs and bantered chat for a moment with each of us as we moved by.

There was no expedition atmosphere about that mess hall – it was a massive naval operation with the buzz of efficiency about it. I turned at the end of the production-line service to face a sea of khaki windproofs and a mural of faces as cosmopolitan as Soho. Nor were they all eating breakfast – many of them were eating supper. The menu was the same for everyone; it was the accepted misfortune of the night shift that they were out of phase.

After breakfast I asked for directions from a lower-deck sailor who was putting on a parka made of expensive-looking material, khaki and shiny, with the letters 'U.S.N.' stamped across the back. He had heard of Scott Base, he admitted, but was uncertain of exactly where it was, so to make sure that he put us on the right path he took us to the Chaplain, who gave us directions and God's speed, and an hour later we walked into Scott Base just in time for a second breakfast.

It was a neat cluster of huts – a centre-trace dog team of yellow-painted boxes on either side of a covered passageway. Scattered about like truant huskies were a few other huts which we presumed housed scientific apparatus too sensitive to be put with the rest of the equipment in the science hut, while the larger buildings were garages for the vehicles: two weasels, three tractors, a bulldozer, a Land-Rover and a Sno-cat in retirement after its trans-Antarctic journey with Sir Vivian Fuchs in 1957-8. The base had been built by the Ross Sea Party of the Commonwealth Trans-Antarctic Expedition in mid-February, 1957, and had been occupied by New Zealand parties ever since. One building dominated the encampment – the aircraft hangar, erected shortly after the Commonwealth Trans-Antarctic Expedition. It is believed to be the biggest building in Antarctica, and as if to advertise its size it was painted a brilliant orange. The irony is that no money was left after that to furnish it with aircraft and it has since been used as a food store, for which it is more than adequate. The air temperature was almost ten degrees colder in the Scott Base vicinity than it was at McMurdo City for, like a white sea the Ross Ice Shelf flows up to the coastline a few yards from the

base and 'breakers' of ice heave themselves up in rows like surf
riding in from the ocean. In front of the base, down on the ice shelf,
I could see the dogs like strings of beads neatly laid out in rows.

The covered passageway was low and the still air in it was chill. At
intervals we passed junctions where short passageways led to various
huts, thus separated one from the other to avoid the risk of total loss
in the event of a fire. A sign pointed to the mess and we followed it
to a heavy refrigerator door. This opened with a metallic creak and
we contorted ourselves over the threshold and into a resonant porch
– a vault of tin – in which hung the anoraks of those who had passed
through another 'fridge' door into the mess. It was a stark box-
shaped room crammed with men. Introductions all round became a
scrum. They were a tough-looking crowd of fellows from whom
Captain Peter Hunt rescued me to show me around the rest of the
base.

I started my conducted tour in the science hut – a box-shaped
building like the rest, but one choked with electronic equipment
ticking and buzzing and penning marks on rotating drums. It was
like being inside an enormous radio set, and the mere sight of it was
more than enough to impress on me the fundamental difference
between Scott Base and my old base at Hope Bay, for here was a
scientific observatory, collecting data in fields of science which meant
almost nothing to me: Geomagnetism, Seismology, Ionospherics,
D-Region observations, 'Whistlers', Auroral studies, Auroral Radar,
and Meteorology. Only the latter had been our small contribution to
geophysical science at Hope Bay, such work being done at other
British bases, but I kept such comparisons to myself as Peter Hunt
strode around the base that had been his home for just over a year.

Down the covered-way I bounded in pursuit of my guide, who
created a slip-stream of cold air which turned sharp left at the first
junction and went outside, across six yards of well-trodden snow to
the main garage. The fleet was out. The cavity left behind was dingy
but warm and the only sound was the dull roar of the stove. Around
the walls were greasy engine parts; on the floor were pools of oil;
above our heads glowed naked lights coated with a film of grime.

We went back into the covered-way and breezed along to the next
junction, turned left again, through the heavy door and into the
cold-porch with its kerosene air-heater rumbling softly. Our boots

clattered on the metal floor of the porch and over the threshold of another refrigerator door into the almost seductive atmosphere of one of the living-huts. The floor was covered with linoleum, and curtained cubicles cuddled each other on both sides of the corridor. We peeped shyly in at each one; a cosy shambles some of them, others were neat and antiseptic; and breathing warm air into all of them were the pale pink mouths of the air vents.

On we went with scarcely a moment to shudder; down the covered-way and into the hut with the toilet, spare generator, and photographic darkroom. Out again and down the covered-way, past another junction leading, so I was told, to another sleeping-hut; through another refrigerator door at the end of the covered-way, through another cold-porch and yet another heavy metal door, into the sledge workshop. It was a clutter of equipment and vacated sleeping-bags of the summer men who had no room elsewhere to sleep. Near by was a poky little survey office and a big bare washroom. Partitioned off the washroom was a pine walled bathroom, and following its plumbing we went out of another door, along a short sleeve-like passage into the rumbling generator hut. Two enormous 48 kVA generators sat gleaming, one resting, the other throbbing.

We retraced our steps to the mess room, off which went a steamy, food-smelly kitchen, a radio room and the base leader's office; and Peter Hunt let me relax, exhausted with my first impressions, with a cup of coffee while he stood at one of the square porthole windows gazing south.

CHAPTER FIFTEEN

The whisper of discontent

On the fourth morning after I had arrived at Scott Base four of us loaded our two Nansen sledges, hitched up the dogs, and burst away on the start of our journey to Scott's farthest south latitude of 1902.

Amongst the two teams of dogs were the pick of the animals I had brought from Greenland, and once clear of the base on the crisp unmarked snow I felt the surge of exhilaration I had missed for so long. The freedom of open country lay ahead – but something was lacking. There had been no build-up of expectation for me; no long winter months of preparation, or spring months of training and final checking – all that had been done by Peter Hunt who had spent the previous summer in the field with dog teams and the winter at Scott Base.

Nor had I yet felt completely at ease with my new sledging companions, who only four days before had been strangers to me. Our last few days had been so hectic that there had been little time to get fully acquainted. Neville Cooper, who was to be my tent mate, had spent two months of the previous summer with the New Zealand Alpine Club's man-hauling party working in the foothills near the mouth of the Beardmore Glacier – I had been fascinated by his description of that great sweeping torrent of ice, and was determined to question him more closely during the weeks ahead. Malcolm Laird, the geologist of our party and a keen pot-holer, seemed to be a most companionable fellow. Neither Malcolm nor Neville had enjoyed much experience of dog-sledging, but the time had surely come for them to learn during the journey on which we were embarking.

It was not a long journey out to the airstrip – in less than an hour our teams were picketed alongside an American Dakota and we were busy loading our gear and dogs into the aircraft at the direction of its pilot, Lieutenant Don Angier of the famous U.S. Navy VX-6 Squadron, and soon we were roaring into the air on our way south over the great Ross Ice Shelf.

Basically their techniques of sledging were the same as ours, for they had been established by Dr George Marsh, an ex-Hope Bay man and dog expert with the Ross Sea Party of the Commonwealth Trans-Antarctic Expedition. But modifications had evolved over the years, and my second big shock came on the very first evening. The Dakota had touched down to a perfect landing on an ice-field at the edge of the Nimrod Glacier at Latitude 82° 15′ S. We had off-loaded the stores and spanned out the dogs, and the aircraft had taken off with a roar of rockets blasting the snow into a plume of blizzard. We had pitched the tents; the evening was warm but the sky was slashed with cirrus clouds hooked by the high winds of the stratosphere. Instinctively I prepared for the violent storm and was amazed that my companions were so unconcerned. Small items of equipment they left lying around as if blizzards were unheard of. They watched with interest but without a word – they had no doubt thought 'a queer one we've got here!' – and when I had finished Neville informed me that they had not had a blizzard the previous summer!

It took me fully two months to adapt myself to the new environment; a summer of sledging over easy, safe country; a summer of adjustment to a broad terrain, big and pure, snow plains and low hills, mountain ranges serrating the edge of a blue sky dome, spectacular icefalls, sweeping glaciers, high climbs on bare rock above clouds which churned in the valleys below, and sledging in mist on iron-hard snow. Two re-supply landings were made by the Americans to save us relaying stores. Not even the radio gave us trouble – we made contact with base 300 miles away without fail once a day. The summer was spent surveying with much more precision than was possible in hostile Graham Land, and which resulted in a map covering over 10,000 square miles of unexplored territory: It was a great success, a credit to everyone connected with it, and the most boring and frustrating two months I ever spent in the South.

It was not until the last two weeks when the weather deteriorated and the first blizzards blew, when we ran into crevasses on the Ross Ice Shelf and crossed the track of Scott, Wilson, and Shackleton in their farthest south bid of 1902, that I found a better harmony with my companions. They had been very tolerant, but one cannot form deep bonds with men on a picnic.

The last two weeks had brought us together and given me a slight

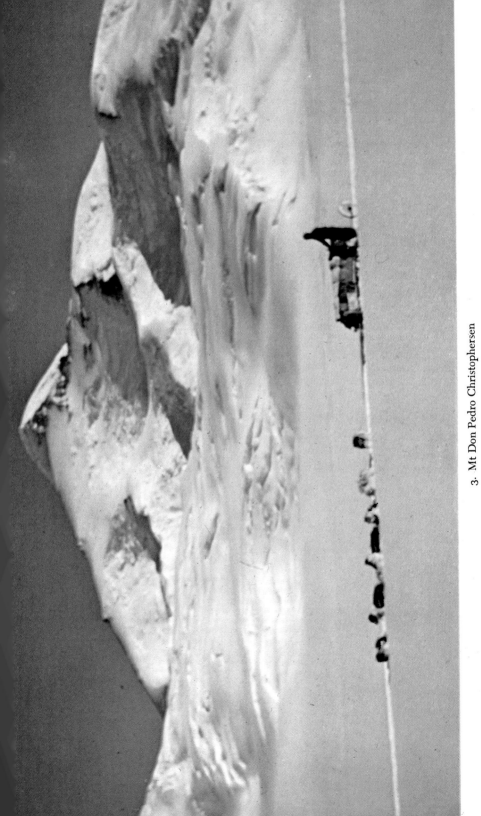

3. Mt Don Pedro Christophersen

hope for the near future, for I had seriously thought at one time of resigning as soon as I had completed the sledging – it had seemed to me that precious time was slipping by, but exciting ideas for the following summer began fermenting in my mind and I grew anxious to see the winter.

We were picked up by the last flight of a Dakota that season and landed at McMurdo airstrip in the early hours of 9 February. Unloading and organizing our dogs took a long time and the first part of the route was rough, but as we drew away from the snow ramps, huts, and general debris at the airstrip, and our field of view extended, we saw that the open water in McMurdo Sound had eaten to within a mile of the runway, and moored alongside the ice edge were two large ships and a tiny one. At first I did not recognize her. She looked rusty and dirty, but her profile was too familiar to keep me guessing much longer – it was the old *John Biscoe*. Nostalgia which I had only so recently dispelled came flooding back to me. She was a worn old girl, a tired old girl; trying to hide her shame under a different name – H.M.N.Z.S. *Endeavour*. How callous to burden her with such a grand title and not dress her with dignity in her old age. Nine years she had served the British bases in Graham Land as the *John Biscoe* and four years she had sailed for the New Zealand expeditions as the supply ship for Scott Base. I remembered her purring in Duse Bay, her well-deck aglow, the night dark and still – my first night ashore on the Antarctic mainland. But my companions were hungry, breakfast was waiting, the breakfast we had longed for during the last two months: fresh eggs and bacon.

We cheered and drove on. Those last miles slid by – the last miles of dog-sledging for my three companions. No one came out to welcome us home, but breakfast was what we looked forward to most. We stumbled along the covered-way into the mess. A few men grunted as we passed through to the kitchen, where on the stove sat a big bowl and a ladle. The bowl was full of a greasy mince, the eggs were locked away and the cook was sulking.

Many of the summer men had already gone back to New Zealand, and of those that were left at base, few spoke to us unless spoken to and those who spoke were curt. Men sneaked about the base or marched with a show of truculence. Men talked in whispers like conspirators or sang at their work with bellicose force. The pure air in our lungs choked on this atmosphere, but we spent the rest of the day down at the dog lines checking our equipment and chopping up seal meat and did not breathe it again until five o'clock, when a man crept up to us whispering 'do you want a beer?' We whispered 'yes!' and followed him on tip-toe to the rendezvous in the garage. There we met most of the others we had seen about the base during the day, but they welcomed us afresh into the fold – the air of mutiny was rife. For an hour we listened to petty grousing boiling into burning hatred. And at six o'clock the beer cans were hidden and the men crept in twos and threes off to dinner.

Over dinner hardly a word was said, but men caught each other's glances, and the mess cleared the instant the meal was over. It was almost too incredible to believe. We were fresh from the field, innocent and slightly puzzled, but we were indirectly to blame for the choleric atmosphere, for according to the fellows at base we had been having an easy time and getting all the glory. Not one of them would have swapped their job for a summer's sledging: they were not frustrated explorers, they were disgruntled maintenance men and technicians whose morale had sunk to the ebb at which only their grievance was in sight. But low morale is infectious and in spite of our hard work during the next few days killing, gutting and stock-piling seals, I too became depressed.

My three sledging companions flew back to New Zealand. The *Endeavour* sailed away at the end of its career as a polar ship. The sun was dipping below the horizon, the curtains were closing on my fourth summer South, and the prospect of winter was miserable. But we gathered in the mess for breakfast one morning and found two new men in our midst. The last aircraft of the season had flown in from New Zealand bringing us a new base leader – the old one had flown at dawn. We breathed an enormous sigh of relief. Momentarily there was a ray of hope, but the awful turmoil of autumn was on us – a testing time for a new leader with no previous Antarctic experience.

Two ships were still alongside the ice edge frantically off-loading cargo as the ice broke up. Vehicles and equipment rode out to sea on pans of ice, and helicopters thwacked the air above them, pin-pointing their position for the icebreaker *Eastwind* as it rounded up the rafts of ice to retrieve the drifting stores and plant. The flagged routes from McMurdo City cracked and breathed as the pace of unloading grew to fever pitch. The new Scott Base leader in his enthusiasm offered my assistance to the Americans as an ice expert, which I found acutely embarrassing, but the Americans were too busy with their helicopter shuttle-service and rescue operations to take the offer seriously. At that time of stress Peter Otway and I were busy moving the dogs on to safe ground and bulldozing their winter food – twenty-five tons of mutton and seal – up above the tide crack, while the maintenance men and technicians in their rattling vehicles drove to and from the ice edge ferrying stores with desperate urgency and at considerable risk of floating adrift. Only the radio operator and the cook were tied to the base by the nature of their jobs. Our new base leader, tingling with importance, was at the nerve centre of activities – the bridge of the U.S.S. *Arneb*. Every radio set in McMurdo was tuned to the ship-to-shore frequency. It carried only messages of urgency. It was a radio drama encroached on in the height of suspense by our leader's bleating orders of mundane significance sprinkled with curses at his men. It must have curled the lips of our courteous American friends to hear those extraordinary tirades, but they were a cause of anxiety in our camp. Were we in for a bad winter after all? If we were it would be my first.

The last ship sailed on 12 March and the sea continued to gnaw its way relentlessly into the Ross Ice Shelf, but there was no longer the risk of losing men or equipment. All American aircraft had been moved to safe winter quarters and the route between McMurdo City and Scott Base now went overland. Tensions eased and men looked around at the fellows with whom they were to winter. Our leader, conscious of his inexperience in polar regions, set up an advisory committee of five men of which he was chairman, but it was looked on as a farce at a base of only thirteen men and was disbanded in the middle of March after a heated debate on what should be done about the two American 'Yogs' – the 600-ton oil-storage vessels – that had broken free from their moorings at Hut Point and were slowly drifting out to sea. They had been towed to the Antarctic in 1955 and were filled up each summer with aviation fuel to supply aircraft during the spring flying activities. One of the 'Yogs' was empty but the other had aboard 200,000 gallons of aviation fuel. It was suggested that I, with one companion, should load up the pram dinghy (which was not in a seaworthy condition), and with an outboard engine we should take it out to sea and board the 'Yog' with our theodolite and radio, and from thenceforth until we were finally rescued transmit her position during the drift, thereby making certain that it was not lost on the high seas. I declined, and the 'Yogs' drifted beyond range of the helicopters and were never seen again.

By the time the sea ice had re-formed at the end of March, autumn was closing fast. The air temperature had plunged and outside tasks became a race against the fading light. The maintenance men, besides their regular jobs, had to transfer 30,000 gallons of fuel oil from the American storage tanks at McMurdo to the rows of 44-gallon drums that nestled together like the thick pile of a tin carpet over the nearby outcrops of rock. Night and day they pumped from the tankers that had been towed by bulldozers the three miles from McMurdo to Scott Base, while Peter Otway and I worked on the meat pile, digging into it with the blade of the bulldozer. We quartered each frozen carcass with a chain saw, and reduced them to seven-pound blocks with the power saw driven by a Ferguson tractor. Not for us the swinging axe and sweat we used at Hope Bay, but then at Hope Bay we were all sledging men in competition one with the other. At Scott Base there were only the two of us to look after the dogs, repair the equipment and prepare the field rations for the next field season. We were, in the eyes of the other fellows on base, 'redundant field men' just filling in the time until the following summer. They had no intention of helping us because we had not the ability to help them in return. The technicians conscientiously did their work and collected scientific data by the ream; the maintenance men kept the base lit, warm and working; the radio operator kept his morse key tapping; the cook kept us fed and the base leader requisitioned for the coming year's stores. We were a base split by taboos on each other's tasks.

But I found it hard to reconcile the lack of friendly co-operation with the tremendous feeling of satisfaction we gained from doing arduous tasks on our own – those twilight days at the whirring saw, screeching in a descending scale as it chewed through the frozen meat; dust and exhaust fumes swirling around, blocking my nostrils, matting my beard; the thunder of the bulldozer near at hand digging up more carcasses to be cut up and stacked; the physical ache at the end of the day after the tractor and bulldozer had been put away,

when Pete and I would stumble into the sledge workshop and strip off
our blubbery anoraks; the glow which came with the wash before
dinner ; a row of men each with different grime on their hands and
different motives in their hearts for committing themselves to a long,
dark winter.

There came with the fading light an air of expectancy. It was in the
first blizzards that swept from the south, it was in the long shadows
and the glow on the clouds, it was in the first stars, the beams of the
headlights and the swinging lanterns carried around the dog lines. It
was in the full drums of fuel, the laden meat sledges, and the
reflector lights on the marker flags. It was in the very smell of winter
which alerted the senses. And when the shadow of the earth crept
above the horizon we slipped from twilight into darkness.

CHAPTER SIXTEEN

The thunder of the elements

Our work went on without the sun. But we began to see each other differently. We knew those men would gather every meal-time, and next week, next month; right through the winter we would see each other every day. The prospect was so horribly inevitable that we began to study each other with new interest. Each man who spoke was listened to. Sharp edges scratched and cliques were formed. There were interests which bound men together, and they would sit at the same table for three meal-times or more drinking at the fountain of new ideas until it ran dry or their interest waned. It was the fickle relationship of men thrown together whose common motive for going to the Antarctic was 'to save money'. When I asked them if they would still have gone South had there been no generous salary (about £1,500 p.a.), most of them had looked askance and asked if I was serious. When I said 'of course', they had given no reply – their answer was in their silence: 'the man's a fool' their eyes seemed to say. Others had defended their mercenary motives, but only three men had firmly denied that it was the money that had attracted them.

Most of them scorned the romantic conception of a continent ablaze with heroic deeds – a world of men ascetically disciplined.

> Whom shall we send in search of this new world,
> Whom shall we find sufficient?

My comrades at Scott Base were 'sufficient' – they proved it to me. Ordinary men – not poets or aesthetes. They saw no paradise in snowscapes, they heard no colour-music in the wind and found no sense in challenging the elements for they were being paid to run a geophysical observatory, and could do so better if they were comfortable. Ordinary men – not dedicated scientists: some had degrees, but not in the subjects that filled their time profitably from breakfast to dinner with an hour's break at lunchtime. Ordinary men – not hardened explorers. Few of them had read a polar book – they were bored by the literature of adventure, and yet they were 'sufficient' for a scientific outpost. They were ideally suited to the monotonous task of collecting data from ticking, light-flashing, whirring mechanisms. If they had been less qualified and fired with the urge to explore the surroundings their work would have suffered: if they had been research scientists they would have been tempted to nurse their own interests and neglect the routine of the observatory. Scott Base was an Antarctic society of ordinary men in which the explorer was an alien – the exact opposite of the Hope Bay crew of dare-devil wandering romantics, and different again from the dedicated scientists wintering at the American bases who had an academic stake in the Antarctic, and the American servicemen, for many of whom the Antarctic was a miserable posting. Each contributed in his own special way to the unveiling of a continent.

The ordinary man demands compensations for wintering in the Antarctic: he wants money and comforts and radio telephone contact with his friends and relations at home. These were provided for the men at Scott Base; but comfortable men are often dissatisfied men. Drained, after a monotonous day's toil, of the energy necessary to find something more interesting to do, their evenings were filled with canned entertainment. Eight films a week were sent over from McMurdo City. They fought against them like addicts each evening: 'I'll watch the first reel to see if it's any good,' then at the end of the first reel 'it might improve' they would say, and despising themselves they would stick it out to the end swearing that they would never watch another. Some with a major effort of will would go over to the American base to see their friends, and invariably they would sit through another film, which on its circuit would reach Scott Base the following week and face those who had seen it with the awful dilemma of whether to watch it a second time. What else could they do? They could go back to work; they could go to bed and read a book; they could 'paint by numbers', play a game of cards, construct a model from a children's plastic model set – a very popular line at the American store; or they could sit through a scientific seminar – a social occasion which became very popular as the winter drew on and was held in alternate weeks at Scott Base and at the science laboratory at McMurdo City. But relaxation became a strain – men enjoyed their working day far more.

Once a week the base was re-fuelled, and every week two new men took their turn at supplying the base with snow. It was a far more advanced operation than its equivalent one at Hope Bay where we would draw the snow blocks on a small sledge, carry them on our shoulders through the hut, climb on to a chair in the kitchen, drop them into a copper tank and light the anthracite boiler stove. At Scott Base we used a tractor to drag the sledge to the snow-mine, and hatches opened in the sides of the huts directly above the snow-melters into which a man outside the hut could feed his blocks of snow. Only the cook was let off this chore, which in any case took only about an hour a day, and was for the technicians, radio operator, and base leader the only time they had any physical exercise. But for Peter Otway and me, with fifty-four dogs to look after, our daily routine involved at least an hour a day down on the shelf ice where they were spanned out.

It was there that we felt the moods of the winter. It was as if we had left the safety of our ship and rowed away deliberately, tempting the seas to swallow us. Beyond the dog lines in the pressure ridges this sensation was even more powerful, for there the swinging lantern cast small shadows and light specks which played on the surface of those ice waves and made them shimmer with animation. Among those silent waves in the stillness of the night we could hear the throbbing of the engines – the breathing of our base – and pricks of yellow light at the windows of the huts suffused the vapour of her breath with the faintest hint of colour. Below the windows, the wave crests of snow were turned to glowing golden foam, and the swell of the snow mounds, bathed in purple, sank deeper into indigo. Among the dogs we walked with a lantern casting its pool of light, long shadows sweeping behind the animals – white ghostly creatures they looked against the heavy blackness of the night. The still air would split with dog noise, each animal lunging at his chain, racing around in circles, leaping in the air demanding to be visited, and their piercing yapping would mould into a long plaintive howl as we left them to return once more to the safety of our ship.

There were days when the heavens were moonless and not the gentlest breath moved the air over the rocks; cold days when moisture in the nostrils froze and beards matted with feathery crystals. Snow, iron-hard under footfalls, squeaked. Fingertips tingled. Seal meat was like a greasy stone. Aurora breathing a glow in the sky would swell across the heavens like a pale green mist – a faint curtain through which the stars gave it a weird dimension. Then suddenly it seemed to writhe into rolls and shoot out flashes which spiralled towards the zenith convulsing and raining spears of shimmering light. The whole icescape, a moment before in the grip of darkness, would be lit by a green-grey lambent light – a shower of light which drifted over the scene and faded into the darkness again. There were the moonlit scenes of soft light on the snows when vapour drawn off the chimneys of the base became flowing veils stained pale ochre in the lunar glow. Palls of vapour hung over the dog lines, the breath of the huskies, with no breeze to dissipate the fog.

There were the winds and blizzards – violent onslaughts which shook the huts and hissed at the windows. Out into it we would stagger, heads bowed, down to the dog lines, six steps between each marker flag. Stinging, stabbing, blinding drift would clog the eyes and smart the flesh. We would find the meat sledge a swirling inferno of choking snow. There, on top of the pile of frozen meat, we would shake loose chunks and pitch them up-wind into the night. We would scramble down holding our breath as if submerging into a breaker of foam around the cliffs, and loading the sledge we would lurch around with the torch beam pressed back by the blizzard until it was only a stump of light. The spans were laid out in perfect symmetry – we would count our paces, count the dogs and when all were fed we would turn for home. The wind from the south would catch our backs, whipping us along and up the hill and thudding us against the door of the covered way. We would fall inside, a hissing whirl of drift coming after us, and putting our shoulders against the door we would fight against it, squeezing the blizzard out, clamp the door shut, then sigh with relief.

Those were the days when men came together. The vibrating huts seemed to shake them into a new consciousness of each other. You could see it in their eyes and hear it in their voices. They needed the reassurance of their fellows, and reached out for support, disguising their need as the hand of friendship. The thunder of the elements awoke them. The pressure in the huts pressed on their ears. They felt buried in the spume of the winter's vengeance and the experience was new to them. But those blasts of blizzard were only short spasms in the long, still, cloudless days that preceded our mid-winter. Each day was like a pulse beat, slow and regular, ticking off our life together, seldom stimulated by excitement to beat a little quicker until the time-mark of our winter.

My colleague and I had spent the darkening days working on my map of the previous summer. Pete Otway had been one of the three surveyors with the Northern Party bordering my territory, but his field books had been taken back to New Zealand at the end of the season, so together we had worked on my survey, dividing the routine jobs between us. I could not have had a more amiable and considerate colleague. He was an Antarctic enthusiast in a most natural and unassuming way, and his pleasantly mellow sense of humour and cheerfulness were a source of great comfort. He had a natural charm rooted in gracious upbringing and a well-balanced perspective of society. He accepted a man for what he was and was equally polite to all. He was without enemies. He had not the spiritual depth of Dr Edward Wilson nor the robust humour of Lieutenant 'Birdy' Bowers, who had both perished with Captain Scott in March 1912. He sang no psalms, he thumped no tables, but he watched with interest as my plans evolved for the coming season, and by mid-winter they had blossomed.

As early as 12 May, after much careful thought and discussion with the Americans at McMurdo, I had sent a cable to Mr Markham, the Director of Antarctic Division, proposing a four-man expedition to the area east of the Beardmore Glacier. I had not specified this area exactly because the only maps I had, indeed the only maps that existed, were those of Shackleton and Scott which did not extend beyond the range that walled the east side of the Glacier. I had visualized a dog-sledging party of four men, supported by air-drops, ascending the area left blank on Scott's map from the shelf ice to the polar plateau where we would meet the Dominion Range. This range did not look at all formidable as a barrier to the polar plateau on the two maps I had studied so closely. It was drawn on both of them as a narrow strip – a streak of cloud which petered out; so I proposed to finish my map at the tail of that range and then head due south for the Pole! I saw this dash as a fitting celebration of the fiftieth anniversary of the attainment of the South Pole and as a sensible way of getting back to McMurdo, for my friends in VX-6 Squadron had assured me that there would be no objection to loading my party aboard an empty Herculese aircraft returning from the American South Pole Station at that time of the season. Mr Markham's reply was two weeks in coming: 'Your initiative and enthusiasm to enlarge next season's programme and capitalize on Scott anniversary appreciated and commended, however . . .' – the cable went on to cut my proposal to shreds. Mr Markham also pointed out that I had not yet been appointed leader, but he kindly agreed to consider my proposed journey as an application for the post 'along with others received'. I was not put out of the uncertainty about the post of leader, and the field area that I wanted, until mid-winter – and then the spirit leapt.

To winter in the Antarctic is to climb a hill in the dark; a long, hard struggle because the mind and body are unfamiliar with the experience. At the summit – mid-winter's day – there is a feeling of elation, the climb up is momentarily forgotten in the intoxication that accompanies the shaking of hands and slapping of backs. For some men the descent is worse than the climb – for others the run down starts easily, a soothing rhythm, a delightfully carefree loping movement which gathers speed and jolts a little, and the breeze of action ruffles a man bounding faster, and faster still. Sunrise at the base of the hill looms up to meet him and he sees the plain of summer sweeping away in the distance; but he is careering so fast he cannot stop and the winds of spring are ripping at him as he bounds on to the plain – exhilarating!

That delightful post-mid-winter rhythm awakened the minds of men who had been dormant and insensitive during the darkening period. It started with a simple experiment – throwing boiling water into the air when the temperature outside was $-50°$ Fahrenheit. The water exploded with a hiss and rained minute crystals down on us. We dug out cameras and photographed it, and so started a hobby which inspired a searching interest in the winter scene around us.

Men prowled around with cameras taking shots of everything that was considered unusual or unique to our latitude. Spurts of 'daylight' from electronic flash equipment became an accepted winter phenomenon. It was directed on every outside activity to record it on film for posterity. Even the cook was caught up in the craze and was seen taking flash-gun shots at the moon! The more skilful photographers developed their own colour film and within a few hours of taking their shots would be projecting the results on to a screen. If the results were not good enough they would go out and improve on their first attempt. There were multiple-exposure shots of the moon – six images of the moon on the same picture as it made its lower transit on our southern horizon. There were many attempts to photograph the aurora, and cameras were directed at the Southern Cross, taped on to a rotating mechanism which kept pace with the apparent movement of the stars, enabling a long exposure to be given without the image of the stars appearing as short arcs on the film. With such clarity of atmosphere our photographic results were astounding. There were 24-hour exposures of the 'night-sky' in which our cameras were left on the flat roofs of the huts. These cameras were left pointing at the zenith with their shutters held open by a rubber band which kept pressure on the shutter release. As the earth rotated the stars inscribed their track on the film in circles around the celestial pole. The colours of the stars ranged from mauves and blues, brilliant silvers and yellows, and warmed through pastel shades of orange to purple. With the naked eye we could only just detect these colours, but the film confirmed and intensified them. We would not have noticed the pre-dawn glow in the northern sky had we not been prompted to take 24-hour exposures of the stars, nor would we probably have discovered the animation and colour in the polar night.

We were racing towards spring. The survey office and the sledge workshop came alive with atmosphere. The smell of wood and linseed oil, rope and canvas, dogs, dope, blubber, tobacco; the clutter of brightly painted boxes, half-built sledges, field rations bulging in polythene bags; the soft rumble of the generators in the nearby hut and the purring of the fans; the classical symphonies on the tape-recorder, the buzz of conversation, and the chatter of the sewing machine built up this atmosphere of urgency, of expectation, of joyous momentum which attracted men like a magnet. It was a pocket of the old expedition spirit, where through its sledging, its chattels, its smells and sounds, men felt themselves drawn into the slipstream of their two field men who had broken away to race towards spring. Only two men were left far behind slowly plodding down the hill. We had no time to wait for them.

A dead sky flushed with a rosy hue. A pink moon floated full and slow on its last circuits of a silent world. Our preparations went on apace and the air temperature sank to −72° F. It was still, very still. Each breath we drew in was cold, brittle steel. The air seemed to crack if we walked through it quickly. Dogs fed on low-grade mutton began to show symptoms of scurvy. Their hair fell out and suppurating sores developed; they stuck to the ice in pools of their urine and tore off flesh if they jumped up too suddenly. The symptoms came with the pre-glow of dawn, and even as we rushed to them the warm seal meat that we had been saving for the pups, the clouds moulded in a wash of pale colour and deepened into flames of red. The rifle-shots were strangely muffled that ended the lives of those poor creatures, and we dragged their bodies to the pressure ridges to be chewed up by the grinding ice. To conserve the seal population we had been sent mutton. It was an experiment in dog food we had been told – an appeasement to the influential nature lovers – the preservers of Antarctic wild-life who consider the ration of three seals to one husky for winter dog food an unjustifiable slaughter. The blood of those dogs was in the dawn sky.

The sledges were ready, the food boxes were packed and careful lists of equipment prepared, and at noon each day, as we worked down at the dog lines, the sun wrote its message on the clouds. The shadow of Mount Erebus reached over us. The northern sky was a summer approaching, its heralds were the clouds, but the hills behind us would steal the first rays that should have been ours, so we climbed them. The northern horizon was a brilliant yellow which moistened into orange and purple in whisps of fleecy vapour; the sea ice in McMurdo Sound was a green-grey table set to receive the first grazing ray. Our expectations for the summer, the ardent hopes for success, the future, the whole life ahead of us seemed to rest in our silent fixation on the brightest part of that horizon. For a second it fired a golden edge – then it climbed in its glory – an orb of pure joy.

CHAPTER SEVENTEEN

With a feeling akin to awe

Scott Base remained in the shadow of the Hut Point Peninsula for another two weeks, but each day at noon the sun curved nearer. It caught White Island to our south in a flush of rose, incredibly beautiful against a backdrop of twilight sky and the foreground of shelf ice still blue-grey with cold shadow. It was like a steel bar heated by a furnace, thrust across our southern horizon – and the air temperature soared. A few days before sunrise the temperature on the shelf ice in front of Scott Base had sunk to the record low for that place of –76° F, and in the soft light of dawn our interest in throwing boiling water into the air found new impetus, for there was then enough light to use slow colour film to record those spectacular explosions of water. But within a week the temperature had risen eighty-six degrees and still we waited for the sun to creep over the hill. We saw our first glimpse of it at Scott Base on 3 September – five months after it had set behind Erebus. The .shadows of our sledges and straining dogs shot out like feelers over the snow. The wind of the gallop, the creak of sledge timbers, the panting dogs and trails of vapour were sensations of re-birth.

But with the sun came merciless blizzards. We were pinned at base for almost a week by the first blast of storms that heralded summer, and it was not until 11 September, when they paused for a day to gather more venom, that we set off with two teams of dogs for a training run north to visit the old huts of Shackleton and Scott. It was early in the morning; the sun had not cleared Hut Point Peninsula but it blazed past Cape Armitage like a curtain of gold and etched a rim around Observation Hill, on which stands the cross in memory of Scott and his four gallant companions. It was cold in the shadow and the scene was stark, but as we reached Cape Armitage and cut into the sunlight the scene burst into orange flame. We felt consumed by it.

The dogs had reached the steady trot that comes at the end of the first three miles of a smooth sea ice journey. We rounded the cape and headed across a small bay, bumping over rough tracks made by the 'weasels', past busy American mechanics tinkering with aircraft – black silhouettes against a sky burning in the morning glow. The preheaters and exhausts of the rumbling vehicles puffed plumes of vapour as men leaned from their cabs or stopped work on the wings of cold aeroplanes to shout 'Hi!' The day was friendly. Men felt alive. McMurdo City throbbed with activity.

We bounced over cables and pipelines snaking their way from the American base to the airstrip three miles away, and passed close by Hut Point where in the shadow of two huge circular fuel tanks sat Scott's 'Discovery Hut'. It looked in a dilapidated condition from a distance as we drove by on the hard ice near the point. We would have stopped had there been good picketing ground for the two teams of dogs, but we knew there was little to see as the interior of the hut was almost completely filled with snow and ice which had been rising like a tide since 1916 when it was last occupied. The hut had been roofed on 26 February 1902, which was six days after Dr Otto Nordenskjöld's party had slept for the first time in their hut at Snow Hill Island on the other side of the Antarctic: but the 'Discovery Hut' was never used as a 'home' – it was intended as one, but Scott found such good winter quarters for the expedition ship in the little bay south of Hut Point that he decided to use the ship as his base and the hut as an emergency base, which he hoped 'would come in useful as a workshop or as a play-room, or for any purpose which might tend to relieve the congestion of the ship.'*

The old hut certainly had its memories, but they were well guarded by the ice. From the outside it was hard to visualize the men that hut had sheltered and the hardships they endured. It had started out its life as a most commodious building and was used for a variety of purposes: drying tents, skinning birds, weighing and distributing food and equipment, sailorizing jobs and gravity observations; it was even used in its hey-day as a theatre, complete with footlights and scenery! But it was to serve a more sober function in the years ahead. It was used as a staging post for the expedition of Shackleton in 1907–09, and again by Scott on his last expedition of 1910–13, but the most poignant memories the old hut had buried under its high

* Scott, Captain R. F., *The Voyage of the Discovery*, Vol. 1 (1905), p. 216, Smith, Elder & Co., London.

tide of ice were those of the Ross Sea party of Shackleton's abortive Trans-Antarctic Expedition of 1914–17.

It never had been a warm hut, but men in good health could tolerate it, and men in poor health were at least protected from the biting winds which shook the hut and drove snow through the chinks in the boarding. For one brief spell it was connected by telephone to Scott's hut at Cape Evans fifteen miles away, but the cable, which ran over the sea ice, was severed when the ice broke up. It became once more an isolated, comfortless advance base and served as a refuge for Captain Aeneas Mackintosh and his five companions, who were cut off by open water from reaching Cape Evans after three of them had laid a depot at 80° S.* They were the support party for Shackleton's ill-fated attempt to sledge across the Antarctic from the Weddell Sea to McMurdo Sound. They did not know that Shackleton's ship the *Endurance* had been crushed in the ice and that the whole party were struggling for their lives. Nor did they know until the sea ice re-formed two months later and they were able to sledge back to Cape Evans that their own expedition ship the *Aurora* had been blown out to sea. Ten men were marooned and spent a hard winter, but nine of them set off the following spring, ill-clad and in spite of their poor condition, to lay depots at sixty-mile intervals all the way south to Mount Hope at the foot of the Beardmore Glacier – depots that Shackleton would no longer need. Six men went south from the 'Discovery Hut', five men returned two hundred days later stricken with scurvy after making an incredible journey, which totalled (including relays) just over 1,600 miles. In that hut they lived a hellish existence for two months while they waited for the sea ice to form, but Mackintosh and Hayward, impatience getting the better of sound judgement, had set off on weak sea ice to reach Cape Evans and were never seen again. The remaining three men waited two more months before making the attempt to sledge the fifteen miles to Cape Evans. They were the last men to occupy that old hut, and they had left it on 15 July 1916. A hut of tortured memories now, preserved in ice, a shell worn by the winds of many years.

As our sledges rattled past Hut Point on bare patches of ice and the peninsula swept away to our right, there was a sudden and tremendous feeling of exposure. A vast scene opened up. There was

* Joyce, E. E. M., *The South Polar Trail* (1929), Duckworth, London.

no foreground except bay ice: nothing to restrict the imposing view of Mount Erebus' classical volcanic profile, smoking white steam in lazy clouds, its slipping cloak of ice rippling, cascading and splitting into wart-like areas of crevasses. Away to the north-west the horizon was flat – a seemingly limitless expanse of fast ice contrasting impressively with the smoking monster to our right, and the western mountains, a rugged and beautiful chain, stretching as far as the eye could see, to our left. Behind us and out of sight was the American base busy with its machinery and men, but ahead no foot had trodden since winter. The dogs' pads beat clean snow and the wind of movement cut into our flesh. Spring sledging was invigorating!

We closed on a long low tongue of ice which thrust into the bay from the slopes of Erebus like a serrated sword and stopped at the tip of it for lunch. There was no tide crack where the glacier tongue met the sea ice for the whole tongue was floating. Shackleton's expedition ship, the *Nimrod*, had moored alongside it on 13 February 1908 and landed a depot of sledging stores. Their soundings gave the depth of 157 fathoms, but it is easy to forget there is water beneath a compact cover of sea ice. The ice converts the sea to a terrestrial element – at least as far as travel is concerned: the shock when sea ice breaks up is not the fear of falling into the sea, but the surprise that it is there!

It was five miles from the glacier tongue across South Bay to Scott's winter quarters of 1911 – a delightful run with the monotony of perfectly flat sea ice broken up by drifts of beset brash, pressure cracks, bare ice and islands. It somehow reminded me of sledging in the Prince Gustav Channel south of Hope Bay, but I was only vaguely conscious of this for old huts are very possessive. There were one or two grounded bergs near Cape Evans occupying roughly the same position that the 'castle berg' had in Scott's day and around these we ran the two teams like a thread, and burst clear. We drove the dogs above the tide crack and camped on a narrow ledge of snow about sixty yards from the hut. The evening was very still and the long shadows were shredding the scene in strips of light and shade. We moved about silently, but the dogs without reverence made their usual hungry sound until they were quietened with pemmican. All four of us kept glancing across to the hut throughout our camping ritual, but not until all was done did we stroll on to the sea ice, along the beach and across firm, fresh, printless snow up to the door of that timber shrine.

It had been restored by a New Zealand party the previous summer under the leadership of Les Quartermain, an Antarctic historian who grew a grisly grey beard and inspired his six virile young helpers to toil for three weeks with pick and shovel to clear the hut of 250 cubic yards of ice. Relics embedded in the ice were thawed loose outside in the summer sunshine and taken back into the hut by Les after it had been tidied and the shelves and bunks had been shored up: then with his historical eye and a passion for relics, he had allocated each piece to its rightful place while his men spent a further two weeks weatherproofing the hut and tidying the environs. We were privileged to be the first to see that hut mantled in spring snow, lit by a low sun; a hut restored, standing as proudly as it had in its first spring fifty years before. Thanks to Les Quartermain and his men there had been space for the spirits of men who had lived there to move around, and everything was in its place for their fiftieth winter in that hut.

Scott's *Terra Nova* expedition had spent their first winter to the time-mark of mid-winter when they made vociferous din and revelry as they started down towards spring. 'We are all adventurers here,' Scott said. 'Of hopeful signs for the future none are more remarkable than the health and spirit of our people. It would be impossible to imagine a more vigorous community and there does not seem to be a single weak spot in the twelve good men and true who are chosen for the Southern advance. All are now experienced sledge travellers knit together with a bond of friendship that has never been equalled under such circumstances.'* They had spent their run down towards spring punctuated only by sleep and seminars. They produced two volumes of the *South Polar Times*, the second appearing on 8 September: their ghosts were probably still jockeying to read it when we barged into the hut, our eyes unaccustomed to the dim interior, for only a fading glow was framed at the two windows, and they were at the far end of the hut.

To the right, dark and dingy, was the kitchen, open to view once our candles had been lit for no wall separated it from the rest of the

---

* Scott, Captain R. F., op. cit., Vol. 1 (1914), p. 404.

hut. We saw shelves loaded with old tins, cups on hooks, a cook's table scarred with the thudding meat axe, and a dirty stove cluttered with great pots and kettles stained with time and stews. We were in the 'men's quarters' – we thumped into their table, and the creak of the floorboards and leaping shadows brought the place alive with movement. It was cold and eerie, but we stayed close together and passed on to the 'wardroom', once separated from the 'mess-deck' by a wall of food cases through which a door-sized gap gave access. Chairs sat to attention at the bare, big, austere wardroom table. Behind them the cubicles, ramshackle structures stained with blubber smoke, were cluttered with remnants of worn-out clothing, grimy and musty. Herbert Ponting's darkroom, a squat black box, stood with its door ajar, choked with ice crystals, spear-racks of icicles, and shelves full of frosty bottles of chemicals. In the right hand far corner of the old hut was the science lab; in the left hand far corner we found Scott's cubicle, and as we sat on Wilson's bunk looking across the chart table we could clearly visualize Captain Scott writing his journal.

The marooned men were amongst them – the survivors of Shackleton's Ross Sea party. Traces of their struggle for survival were in every rag that lay about and the grime that impregnated every magazine and book, every home-made scrap of canvas clothing and the sandals soled with bits of wood. Their privations permeated the atmosphere of boisterous fun and serious debate of Scott's 'amiable argumentative' party who had wintered there a few years earlier, and as the darkness closed in and we stumbled towards the door it was as though we were pressing through a crowd of unseen people. We reached the door and drew a deep breath, turned and barred the door behind us and made our way silently back to the tents: frail, small, but friendly they seemed, and the roaring primus soon warmed our chilled bodies.

We all four gathered around in my tent that evening and as a breeze drummed the fabric and steam rose from the pot our conversation bounced merrily from one to the other. We reminisced on the winter we had just passed through and compared it to the winters of long ago. We dug up old stories freshened with the gaiety of a tent crammed with good friends – the first camp of spring. Only one man we wished could have been with us then – Les Quartermain, who had been in his element the previous summer, scratching and chipping his way towards the bunk of his boyhood hero Captain Robert Falcon Scott. Every half hour or so during every working day one of his virile young helpers had let out a yell of excitement and slithered over to Les bearing a relic. We could picture the old man holding up the Tilley lamp his eyes and grey beard gleaming in the lantern glow, as another piece of the puzzle was reverently placed on a pile of what looked suspiciously like junk to a less experienced eye. Many little jokes had been played on Les, and not a few arguments raged on the subject of Scott's immortality. But Les, in a philosophical and academic manner, had defended his hero until one day when a heartless blow was struck. It stopped poor Les in his tracks.

Bob Buckley had been working away in the corner which was known to be Scott's bunk, while Les was down the far end of the hut sorting out relics. After a few hours Buckley uncovered half of the bunk wall, exposing a few old bits of junk: a pipe, a small calendar, but nothing that had not been expected. An idea then came to Bob in a flash, and delving through a pile of 1909 magazines he found the photograph he was after: it was a fine picture of a buxom bathing beauty with a saucy smile and a theatrical background. With rusty drawing pins the picture was secured to Scott's bulkhead, then with a yelp of delight he shouted 'come and see what I've found.'

I doubt if ever before in the history of that hut had men run so fast towards Scott's bunk. They all gathered around jostling for position and gazed open-mouthed at the pin-up. A look of horror came over Les's face, while everyone else shook with laughter. At last with tears rolling down his cheeks, Bob managed an enormous wink and said: 'there you are Les – so Scott was human after all!'

We could have used Les as an intermediary that night for, as we sat chatting, the wind increased and the hiss of drift spinning past our tent foretold the coming of a blizzard. We had no reading material with us, but had noticed in the hut the 1909 magazines that had been brought over from Shackleton's hut by the Scott men, so we drew lots to decide who would go and fetch them, and the unenviable mission fell to me. It was a nasty night. The torch batteries were cold and the bulb gave only an orange glow. I felt my way along the coast and up to the hut where the drift was sweeping a scoop near the door. I entered the porch. The door to the main hut went off that porch and

I stood on the threshold feeling cold, and fumbling for a match to light my way to the table where the candles lay. The whole hut softly creaked like a wooden ship labouring in a gentle swell and each spurt of a match gave that place a dim form before the light snuffed and I was plunged once again into darkness thick with unseen shapes. Fifty years before, to the hour, the whole party had been there except for three men who had set off to lay a depot at Corner Camp. That night in the hut they had been working hard on the final preparations for their spring journeys: '. . . a very demon of unrest seems to stir them to effort, and there is now not a single man who is not striving his utmost . . .'.* The candle flame leapt and its glow penetrated the darkness. I shielded its glare with my hand and moved forward slowly. Shadows crept around the room, the pale light moved over sleeping-bags bulging on bunks, breathing it seemed, fusty with age.

I gathered up an armful of magazines, disturbing an odour which rose off them, and around the hut beyond the weak pool of light groans came like whispers of reproach. Two chairs had been moved – they relaxed at an angle compared with the rest, so I gave them a wide berth and brushed past two furry 'hands' dangling limply from the side of a bunk and stubbed my foot against something sitting on the floor. The shadows circled as I moved towards the door; they seemed to float just out of reach then creep up behind me and rest on my back. It was a thoroughly unpleasant experience, and yet the men were friendly enough, and our hearts were kindred – it was only the age we lived in that was different.

My sledging companions were amused when I told them of my experience, but the subject was dropped before I was provoked to challenge them to go and feel it for themselves. The next day a blizzard raged and the only sorties we made from our tents were to visit each other to exchange magazines. They were fascinating reading but the smell they gave off was repugnant, and on the third morning early we dutifully returned them and continued on our journey as soon as it was light.

But the daylight was short-lived. Even as our sledges rattled over the rough sea ice past the Barne Glacier tongue, her towering ramparts flushed pink and shadow seeped up through the snow

* Scott, loc. cit.

beneath our skis like a violet stain. For a few seconds the dogs glowed like burning embers, and into the shadow of the earth they sank until they were submerged and only our heads were still above the climbing twilight. We glanced to our left, to the western mountains – the sea of jagged peaks into which the sun slipped. It had gone till the morrow, but the precipice of ice was still catching its glow – polished pink alabaster, serene smooth facets, echoing the panting dogs' padded trot and the trundled rattle of creaking sledges. But the relentless stain crept up the ice-cliffs, and up the tumbled spate of snow that slipped down the sides of Mount Erebus until only the plume of vapour caught the sun; by which time we were fumbling, stumbling, grumbling in dusk.

We ran into a field of small brash ice which chattered the sledges and threw us about, but we persisted on our course for Cape Royds and were trapped by the darkness in a chaos of ice which capsized our sledges and knotted the dog traces. We staggered around feeling for a way out, slipping and crawling over great glassy boulders and calling to each other through the night. By a foot at a time we retreated; heaving, lurching into pitfalls and walls until the feel of ice flattened out and the sledges juddered over ice-flowers and small knobbles on to hard snow. We had retreated and swung around closer to the coast but the night by that time was pitch black, so when we reached a snow strip which rose up in a bank we decided to camp and wait for daylight to see where we were.

I was up at the first light of dawn the next morning, but through the tent door I could see only back the way we had come. I had to crawl out of the tent to get a view in the other direction, and looming there, not twenty yards from the lead dog of my team, was Derrick Point where Shackleton's party had hauled their stores up the cliffs from the sea ice on 10 February 1908! My companions tumbled out to see for themselves, and while they prepared breakfast I set off to find the hut, for none of us knew exactly where it was. There was a small ice-foot – a miniature glacier split with crevasses and tumbled in blocks; up this I scrambled and on to a hard snow col between two rocky hills, across a small frozen lake and there it was to my right: a neat, warm ochre, sun-soaked hut nestling in a dip, as snug a little hut as ever I have seen. It brought from me a gasp of joy – it was a delight to the eye. Behind it, rising above a rock ridge, the white cone of Mount Erebus cut a fine profile against a blue sky, and the warmth of the sun was sensual.

It was a small pocket of kindly feeling – a shell of timber with few relics left to taint it with the odour of age, and yet I entered that hut as Herbert Ponting had done: 'with a feeling akin to awe'.* It was from that little hut that Shackleton and his three companions of the Southern Party had set off for the South Pole on 29 October 1908. Four men and four ponies nine days later watched their support party 'dwindling to a speck in the north'. To their south lay almost four months of dire hunger and, as Amundsen said, 'the most brilliant incident in the history of Antarctic exploration'.† They sledged to within ninety-seven geographical miles of the South Pole – an advance of 363 geographical miles beyond Scott's farthest south record of 1902. They discovered and pioneered a route on the Beardmore Glacier and discovered nearly 500 miles of a new mountain range. The hut seemed too small to have housed such men.

Even Sir Raymond Priestley, who had been a member of Shackleton's expedition, was affected by the occult atmosphere of that place. He wrote in his diary when he visited the hut as a member of Scott's expedition in 1911: 'The whole place is very eerie, there is such a feeling of life about it. Not only do I feel it but the others do also. Last night after I turned in I could have sworn that I heard people shouting to each other. I thought that I had only got an attack of nerves but Campbell asked me if I heard any shouting, for he had certainly done so.'‡

We adopted that little hut, my companions and I. It was set in a delightful environment and all day we strolled around soaking in sunshine, aware of the impulsion that had driven the Pole-seekers to exercise hard where we lazily ambled. Was it any wonder that thoughts of them re-kindled my idea of dog-sledging to the Pole at the end of the field season. There, in Shackleton's hut, it was easy to dream. Time was turned back half a century by the adventurous spirits that dwelt in that place and I was unashamedly in sympathy with them. I was more aware of atmosphere there than in any other

* Ponting, Herbert G., *The Great White South* (1921), p. 97, Gerald Duckworth, London.

† Amundsen, Roald, *The South Pole*, Vol. 1 (1912), p. 40, John Murray, London.

‡ Priestley, Sir Raymond E., *Diary* (unpublished).

place I have visited. It was for me a stimulating experience, although on another occasion it might not have been so, for it had caught me that day with a rising 'Pole fever'.

But a man who admits an attraction for the Pole is now usually looked upon as mad or over-sentimental; the emotionless assault of the South by machinery is a sign of our times and is regarded with approval by all men, except the romantics who want more than cold, efficient, callous success from their Antarctic experience. I was sure I would meet ridicule if I pressed my idea, but I felt impelled at least to give it a try. Our sledge journey back to base could not slip by quickly enough for me.

CHAPTER EIGHTEEN

The forbidden journey

The bustle of spring had us all in its grip.

There was talk of the 'padded 'plane' and who would go on it: the first aircraft homeward-bound was always reserved for the men who had not enjoyed the long dark winter. It was a standing joke (grossly exaggerated) that the passengers jabbered and giggled all the way north, and were met at Christchurch Airport by big men in white coats.

Four days earlier in the season than in any previous year, on 27 September 1961, the first four aircraft of 'Operation Deepfreeze 62' touched down at McMurdo Sound after their flight from New Zealand. On board the leading aircraft was the Commander of the U.S. Naval Support Force, Antarctica – Rear-Admiral David M. Tyree, U.S.N., who, like the first flower of spring, visibly ended the long winter. He was closely followed out of the aircraft by a bevy of blooming scientists, technicians, engineers and sailors, who spread over the ice around the enormous silver aircraft like a khaki and bright orange stain. 1,327 pounds of personal mail and 1,500 pounds of fresh food and milk was then unloaded for the deprived explorers at the American and New Zealand bases who, at their first contact with the 'outside world', caught colds and grumbled with anti-climax, boycotting the excitement of letter reading in an attempt to prove that they had become self-sufficient during the winter. They felt invaded by the new men. But this feeling soon wore off – the battle with spring left little time for contemplation.

Among those new men was Athol Roberts, our new base leader – a man well padded with health and tact. He had made a study of polar psychology through literature and interviews. He knew the explorers' quirks of temperament. He knew the petty prejudices and parochial minds that lay behind their spring smiles of apparent contentment. He knew about their cliques – men swept along in the full spate of their grievances. He knew how to smile with them and his research paid him great dividends; for within a week of being at base he had won over every man with his charm and understanding. He listened with interest to my arguments for a dash to the South Pole with dog teams, but he reserved his judgement with amazing diplomacy which neither squashed my plan nor cheered it heartily. He managed his men by giving them just enough rein to keep them keen – he was the ideal base leader for a vigorous field season.

The new field men arrived and the sledge workshop filled with kitbags and clobber, spoiling the symmetry of neatly placed boxes and sledging chattels. I tripped over shapeless sacks and their stencilled names in bold red paint glared up at me, intruding the cosy atmosphere created and fostered during the winter. 'Vic McGregor' one shouted, 'Kevin Pain' growled another, while 'Ron Hewson' lay in one corner, clumsily sprawling, and, like the others, asserting himself and assuming the right to take up space in our beloved haven. I saw in those sacks lifeless men, deserving no truck; least of all the ultimate privilege of a dash to the South Pole on the fiftieth anniversary of the heroic struggle of Amundsen and Scott. Those sacks had never before been to the Antarctic; they were filled with store-scented woollens – gear un-worn by men un-tried – chosen by Mr Markham from a handful of applicants. The mute insolence of those ugly kitbags tainted the meeting with their owners; men innocent and keen to prove that they were more than just adequate. But I thought only of the men more deserving than those three who had shouldered the weight of earlier winters: men like Roger Tufft, Hugh Simpson, and Lee Rice; the Reclus men, Dennis, Dick, and Ray – the real men of the South. It was they who should have accompanied me for they were in sympathy with polar history.

I set off on a training run down the coast with my three new men to break them into the technique of dog-sledging; and the wind blew the newness off their clothes and flushed their cheeks with joy. But my Pole plans meant little to those men. They were too excited by the flood of sensations that had become mundane to me. They could not focus on the dream that had become vivid to me only after years of dedicated reading.

On the night that we reached Scott's Cape Evans hut I was called back to base by radio – a reconnaissance flight over my area in an

American aircraft of VX-6 Squadron had been arranged for the following day – so I only had a few hours in which to judge the mettle of my new companions and I saw no flicker of the spirit which I had hoped to see. But then – I was prejudiced against them from the start.

20 October 1961: the sky was clear and the shuddering aircraft loaded with fuel for a prolonged flight suddenly ceased its rattling as the roaring rockets spent their energy and curled back to earth like falling leaves. It was 5.30 p.m. The Dakota climbed into the air and purred. High above the Ross Ice Shelf we drank sugarless black coffee from cardboard cups and steamed the windows of the plane with faces peering, marvelling at the expansive scene. Below us blue ice, seracs, crevasses and naked rocks slid by; and the serrated peaks of distant ranges – gleaming teeth of a massive jaw – held back the full face of a continent puffed with the ice of aeons. Its tongue lolled from the base of those mountains, textured with the wind-chiselled snow – the 'Great Ice Barrier' – the route to the Pole.

We walked around with reverence, high up in the air, while the flight engineer and navigator studied dials and filled up forms. Warm air breathed from mouth-like vents of an aircraft animated with the vibration of flight; rattling like tin, carrying explorers on a comfortable reconnaissance mission. Hours went by and mountain ranges came and went until the horizon seemed to sink and the aircraft changed its course. The broad white road of the Beardmore Glacier crawled away from under the starboard wing, between bold mountains climbing up to the polar plateau hazy with distance, while our pilot, Lieutenant (Jimmy) Weeks, with a two-day stubble bristling, broad shoulders filling his safety harness, held the stick with one hand and his coffee cup with the other and sniffled with a cold he had caught in Christchurch a few days before.

Flying along the foothills of the Queen Maud Range we lost ourselves on the navigator's map dotted with outlines of mis-shapen glaciers. We were looking for one of them in particular – the Axel Heiberg, Amundsen's route to the polar plateau – but for what purpose I cannot recall, for at that time we had no dream of using it as a route ourselves. The Shackleton Glacier was easily identified even with the imprecise sketch that was our guide; a raking, naked monster it looked. We counted the glaciers marked to its east, then turned up the Strom Glacier, the engines roaring with extra power. Skimming

a massif we caught our breath and were at once lost in wonder. The
faces of rock and yawning blue chasms, snow-fields and chaotic icefalls, spurs and ridges, opaque shadows and brilliant sun-drenched
domes of snow slipped past our steamy windows – then up loomed
the rolling plateau. Not one of us had any idea where we were.

It was not until many months later, when I was showing colour
slides in New Zealand, that we found we had taken pictures of the
Axel Heiberg on that first short, noisy flight up to the polar plateau –
pictures taken with cold, nervous fingers of a spectacular icescape
too immense, we had thought, to be part of Roald Amundsen's route.

From the south those massive mountains looked no more than
shoulders of snow, and between two of them we descended in search
of the Axel Heiberg. So close were they that there seemed to be
barely room for the wings to stretch, and from the side windows we
saw only walls of ice that slipped into the abyss below. We had
descended the Cooper Glacier, but we did not realize it until we had
circled at its base and ascended it again. By that time Jimmy Weeks
was concerned about the consumption of fuel. There was little to
spare and the Axel Heiberg had eluded us once more.

The flight shedule for that reconnaissance had not been made up in
my presence and from the head of the Cooper Glacier Jimmy Weeks
flew directly across the polar plateau towards a massif at the head of
the Mill Glacier (which I later named after Peter Otway). On the
flight deck I begged the pilot to fly off course around the edge of the
plateau where the glaciers started their slide to the coast, but he could
not make such a wide diversion without first asking for permission
from the flight control at McMurdo – and they did not reply to his
radio call. So we flew across featureless plateau forty miles from my
proposed route and watched the miles slip by – victims of a wasted
mission, tied by safety regulations to a useless route, until we reached
the Otway Massif and banked in a loop to fly over the Keltie Glacier.
Back again to the Otway Massif and low over a possible landing site,
we then changed course once more and flew down the Mill Glacier,
which I hoped to cross with dog teams. The Beardmore Glacier lay
ahead and the sun glinted on its massive icefalls. My part of that
reconnaissance was almost over – we were flying out of my area and
into that of the Northern Party which was to be led by Dick Walcott
(my old Hope Bay companion); but Dick was not yet in the South

and his place on the flight was taken by Peter Otway, who was to be his surveyor.

It seemed to be an easy snow terrain and I watched it lazily slip by as Pete leaped from one window to another, steaming up each in turn, his camera clicking and fingers pointing to features of Dick's proposed route. Athol Roberts slumped on the floor, dog-tired (he had that morning flown to Cape Hallet at the northern reach of Victoria Land to visit the base jointly manned by the Americans and New Zealanders). He looked an old man as he snatched a rest, while Vic McGregor, my geologist, flushed with excitement and youthful exuberance, stepped over him with gangling limbs, baggy in new windproof trousers. Those two men seemed separated by more than just their years in life – there was a full life of adventurous experience in the sleeper, and only a longing for it in Vic McGregor.

It was a stark icescape the plane droned above until we flew down the Nimrod Glacier that I had mapped the year before; then like Peter I pressed the window, calling my friends to come and see. There was one point on that long flight across the Ross Ice Shelf back to base from where all land to the north and south we could see from those steamy windows – an area of some 25,000 square miles – had been mapped the previous season by the two New Zealand field parties. If there was any satisfaction from that work too deeply personal to share it was there at that moment in time and space. It was 3 a.m. The sun was still streaming warmth through the windows of our steel cocoon.

Two hours later our aircraft landed at the McMurdo airstrip. It had carried us on a flight of 1,600 miles, and I was wiser about my new area by little more than the certainty of a landing spot 600 miles from base; but I had seen the polar plateau and had felt the dimension of grandeur; I had seen the Beardmore Glacier and my mind was so full of wonder and pride that I could find no expression for my thoughts except in silence.

We staggered back to base and tumbled into our beds. Then, refreshed, I started my final bid to gather support for a dash to the Pole. There had been a meeting of the Scientific Committee on Antarctic Research a few weeks before in Wellington, and its august members had flown to McMurdo as the guests of Rear-Admiral Tyree. Never was such a gathering of prominent men more uniformed than

they. Dressed all alike they were buzzed to and fro, or were blasted
into the air and flown to the far corners of the Antarctic and back in
time for dinner. They scorned the 'dog-rides' delighted in by all the
other V.I.P.s and this endeared them to me. They were above such
entertainment. They were all polar experts. They gave my plans a
sympathetic hearing but I could feel them wishing I had struck on a
more worthwhile idea.

Some of them lodged at our base for bed and breakfast, others
came and went like genial giants thick with accents, pounding hand-
shakes wishing us well. They all had a place in their hearts for adventurers like me, but each man was a diplomat and only hinted their
approval of my plan to Admiral Tyree. Our house guests took a more
personal interest. There was Dr Torri from Japan who spoke few
words of English but whose inscrutable smile was so infectious that
we bowed and smiled each time we saw him. There was Admiral
Rodolfo Panzarini, lean and swarthy, a fluent linguist, a man hard-
cored but coated with humour and stories painted with lavish word-
pictures. He was the Director of the Argentine Antarctic Institute,
and reminiscing about Graham Land with him was a fresh breeze.
Sir Vivian Fuchs spent three days with us, surrounded each time he
sat down with admirers pressing him for stories, but in spite of his
demanding fans he made time to study my plans for the coming
season. My argument that it would be more dangerous to descend
from the plateau than to sledge across it to the American station at
the South Pole (from where I could be safely transported by air
directly back to base), met with his full agreement, and through his
influence I almost got permission.

Only Athol remained unconvinced and begged me not to press the
Pole dash any farther. But with only two days left before my party
was due to go into the field another complication developed. I
wanted Pete to come with me in exchange for Hewson, who had not
found the enthusiasm I had hoped to see in all the members of my
party, and this involved us in a stream of cables to and from New
Zealand. This request was granted after some haggling over salary,
and on what I thought was to be my last evening at base only a
decision on the Pole dash remained still unresolved.

I was invited to the Flag Quarters at McMurdo, and dressed as
immaculately as a man can be in brand new windproofs, Eskimo

'kamiks', and an après-ski sweater of elaborate design, I drove the three miles in a rattling weasel, parked, and walked up to the door and knocked. The door was opened by the Admiral's aide who bade me enter a porch and take off my anorak. My visit was meant to coincide with the grateful thanks and goodnight wishes of the Admiral's dinner guests – a ritual which had been delayed – but a familiar voice called 'come on in' so I entered the spacious room. The men who sat at the Admiral's table wore the contented smiles of spreading men who had just indulged in a bout of eating. I was asked to sit at the far end of the table, opposite the Admiral. A bottle of brandy was placed within reach and smoke curled from fat cigars. But I felt overawed at the table with such important guests and the time I felt was being ill-spent discussing Scott's last expedition while my own gear still needed checking. At last the Admiral's aide with perfect tact hinted that the time was flying and the Admiral's guests got up and left Athol and me alone with our host.

The audience with the Admiral flowed deep and personal. In his soft, slow drawl, he discussed all the points for and against my proposed Pole dash. He was an ageing man, clad in navy-blue serge, baggy trousers, and matching tunic. There was nothing dynamic or impressive in his appearance; he was a kindly, father-figure, comfortable to listen to, compassionate in his argument. With disarming sincerity he admitted to us that he would have liked to see my teams make the journey to the Pole on the fiftieth anniversary of a very heroic struggle, but times had changed and search and rescue in the event of any mishap on my dash across the plateau would involve more men than he could spare at so late a date in the summer season. He had talked with us so frankly that in spite of my disappointment I left Flag Quarters profoundly moved by his concern for every man that came within the scope of his responsibility. Athol and I were so far away in our thoughts as the weasel lurched along the road back to Scott Base that we had not noticed the warning signs that blasting was in progress on the nuclear reactor site half-way up Observation Hill, and suddenly an almighty explosion shook us back to reality. We ducked instinctively and drove like mad towards the mellow wolf-howl of our dogs two miles away.

I worked through the rest of that evening and after everyone had gone to bed I started checking all over again. I checked and re-checked all the gear divided into three separate loads. The bulk of the stores I was going to take with me on the first trial flight up to the polar plateau. It consisted only of the expendable items plus the bare necessities for survival. My three companions were to follow the very next day or as soon after as the weather permitted, bringing the rest of the gear and the two teams of dogs.

I kept a lonely night-long vigil over those three piles of stores. The spell was broken only once when I felt the need to store up music for the months ahead in which I would be without it, but when I went into the messroom to feast on symphonies the jarring strains of bad jazz and clinking beer cans drove me back into the night. Still and silent it was; soft sunlight bathing pressure ridges; shadows fingering the snow smooth and polished by the violent winds of spring. Alone I sat through those hours before departure and no one knew how those hours affected me.

At dawn I hitched the cargo sledge to the tractor and without farewells I started my solitary ride out to the airstrip, keeping well clear of beaten roadways, prolonging to the bitter limit that night of meditation.

Together with Jimmy Weeks and his crew we loaded the aircraft and without delay the plane took off. There were notes left behind for Pete. Everything was in order; but there was no sleep for me in flight, there was too much to think about.

We reached the mouth of the Beardmore Glacier, and flying low for my benefit we retraced the route of Shackleton and his three companions in 1908–09. I saw the four of them in every shadow cluster, and their sledge tracks in every stream of ice sweeping down the west side of that mighty valley glacier. In my imagination I saw their footprints – staggering prints of men exhausted. Pole-seeking for what purpose? Was it worth their lives to risk it? If only they had taken dog teams. If only Frank Wild's pony had not plunged out of sight down that crevasse they would have had enough meat and energy to complete their journey.

I studied with binoculars every step of their route from the co-pilot's seat until we banked and flew up the Mill Glacier, then I went aft to get a better view through the port windows. I saw much more blue ice than I had expected, but few crevasses, and the small tributary flow which I called the Mill Stream Glacier appeared to be

4. The Axel Heiberg Glacier Region

perfect sledging country. We banked once more as I strapped myself in, and craning my neck I could see through the window a white plane rising to meet us. The shadows caught the aircraft up and raced over the snow, which for some reason I expected to cushion the blow, but the skis rattled and screeched on an iron-hard surface. The flight had taken four hours. I jumped out of the aircraft and stumbled a few steps across the polar plateau. The altitude was 9,200 feet. The air temperature was minus 35° F, and the propellers, still shirring to keep the engines warm, drove the cold air into us like sharp knives as we staggered to and fro with the boxes of supplies, piling them into a sizeable depot which we surmounted with an enormous flag.

I had no time to look around at the scenery until the depot was secure, but while Jimmy Weeks and his crew were struggling to rack the JATO (jet-assisted-take-off) rockets under the aircraft I stole a quick glance at the comfortless desert and was filled with foreboding about working for three months on that windswept, featureless plateau. Like remora fish clinging to the belly of a shark the twelve JATO rockets were ready for the trigger, and when Jimmy Weeks invited me to go back with him to McMurdo I needed little persuasion. I satisfied my conscience that on the return flight I could see a little more of the country I would be travelling over in a few days' time, and I could direct the loading of dogs and gear into the aircraft the following day. In only a few minutes after the last man was aboard we were taxi-ing at the maximum speed that the old Dakota could manage at that altitude, when suddenly we were blasted into the air with a rending sound that rasped our nerves. Jimmy had fired all twelve rockets together just to make sure that we got airborne! It scared the wits out of all of us, and the flight seemed so peaceful when the rockets died that even the engineer looked out of the window.

We flew along my proposed route towards the Keltie Glacier down a valley of blue ice streaked and patched with snow, past Mount Usher, and out once again over the Beardmore Glacier. The long flight was soothing and conducive to comfortable meditating. I day-dreamed and drifted back to hard thinking and wandered once more into the realms of fancy. It was a delightfully fluid kind of thought, and while thus engrossed it occurred to me that four years had slipped by since I had stood on the Graham Land plateau – a very different plateau to be sure – but an arm of the polar plateau nevertheless. I

wondered how my fortunes would fare in the bigger theatre south-
east of the Beardmore. It could surely never be as cruel as the abject
misery of suffocating in mist on the spine of Graham Land. But
perhaps the lack of a geographical goal would wear my party down.
I wracked my brains for an alternative to the Pole dash but found no
solution, and slipped once more into the musing thoughts.

McMurdo Sound lay under a blanket of ruffled cloud, dreary and
depressing. I no longer had any feeling for it after the sight of un-
touched country and pure, iron-hard snow; and I found myself telling
my companions about the plateau in glowing terms in spite of the
bitter cold, biting winds, the breathlessness, and the eyesore monotony of that desert of ice.

At 5.30 a.m. the next morning we were scheduled to fly. There was
no time to waste, no time to eat, no time to ease the tensions of the
last few days, but then came one moment of elation. It came as we
beat the back picket loose and the dogs took off with eagerness. Men
yelling, running, leaping, waving; the wind in our faces, our small
base shrinking, the aircraft looming, swallowing us and our growling,
slithering, frightened dogs. Soon we were airborne, and cradled in
gear I slept like a babe in the deepest sleep until Pete woke me up as
we reached the Beardmore Glacier.

It unwound before us like a roll of honour, white in the purity of
endeavour. Miles wide, a sweeping river of ice in spate, pouring from
the polar plateau against the struggle of men who fought it. If only
they had taken dogs. Dogs like ours could have done it. There they
lay – our friends the huskies – fifty years later panting pools of warm
saliva, shaking in an aeroplane above their natural element the
glaciers of Antarctica.

We landed with a roaring shudder and tumbled out on to the
plateau. The sky was clear. The Dakota took off, bursting a blizzard
of snow which gently settled as the purr of the aircraft softened to
silence. Our lungs were burning with exertion, our tents were
pitched, our dogs were spanned – the scene was ours. We were alone.

CHAPTER NINETEEN

In the footsteps of Amundsen

We were landed on the polar plateau about half a mile south of the Otway Massif on 6 November 1961. My party was a small one of four men and two teams of dogs. We had fifty-five days' rations and were to be re-supplied by an air-drop of a further thirty days' food and fuel just before Christmas. We were to be picked up at the end of the season either from the place where we had been landed, or at any other more suitable location on the plateau. Our objective was to map as much new country as we could in three months of summer.

Basically my plan for the exploration of the area was to sledge down the Mill Stream Glacier, where we would lay out a precise base line for the survey and by star observations compute its exac geographic position; then by sledging on across the Mill Glacier to the Dominion Range I planned to set up survey stations overlooking the Beardmore Glacier, and retrace our steps back to the valley between the Mill Stream and the Keltie Glaciers, where a survey station on the summit of Mount Usher at 12,000 feet would give us a grand view of the surrounding country. On our journey eastwards towards the head of the Shackleton Glacier I hoped to set up survey stations on the edge of the plateau wherever possible in order to see down to the coastal ranges, but because I had not flown over this ground on the reconnaissance a strong element of doubt fell on this part of the plan. Our re-supply of food and fuel I hoped to receive somewhere near the head of the Shackleton Glacier, and after occupying mountain summits as survey stations in that region I planned to make for the head of the Liv Glacier and the Axel Heiberg Glacier, completing the control for a map covering at least 20,000 square miles of previously unexplored country.

On my original plan, the party was then to have sledged 300 miles across the polar plateau to the South Pole, but I had been obliged to abandon that attractive climax and settle for a season devoted to survey.

The McMurdo Sound-Scott Base area, including the Queen Maud Range and the
Axel Heiberg Glacier

It was a season of high climbs and gruelling sledging in strong winds and bitter weather; a protracted journey in which (at first) four men with disparate motives struggled towards a goal-less finish, accumulating notebooks full of data wrestled from mountain summits and exposed rock faces. Four men breathless with exertion, unconcerted in their efforts, unadapted to the country, found little respite from the toil or their disunity of thought.

But those first few weeks were a great success as far as our programme was concerned: we mapped 7,000 square miles of country from the mountain ranges overlooking the Beardmore, Mill, and Keltie Glaciers, and geologized the rock exposures, finding mostly mudstones, sandstones, and composite seams of coal. Our first fossil finds were seed-ferns and conifers reputed to be about 200 million years old – the richest collection of plant-fossils yet found in East Antarctica. They were found in an erratic boulder of dark shale at the base of an isolated nunatak on the polar plateau, where the wind chiselled the snow for miles around or polished the surging waves of blue ice. A bleak and bitter spot it was, one of the last rock outcrops not engulfed by the dome of ice which rose to the south. But so many exciting finds were in store for us that only our geologist Vic McGregor maintained his gasping enthusiasm for those imprints of a warmer age. He found silicified branches, stumps of trees, and *Glossopteris* leaf impressions, which he packed with loving care.

Pete Otway's survey work was less rewarding, for all we had to show after staggering down from the mountain-top stations was first-degree frostbite, swelling tongues, and field-books bursting with spidery figures written by a shaking hand. Kevin Pain our field assistant, who, at the ripe age of thirty-three, was the oldest member of the Southern Party, kept our record of the weather, while I kept contact with base by radio.

My companions were conscientious men, content to be part of an efficient and well conducted programme, but, as leader, it disturbed me to be without a geographical goal. At the time of going into the field a pick-up point was undecided – it had been left entirely up to me to find a suitable landing-strip either on the polar plateau or on the Ross Ice Shelf, so I began playing with the idea of exploring the full length of the Queen Maud Range as far east as the head of the

Robert Scott Glacier some 250 miles away, which we would then attempt to descend to the ice shelf before calling on the aircraft to pick us up. The immediate reaction of my companions to this suggestion was a credit to their loyalty, but I could see that they were more intent on surveying than adventuring and so my spirit was subdued. We compromised and plodded on until we were struck by a few misfortunes – which fell like the first blows on a masochist as far as I was concerned.

Without ill-luck, good fortune turns sour – and there is nothing like dogged misfortune for bringing men together. I delighted in it, welcomed it in a perverted sort of way, for I knew it would concentrate the grit in my companions. I wanted a journey with a climax, a gruelling journey; but those ideals are hard to win against radio sets, thoughtful pilots, and conscientious companions. Our misfortunes tipped the balance of comfort and as one followed another, our journey, to my delight, became an adventure. They were minor misfortunes all of them: had they been bigger we would not have been permitted to struggle with them alone but would have been obliged to share them with our superiors comfortably office-bound in Wellington.

They started with the fall of Joe – a poor old husky who slipped on the ice and could no longer keep up the pace set by his younger team mates, so we let him off the trace to follow in his own time along our tracks. Many hours after we had camped we saw the old dog slowly making his way towards us along the trail, resting every few yards of the way. He collapsed exhausted when he reached us – and died during the night.

Within a mile of poor Joe's grave my sledge collapsed under the weight of a twelve-hundred-pound load, a load it should have carried easily across the perfect plateau surface had the manufacturers done their job properly. We repaired the sledge as well as we could but it would only bear light loads from then on and all our sledging had to be done in pitifully slow, frustrating relays.

Dismal – my lead dog – then became lame. He was Joe's brother, and at nine years of age was really too old for such high altitude. One camp site was almost 12,000 feet – Husky Dome we called it – and, although the younger dogs showed no ill effects at that altitude, Dismal weakened every day. We carried him on the sledge for miles, strapped to it so that he could not fall off, but the jolting punched the breath out of him, and when we reached a buttress near the head of the Shackleton Glacier the old leader slumped to the snow. It was 16 December – the fiftieth anniversary of the date that Amundsen and his companions reached the South Pole. We had a party that night to celebrate it.

I made a Norwegian flag from bits of bunting and strips of hand-kerchief, and with the tent gaily decorated in festive streamers and candles struggling to glow through the fug of cigar-smoke, the four of us drank a toast to the memory of the five adventurers who first reached the Pole. But into that festive atmosphere penetrated a shot of bitterness – a message from base came over the radio saying that I must abandon all thought of attempting a descent of the Robert Scott Glacier as Dr Charles Swithinbank, who was working at the mouth of it, had reported the glacier impassable. That I found very hard to believe as Dr Swithinbank was an expert sledger; I could not imagine him being turned back from a route that had been sledged over once before. But I had to accept what I was told, as I could not make direct radio contact with Charles to ask him precisely what he had found. I discovered almost a year later that he had been de-liberately mis-quoted – to put me off!

Our party broke up deeply depressed, and it was not until after we had climbed into our sleeping-bags that a new idea came to me for a climax to our season: we would descend Amundsen's route on the Axel Heiberg Glacier! No one had done it but Amundsen's Pole party. They had made no map of it and had taken only two photo-graphs. I sat up and shot the idea at Vic. 'Of course, of course!' he said, 'Why didn't we think of it before!' I padded across the squeak-ing snow to the other tent, shook it and shouted to be let in. The sleeve entrance was untied, a hand tugged it open and I stuck my head in to see two faces peering at me through the gloom. 'Let's go down Amundsen's route!' I laughed. Kevin just grunted and nestled into the folds of his warm sleeping-bag. Pete beamed and said, 'But we'd never get permission.'

We did not stop to chat about it and the idea did not delay our sleep, but the next morning on my last radio contact with base before the re-supply flight took off from McMurdo I asked for a copy of *The South Pole*, Volume Two, by Amundsen to be free-dropped with the rest of my supplies. With this request I made no comment. Athol made none in reply.

The re-supply drop was precision flying. We had marked a bull's eye in the snow with a flag at the centre and circles stamped around it, each one numbered so that we could 'score' the drop. This turned the job into a sport for the pilot, and with a bull's eye prize of a promised bottle of Drambuie he was less inclined to scatter the boxes and jerry-cans indiscriminately. His very first drop of three boxes fell in the centre circle – one box gouging a pit only two feet from the marker flag – and as the aircraft made pass after pass at the target he found less space to 'place' the loads, so he dropped the rest quite near the tents, flying over us at only fifty feet. We could see Athol in the doorway of the aircraft and hear over the radio the slightly bored voice of the pilot reporting to his base at McMurdo that his mission was completed.

'Dismal Camp' we called the place in spite of the successful re-supply flight. My old lead dog would eat no food and lay groaning for hours while the other dogs whimpered and 'talked' to each other softly. I tapped out a long message on the morse key to Athol back at base asking for his sanction on our change of plan: to map as far east as the Axel Heiberg and descend it to the shelf ice from where an air-craft could pick us up with less risk and less expense. The reply was non-committal. That night Dismal wheezed and coughed while I lay awake and twice I raised myself on to an elbow trying to muster the courage to go out and kill him, but courage failed me each time and I sank back into my sleeping-bag, covering my ears to deaden the sound. In the early hours of the morning I could stand the strain of it no more, and without waking Vic, I quickly got dressed, strapped on my knife, and wriggled out of the tent.

The morning air was cold and still. Some of the dogs looked up, grumbled, then snuggled their noses back into the warm pile of their curled bodies. Dismal raised his head as he lay on his side – he was a pitiful sight. My hand fumbled for the knife but could not draw it from its sheath; instead I took the picket hammer from the sledge and stood above him almost blinded with tears, waiting and waiting until his eyes closed for a moment as his racked body gasped for breath – then my hammer swung and crushed his skull. I swung it again like a maniac until the hammer fell from my grip and I was sick.

I dragged him away about thirty yards, dug a deep hole and buried him. Above his grave I set up a sledge flag and guyed it so that the wind would not move it, then crawled back into my tent. Vic was still asleep.

We moved off later that morning leaving our large depot behind and taking only enough food to last the short survey trip a few days' journey from 'Dismal Camp' back along part of our route and up towards Mount Black. Kari was my new leader – a skittish little bitch I had brought from Greenland. She followed the tracks of Pete's team well, after vicious dog fights had rent the air in a frenzied start. We left behind a trail of blood until the cold air froze a crust over the wounds of our injured dogs, and just before we camped that evening one of Pete's sledge runners snapped in half. For the next five days a blizzard raged and we had to cut down to half rations; but on the sixth day, while Kevin made temporary repairs to the broken sledge, Vic and I sorted out the last of our food, leaving Pete and Kevin all but half a meal and a primus half full of fuel so that they could stay a day longer to complete the survey, then we set off back to 'Dismal Camp'.

The weather had broken and from that time on blizzards, snowfall, low cloud and cutting winds made our life a misery. At each relay of the weakened sledges we stuck in marker flags every quarter of a mile, and many were the days when we travelled 'blind'. We travelled in the isolation of our anoraks – they were the outer skin of our straining bodies in which we shrank, mere flesh and bood, while consciousness became detached, and in a sense we each became dual people battling with ourselves. Near the end of each day when the hissing drift had worn us down, drawn off our strength, and stung us into walking sleep, our consciousness would escape across a void and watch our bodies struggling pathetically. This detached self would not return to us until camp was pitched. Duality would then merge once more into a man co-ordinating mind and body in his need to feed and sleep. There were few snaps of temperament during this testing period; we were under stress and felt it, but we had found a goal at which to aim and we measured our pace to meet it.

Our New Year camp was at the base of Misery Peak on the massif I named after Athol Roberts at the head of the Shackleton Glacier, and as we had missed our Christmas festivities we had a party on New

Year's Eve. I persuaded my three companions to go over to Pete's tent after the bulk of our feast had been prepared, and that left me free to 'lay' my tent with the luxury items I had kept hidden until then. I had carried an enormous iced cake secreted in my personal bag. It was decorated with tiny tents, sledges, dogs, and men, and had a suitable inscription piped across its snowy dome. The cake had been made up to my specification in Wellington and brought down to Scott Base by Athol in time for me to disguise the parcel and hide it amongst my gear. There were numerous other small items and gifts appropriate to a festive occasion, which in our culture we had grown to accept along with crackers and paper-chains. The effect was gaudy but exciting and completely alien to our harsh environment.

We were like boys that evening wrapped in tinsel. No blizzard hissed at our light-hearted laughter or shook our frail shelter. It was a tranquil evening spiced with cake and sticky sweets – an island of ease and luxury in a sea of physical toil. We chatted merrily for hours – four human creatures cramped inside a tiny tent, our tracks across the icy desert already swept clean by the wind. Four men bound together by their dependence on each other, toasting the focus of their new-found dream – the climax to their journey.

1962 crept in muffled in a clinging mist. Skis clattered over hard-packed snow and our rattling sledges were dragged no distance before we camped. Snow fell like eider-down bursting from a pillow. Dogs sniffed for a breeze which did not come. For days we fought for every mile – drunken sledges ploughing through a sea of loose snow pulled by swimming teams of dogs tired and sinking, men hoarse with shouting, their bodies aching. Then, as gently as a ghostly sigh, the breeze played on our tents and set the snow in wraith-like drifts lazily moving towards the west. It was an awful, desolate white world we drove our teams across while the wind snatched at our anoraks and the flying snow's icy stings chapped our lips and numbed our cheeks. But in two weeks of cruel labouring we reached the base of a massive mountain that we had set our hearts on climbing.

On 16 January 1962 – the day, fifty years after, when Captain Scott and his four companions learnt for the first time that they had been forestalled at the South Pole by Roald Amundsen's party – we made the first ascent of Mount Fridtjof Nansen. 'Great God! This is an awful place,' Scott wrote in his diary on 17 January 1912, 'and terrible enough for us to have laboured to it without the reward of priority.' Those immortal words were singing in my ears for the seventeen hours we were on that 13,330-foot mountain, cringing in a stabbing wind, struggling to do our survey, stopping every few minutes to blow into our gloved hands and massage our stiff bodies. The misery and exhaustion we suffered dug deeply into our reserves, and the long, long trudge back down to camp almost claimed the four of us. It was less windy down below and the sun was soothing, but in spite of the risks of resting we were compelled to lie down every few yards. Our last rest was only a hundred yards from the tents, which we reached at 4.30 on the morning of 17 January.

The sledge flags drummed in a stiffening breeze from the south, while we assessed our chances of successfully descending Amundsen's route to the Pole on the Axel Heiberg Glacier. Mount Fridtjof Nansen in one way had been a good mountain to us, for from the eastern side of its massive dome we had been given a glimpse of part of Amundsen's route. The icefalls of the glacier we could not see but the top terrace and the run off at the bottom looked crevasse-free.

My companions were keyed up with the anticipation of those icefalls; so we scorned the radio message suggesting that we retreat to the Otway Massif where we had been landed over ten weeks before, and drove our teams around to the head of the Axel Heiberg Glacier. The evening we reached that spot was glorious. The smooth, soft plateau sank gently towards the brink of a bowl of cloud. Two ice-caked mountains rose on either side catching the sun on their slipping faces scarred with crevasses and gaping chasms. The air was very still. The omen was powerful. We switched off the radio and made ready to descend.

We had read passages to each other every night from Amundsen's book. We handled it with reverence and had re-read until we knew by heart the account of his ascent and descent of that magnificent glacier. But we found many ambiguities, for the narrative of his journey had not been intended as a route guide for future travellers. He had taken only two photographs and neither photograph showed the icefalls. He had made no maps, left no route sketches. We had no choice but to re-discover a route down the Axel Heiberg.

We could only assume that the amount of ice flowing down the valley was the same as it was fifty years before. We could only assume that the crevasses and icefalls, although all different, would be cut in the same general pattern, for the bedrock over which the ice flowed could not have been eroded in a mere fifty years. We could only assume that his account was true until it was proved either grossly exaggerated or, what was more likely, very modest.

Undoubtedly, Amundsen's route up the Axel Heiberg Glacier had been a triumph of courage, experience, and good sportsmanship. The object of his expedition was to beat Scott to the South Pole. On the face of it there was no reason why Amundsen should not have driven his dog teams directly from his base camp to the Beardmore Glacier – a route to the polar plateau already discovered and pioneered by Shackleton. There was no written rule forbidding Amundsen to use the Beardmore route. But the idea of using the same route as Scott scarcely occurred to him. In his book, Amundsen says: 'Scott had announced that he was going to take Shackleton's route, and that decided the matter. During our long stay at Framheim not one of us ever hinted at the possibility of such a course. Without discussion Scott's route was declared out of bounds.'*

By sledging due south he ran the risk of finding his path barred by an unbroken chain of mountains, and since he had no ulterior scientific motive for his expedition as had Scott, the success or failure of Amundsen's expedition depended on finding a new route to the polar plateau. This was the challenge which Amundsen and his companions accepted, and by tackling the Axel Heiberg Glacier, which from every angle looks appalling as a sledging route they proved themselves masters of their own fate.

The Beardmore Glacier, as seen from Mount Hope, had given Shackleton and his companions the opposite impression. It stretched out before them as a mighty highway to the Pole. The glacier was 140 miles long and its gradient was gentle, rising only to 7,800 feet at the plateau. Even its direction was favourable, for the first half of the climb lay due south and the second half lay south-west. But whereas it took Scott and his tough companions fourteen days to man-haul their heavy sledges up this previously explored and relatively straightforward route to an altitude of 7,800 feet, Amundsen

* Amundsen, Roald, op. cit., Vol. 1 (1912), p. 52.

had taken only four days, including reconnoitring, to climb to an altitude of 10,600 feet. His achievement was even more remarkable because he took a short-cut through the mountains, climbing to 4,550 feet, and making two descents totalling 3,350 feet before he even got on to the Axel Heiberg Glacier. His total climb up the glacier amounted to 13,250 feet, and his total climbing from the time he left the ice shelf to the time he returned from the Pole was 19,590 feet, as against 11,470 feet climbed by Scott's party.

The first men to see the Axel Heiberg Glacier after Amundsen's successful Pole party descended it in January 1912 were Admiral Byrd and his crew on a depot-laying flight to the foot of the Liv Glacier on 18 November 1929.* But eleven days later Byrd and his crew – Balchen, June, and McKinley – on their flight to the South Pole, flew up the Liv Glacier in preference to the Axel Heiberg because the plateau altitude at the head of the Liv was a little lower. After a most successful and exciting flight up the Liv Glacier and on to the Pole, they decided to make their return down the Axel Heiberg. Their flight down the glacier took only ten minutes – hardly enough time to study it as a dog-sledging route, and to judge from Byrd's errors in positioning Amundsen's place-names he found Amundsen's account most confusing.

The Southern Geological Party of Byrd's 1929 expedition under the leadership of Dr Laurence McKinley Gould had a far more protracted and arduous journey than the Admiral – whose flight from Little America to the South Pole and back, although courageous, was all over in 18 hours, 40 minutes. Dr Gould's party dog-sledged from Little America to the Queen Maud Range and travelled eastwards along the foot of the range from the Liv Glacier to the Leverett Glacier and back. They penetrated as far inland as the north-east spur of Mount Fridtjof Nansen by sledging up the Strom Glacier, and made valuable geological collections in that locality. From a running survey along the ice shelf and by using the very fine photographs taken on the Pole flight by Captain McKinley, a reconnaissance map of that region was made for the first time. With the exception of the icefalls of the Axel Heiberg, which they could not see from the mouth of the glacier, the topography was well shown, but Amundsen's route remained untrodden.

* Byrd, Rear-Admiral Richard E., *Little America* (1930), p. 315, Putnam.

Amundsen's account of his ascent of the Axel Heiberg was un-dramatic. It created the impression that he had found an easy route to the polar plateau. Even the errors he made on the glacier did not seem unduly to hinder his progress. It was a race he was running for the South Pole – he had been forestalled at the North Pole by Dr Frederick A. Cook and Commander Robert E. Peary; he could not afford to be beaten to the South Pole by Scott. To follow the longi-tude of Framheim to the South Pole would be his shortest route, and this is precisely what he intended to do.

As he was approaching the Queen Maud Range he was looking for a glacier that flowed in a south to north direction, and at first auto-matically ruled out the Liv and Axel Heiberg Glaciers because they were slightly off his set course.* He chose to go inland from Mount Betty, hoping to find a direct route up to the polar plateau. This, I think, was his first mistake, and I still cannot understand his reason-ing – but then I am biased because I now know the country. In any case, he took the easier route on his return.

His party of five men and forty-two dogs left their depot just north of Mount Betty on 17 November, travelled 11½ miles, and climbed 2,000 feet. It was an uncomfortable day's sledging, hard work and hot. After camp had been pitched, two parties set off to investigate the route ahead; Wisting and Hanssen as one pair, and Bjaaland ski-ing off alone in another direction. It was perhaps just as well that Amundsen insisted on the prerogative of making the final decision, for a healthy argument developed over which route was the better. On 18 November they sledged just over 2,000 feet up to a sad-dle from where they had their first view of the Axel Heiberg icefalls. Amundsen wrote: 'We now saw the southern side of the immense Mount Nansen; Don Pedro Christophersen we could see in his full length. Between these two mountains we could follow the course of the glacier that rose in terraces along their sides. It looked fearfully broken and disturbed, but we could follow a little connected line among the many crevasses; we saw that we could go a long way, but we also saw that the glacier forbade us to use it in its full extent. Between the first and second terraces the ice was evidently impassable. But we could see that there was an unbroken ledge up on the side of the mountain; Don Pedro would help us out. On the north side of

* See map of the Axel Heiberg Glacier region.

the mountain there was nothing but chaos, perfectly impossible to get through.'*

I believe that from Amundsen's altitude and distance he was only able to form a general impression of which way to go; he could not possibly be sure that there was a route. The Axel Heiberg was in his way. Amundsen was in a hurry. This to me is the most impressive example of his determination in the face of an obstacle that would have turned away any lesser man.

The next part of his narrative is easy to follow on the map, but after he had reached the Axel Heiberg his description becomes vague, and his ambiguity over this part of the route caused us great anxieties. Knowing as we now do exactly where he camped on the evening of 18 November, and approximately where he got down on to the Axel Heiberg, it all fits in very clearly. It is obvious that he went right out on to the middle of the glacier, along one of the ice-streams, and up to a point just below the chaos of the bottom icefall.

They had difficulty in pitching their tent in the soft snow, and in the evening Bjaaland and Hanssen went off to reconnoitre a route up to the middle terrace. Going up this terrace the next day Amundsen found a fine hard surface on which the dogs got a splendid hold, and although the route was riddled with huge crevasses and they had to relay up the steep climb they made very fine progress, sledged across the middle terrace, and took a rest just at the base of the middle ice-fall. He started off from there using double teams, but soon climbed into difficulties. He found himself 'under a ridge among the many open chasms', and decided that it would be prudent first to make a reconnaissance. They set up their tent at 5,650 feet above sea-level, and then set off. As usual Amundsen tried the shortest way first, and there he made his second mistake on the glacier: 'The shortest way,' he said, 'was awful.'

They returned to the tent, where everything had been put in order and the dogs fed. Then three of them set off to see if another route could be found. This time they took a slightly longer route and went right up under Mount Don Pedro Christophersen, where they found a good safe passage between the huge crevasses. They pressed on-wards until they could see before them the last slope to the plateau. They in fact went right across the top terrace of the glacier until they

* Amundsen, op. cit., Vol. 2 (1912), p. 44.

could see around the corner of Mount Ole Engelstad towards the icefalls between it and Mount Helland Nansen, and from that point they returned to their camp site 2,500 feet below.

Amundsen's description of the scenery that met their eyes on their return deserves to be quoted: 'It was a grand and imposing sight we had when we came out on the ridge under which – far below – our tent stood. Surrounded on all sides by huge crevasses and gaping chasms, it could not be said that the site of our camp looked very inviting. The wildness of the landscape seen from this point is not to be described; chasm after chasm, crevasse after crevasse, with great blocks of ice scattered promiscuously about, gave one the impression that here nature was too powerful for us. Here no progress was to be thought of. It was not without a certain satisfaction that we stood there and contemplated the scene. The little dark speck down there – our tent – in the midst of all this chaos, gave us the feeling of strength and power. We knew in our hearts that the ground would have to be ugly indeed if we were not to manoeuvre our way across it and find a place for that little home of ours. Crash upon crash, roar upon roar, met our ears. Now it was a shot from Mount Nansen, now one from the others; we could see the clouds of snow rise high in the air. It was evident that these mountains were throwing off their winter mantle and putting on a more spring-like garb.'*

On 20 November they set off on what proved to be the biggest climb of the journey to the Pole. They did not take exactly the course they had reconnoitred the day before, and Amundsen does not say clearly which way they went. I would guess, however, that they sledged closer under Mount Don Pedro Christophersen. The surface was not good up on the top terrace and it was very hard work getting up the last slope. Amundsen writes: 'The dogs seemed positively to understand that this was the last big effort that was asked of them: they lay flat down and hauled, dug their claws in and dragged themselves forward.'

They continued their march after they had ascended the last icefall determined not to stop until they had reached the flat plain of the polar plateau, and they finally camped on the summit of the spur running on to the plateau from Mount Don Pedro Christophersen. They had travelled 19¼ statute miles with an ascent of 5,750 feet – a

* Amundsen, op. cit., Vol. 2 (1912), pp. 56–7.

remarkable achievement for men and dogs. Twenty-four dogs were slaughtered that night, and the site became known as the 'Butcher's Shop'. Amundsen has often been criticized over the years for slaughtering so many of his dogs, and it was perhaps unwise of him to be so frank in the English version of his book about how he and his companions enjoyed eating the fresh 'dog cutlets'. The English as a nation of dog-lovers could not tolerate the thought of man eating dog. Amundsen was a practical man with a mission to fulfil – he took his mate on the hoof, as indeed did Shackleton and Scott; the technique only differed in choice of draught animal.

On 25 November Amundsen's party set off into the teeth of a blizzard, heading due south, and after a while they started to descend. This worried them for they knew from Shackleton's account that he had kept climbing for a long time after he had reached the plateau. Amundsen, in travelling due south from the head of the Axel Heiberg had descended into the basin-like névé of the Isaiah Bowman Glacier, but since visibility was practically zero and remained very poor for the next few days they did not realize this. In fact the third mistake that Amundsen made on the way to the Pole was that he ran into some of the worst crevasse systems on this part of the polar plateau by travelling due south from the head of the Axel Heiberg. All three mistakes were quite understandable – I mention them only to show that in each case there was an easier route, and had Amundsen only known of it at the time, he would have saved himself and his companions a lot of anxiety and hard work, and would have reached the Pole sooner.

His trip down the Axel Heiberg on his return from the Pole was so uneventful and straightforward that it barely gets a mention in his book, and yet by reading between the lines of this master of understatement I can see how breathtaking that trip down must have been. He covers the crux of the descent with no more words than these: 'On the ridge where the descent to the glacier began we halted to make our preparations. Brakes were put under the sledges, and our two ski-sticks were fastened together to make one strong one; we should have to be able to stop instantly if surprised by a crevasse as we were going. We ski-runners went in front. The going was ideal here on the steep slope, just enough loose snow to give one good steering on ski. We went whizzing down, and it was not many minutes

before we were on the Heiberg Glacier. For the drivers it was
not such plain sailing: they had to be extremely careful on the steep
fall.'*

It was an overcast day, oppressive with tension; shadowless; still.
The brink of the first drop could not be seen, but we could feel it
waiting to swallow us. Amundsen had called it the 'severe, steep
slope' and I skied towards it to judge for myself, while my companions sorted out the gear we would take down with us on our
reconnaissance. We dared not commit ourselves to the glacier with
our full loads as we might have met an impasse and had to return;
nor could we risk an accident on the glacier, for we had not been
given permission to attempt the descent. It had to be done in less
than four days. We had no intention of taking the radio, which
weighed almost seventy pounds, and four days off the air was the
mute clarion call for search and rescue to begin. A route had to be
flagged through the icefalls and we had to be back on the plateau by
7.30 p.m. on 24 January.

At the edge of the drop I waited – and as spears of weak sunlight
fell through the rotting cloak of thick cloud overhead and pierced
the soft mist in the basin, I skied cautiously over the brink. At first I
skied too slowly to feel the wind of movement; but the slightest
ripple in the surface moistened in that spectral light looked like a
gash – the livid lip of a crevasse – and distracted, I went sweeping
past them, the slope taking charge and tilting me in a gliding plummet
into the weird, silent, mist-swirled bottom of that basin. I had
descended just over 1,000 feet – the run was safe – but it took me
an hour and a quarter to climb back up to our camp.

My friends were ready to move off. We fastened our home-made
Norwegian flag to the front of the leading sledge, prepared the rope
brakes, called to the dogs and lurched forward along my ski tracks.
We over-braked the sledges and descended that fall in perfect control,
not taking the slightest risk that would jeopardize our success. By the
time we reached the base of that drop, sun was streaming on to the
glacier in a patchwork of light and shade. Ahead, a ground mist lay
thick and grey, with only the dazzling crown of Mount Don Pedro
Christophersen piercing it. We felt squeezed by crumbled buttresses
of ice, sun-soaked and shadow-smudged, that towered on either side.

* Amundsen, op. cit ,Vol. 2 (1912), p. 157.

We were four trespassers in a paradise of ice-form, but Amundsen and his men were our advocates. Their presence we could sense.

Only hard work and worsening weather disturbed that feeling and chilled us back to reality. We struggled through the deep snow of the top terrace, our shouts profaning the silence, our tracks scarring the purity of that soft field of snow until they were shrouded in haze. The tents went up on a shadowless ledge with a sensitive mist swirling around us, handling us, breathing depression over us for the next thirty-six hours. Six inches of snow fell on our outward tracks. Time trickled away.

Pete and Kevin volunteered to make their way back, feeling their way up to the polar plateau, leaving Vic and me with the remainder of their food. Slowly the cloud began to lift and while Vic and I snatched a few hours sleep, Pete and Kevin did the survey. At 1 a.m. on 23 January we whispered good luck, and parted from our friends. We skied off the ledge and down a thousand-foot drop on to a smooth table of snow which reached out towards the icefalls. There was not the slightest breath of wind – the sky was a dome of deep blue. On our backs we carried forty marker flags, ice-axes, climbing ropes, crevasse probes and plenty of chocolate. The swish of the skis, the rustle of clothing and the gentle breathing of two men were the only sounds. The warmth of the sun soaked us with sensuous delight.

We reached the corner of that table where the ground fell away in a gaping precipice. Before us was such a scene of turbulence and ice chaos that words were stifled by emotion – I had seen nothing to surpass the power, the beauty in that scene of turmoil. Into the cwm, walled by frowning rock and capped by mountains of sliding ice, fell thundering, grumbling avalanches, exploding snow in white cushions, curling, settling, staining the floor with debris. We were too small to dare exclaim. No words of man could measure the might of what we saw. We stood transfixed and stared in horror at the lacerated wounds and torn white flesh of that glacier far below. The knives of nature had slashed that valley with such viciousness, that mere man we thought – so insignificant – could surely not creep through it. But Amundsen and his men had done so fifty years ago.

Which way had they come? We studied the icefalls through the binoculars for almost an hour trying to imagine a route, but scale was impossible to judge – we were at least 2,000 feet above the chaotic ice that was the crux of Amundsen's route. We had no hope of finding a way, but in order to get some photographs among those spectacular icefalls, we set off from that corner and free-skied down a switch-back fall on to the middle terrace. It looked stabbed and scratched from high above and darkness filled the wounds to the brim with indigo blood, but once on that terrace there was space enough to move between those wounds across the smooth white flesh and roped together we probed our way with some trepidation towards the head of the bottom icefall.

We swished over small bridged crevasses, and in amongst gigantic blocks of marble ice, cut and heaved up, heeling over, leaving their roots stained blue-green in the gaping cavities. We crossed a hump-backed bridge of snow with a yawning crevasse on one side and a chasm on the other. That bridge led on to a traverse which sloped steeply down to enormous pits like puffy blue mouths open and waiting to be fed. Across this traverse Vic and I skied, roped together, but first he shot past me out of control, jerking the rope as he reached its end, which shot me forward at a tearing pace past Vic until the jerk sent him plunging past me once more. Thus we descended like chain shot on truant skis and in the cold grip of fear we hurtled towards the yawning mouths and came to a trembling rest on the tip of a chasm. We picked ourselves up and as we dusted off the snow we felt the leaping pride of having safely negotiated the crux of Amundsen's route.

At the bottom of the traverse our meandering course began. Up and down we went and around the lips of monstrous pits and chasms, until we came on to a comparatively undisturbed tract of the glacier, then across this and into another region of awful pits. Sometimes we had to go down into the belly of these depressions and steeply up the other side, but more often we were able to find a route that took us around the rims of these unpleasant-looking places. At 6.30 a.m. we were through the worst of the icefalls. Ahead we could see a clear route on to the main stream of the glacier. We stuck in a marker flag at the only spot near at hand where there would be enough room to span out two teams of dogs and erect a camp. The altitude of that spot was just under 3,000 feet – we were 6,000 feet below our depot on the polar plateau.

On our way back up the icefalls we stuck in marker flags at every distinct change of direction, so that on the descent with the dog teams, should the weather be against us, we would be able to feel our way between the crevasses by taking a straight line route from one flag to the next. Each crevasse bridge we probed and tested thoroughly – we could get down with the dog teams I felt sure.

Vic and I separated when we had safely crossed the middle terrace. He took the more direct route, placing the remainder of the marker flags, while I detoured to visit the corner vantage point to take more photographs and to see the icefalls in a new perspective. We were both by that time exhausted, and the last 1,000 feet of the climb to camp was a desperate struggle. Resting every few paces we eventually reached camp at 12 noon, crawled into the tent, and slept off our fatigue.

The next day we sledged back to the top of the plateau with the good news for our companions that we had found a route. They had been far from idle while we were making our reconnaissance of the icefalls – they had climbed Mount Ole Engelstad and completed the survey of the Axel Heiberg, and had been on the move for thirty-four hours without a rest.

That night we were all in high spirits as we sat in my tent while I tapped out the radio message to Scott Base jubilantly announcing that we had flagged a route through the icefalls of the Axel Heiberg, and asking for official permission to descend the glacier and be picked up from the shelf ice. Surely, we thought, this permission would be given for there were no suitable landing sites on the polar plateau within a hundred miles of our camp, and it was too late in the season to sledge all the way back to the Otway Massif where we had originally been landed. Fortunately the radio reception faded after I had passed my message, so we were spared, until the following evening, the start of our frustrations.

All four of us were getting very tired. We had been on the plateau for eighty days, the weather had been bad for weeks, and the temperature had started its autumn plunge. We had spun out our rations over a long period, so that we would have a surplus of about two weeks' food. We were now living on that surplus, and yet still planned to sledge on to the head of the Liv Glacier and down the east side of the Shackleton Glacier to complete the survey of that area before descending the Axel Heiberg. Our celebrations were brief – we needed sleep.

The following morning Pete and Kevin set off for Barnum Peak at the head of the Liv Glacier, while Vic and I persevered with the radio, trying to make contact with base. We could not get through at 8 a.m. so we tried again on the emergency schedule at 12.30 p.m., but radio reception was even worse then so we broke camp and chased after Pete and Kevin. They had many hours start on us and by 6 p.m. as the drift started blowing we camped six miles short of them, laid out the radio aerial, and prepared for another attempt to contact base and get the official permission to descend Amundsen's route.

Athol came on the air with the astonishing reply that there was an icefall at the mouth of the Axel Heiberg Glacier that he had seen on a reconnaissance flight which was absolutely impassable. He argued that we had turned back too early and therefore not seen it. Cold fingers and a field radio give little assistance to an amateur telegraphist. To these natural burdens were suddenly added a disbelieving base leader, a belligerent tent companion demanding his share of the base leader's blood, and a situation so ludicrous that words could not come off my morse key fast enough. I was told after my furious burst of tapping that I would get an answer the following evening after Admiral Tyree had flown back to McMurdo from Wellington where he had been discussing my claim and proposal with Mr Markham. I did not like the implication of that – it was growing completely out of proportion.

How Amundsen would have laughed if he could have seen us, beating our knees with frustration beside a radio set, listening to garbled reports on conferences held between our superiors on whether or not to give us permission to descend the Axel Heiberg Glacier. How very different was the heroic age of polar exploration! In those days a party many hundreds of miles from base and without radio would take their calculated risks with almost a gay abandon. No longer are polar explorers permitted to face their dangers alone. Nor are they permitted to go off the air and take their calculated risks in peace and quiet. The humane society in which we live insists upon a multitude of men, most of them strangers, waiting beside a radio for the signal to scramble and risk their lives in flying to the rescue of an explorer in trouble. What a relief of responsibility it would be for the modern explorer if he had only the safety of his companions and himself to worry about!

The radio, that wonderful piece of apparatus, became our burden.

With only a few days' food left and the winds cooling, the polar plateau became an awful place. We trudged into the headwinds as long as we could tolerate it and camped as our flesh began to freeze. Our faces became sheets of ice, our hands and feet died as fatigue slowed our progress to a halt. Unconscious habit pitched our camps, half-conscious bodies crawled inside the tents, frozen fingers switched on the radio, disgust twisted our faces as we heard more excuses – 'they are still in conference'. Our sledging time crept out of phase as blizzards pinned and then released us. Even Dr Charles Swithinbank was lifted from the field two days early so that he could pass his expert opinion at a high-powered conference held at McMurdo on 'what should be done about Herbert's party?'.

'He says he has flagged a route down the Axel Heiberg icefalls and claims that he could get down the glacier safely with dog teams – would you believe that, Charles?'

'If he says so, of course I believe it,' said Charles. So I was given permission to descend Amundsen's route on 1 February 1962 – fifty years and one month after Amundsen and his companions.

We left that infernal plateau hissing as its body chilled, and with loads of nearly 900 lb on each sledge we sank into a cosy pocket of windless, warm, soft-snuggling peace. Our camp was pitched less than a mile from Amundsen's camp of 4 January 1912, but the following morning my radio packed up and Pete felt very ill. I had been given permission to descend the glacier with one proviso: that I made contact with base by radio no less than three times a day! During the night I had woken up and the weather had looked promising. I felt confident that with our route flagged out we would get down in a day, and had no intention of stopping at noon to set up that confounded wireless. But the turn of events had us all worried.

We postponed the start until 1 p.m. by which time I had dried out the radio by hanging it in the apex of the tent above the primus stove, but without making the slightest difference. However, Pete felt a little better, and for the first three miles we went very well. Then the heavy sledges began to plough, and then to float in the deep snow.

Men and dogs gave up the struggle after sledging only six miles that day.

The next day was even worse. We descended over 1,000 feet but only sledged 4·3 miles. The sky was overcast. The scene was drab. We could pick up no stations on the radio. Our camp that night was a hundred yards from the crest of the drop down to the middle terrace, and not half a mile from Amundsen's camp site of 19 November 1911. With the prospect of descending the icefalls the next day, that night should have been the most exciting one of the whole season for me – but it was not. Every minute I expected to hear the search and rescue planes roaring overhead, disturbing the tranquillity of our camp. The sky had cleared by the time we turned in.

At 6.30 on the morning of 4 February we had breakfast, then three of us set off on skis to the corner from where Vic and I had caught our first glimpse of those spectacular icefalls. Kevin did not wish to study them, he was prepared to take them as they came; for him the descent was just one stage nearer home. Pete had recovered completely and was raring to go, and Vic took a boyish delight in pointing out the route.

At 10 a.m. we quietly moved off, over the crest and down the long fall to the middle terrace. But what a struggle it was. The snow lay so deep that we had to push down the slope which Amundsen went 'whizzing down'. We gathered a little speed as we sledged across the middle terrace, and shot over the hump-back bridge on to the traverse. Sledging was a little more exciting there, but from the bottom of the traverse to the chosen camp site we found the going hard.

One moment we were careering around the lips of gigantic chasms, and the next moment we were pushing and struggling to get our sledges up the stiff rise from the sunken bridge of a crevasse to the safety of the lip again. Some of the short climbs back on to safe ground were so steep that all four men had to lend a hand, then at last, reluctantly, we decided to relay. We had only two scares amongst those chasms and both were the result of inexperienced men handling stupid dogs. Neither the men nor the dogs could be blamed for almost driving straight over the lip into a yawning chasm, for although we had sledged nearly 800 miles since being landed on the polar plateau, my companions had tackled few hills and no icefalls before – the plateau is no training ground for hazardous glacier sledging.

I stood and raged at poor Vic for almost five minutes on one occasion for making a dangerous mistake – one which I had made many times myself in my early days of sledging. Tension in me was at snapping point. Nothing must go wrong. Far too much was at stake. Our descent of the Axel Heiberg had become a controversial issue – people were worried about us in case we 'let them down'. The season was rapidly drawing to a close. All distant field parties had been safely brought in; many had already flown out to New Zealand. Rescuing us would have been an extremely hazardous operation – we were, after all, the experts. How thoroughly delightful that descent would have been if no one had known we were there!

We camped that night at the spot where Vic and I had turned back from the foot reconnaissance. We were unable to get through to base by radio to tell them our position, but we had concluded that there was a radio 'black-out' and had ceased to worry for we knew that no aircraft would take off from McMurdo until radio conditions improved.

The following morning, to our delight, we discovered that we had camped on almost the exact location of Amundsen's camp site of 18 November 1911 and 5 January 1912. We made this discovery when comparing photographs in Amundsen's book. On which of those dates he took the photographs we could not be sure, but by using them to get a photographic resection, we found that we could not move more than a hundred feet in any direction without upsetting the comparison between the scenery and Amundsen's photographs.

We saved our celebration for the evening of 5 February, by which time we had sledged ten miles out along the glacier towards the mouth, and had contacted base with the news that we had safely descended the glacier and were heading for the shelf ice to look for a pick-up point. Our last day's sledging was a pure delight. The relief from anxiety and the glorious warmth of sledging at low altitude was a tonic. By lunch-time we had reached the mouth of the Axel Heiberg near Amundsen's camp of 6 January 1912, and a few miles farther along the coast we found the perfect landing-site.

There we spent two lazy, happy days waiting for the aircraft. Vic re-packed with loving care the 150 lb of geological specimens and fossils he had collected, while his heart burned more than he would admit for the ones we had been obliged to leave behind. We had carried some of those rocks almost eight hundred miles, but they were more precious than diamonds, we had been told. Kevin's record of the weather and Pete's survey observations filled several notebooks with cold spidery figures, each one part of a gigantic scheme which would provide control for a map covering 22,000 square miles of the Beardmore Glacier and the Queen Maud Range. It had been a successful season, and the glow of its climax warmed into deep gratitude as I watched my three companions relax and laugh easily once again.

Our tracks had converged on a glacier in Antarctica. We had met in spirit at the head of it and had descended it together. The short journey done, we would now break free and each voyage on alone.

Six and a half years had passed since I had sat above the mudbanks on an estuary near Shoreham-by-Sea, watching the water trickle seaward. Seaward had sailed my hopes with the matchsticks I had pitched into the stream: hazy dreams of youth they were that had drifted slowly out to sea while a church bell clanged the hour of day, marking the passage of wasted time. Those dreams had no pilot, no set course, no destination this side of the horizon. But the horizon pulled more strongly from the foot of the Axel Heiberg than ever it had done at the tender age of twenty.

To the north the world lay – there was nothing to the south of me except the warm memory of a just-completed journey, and the Pole, prohibited to me, which had now lost its appeal. To the north, the Ross Ice Shelf spread out like a mighty ocean. From beneath our feet to the horizon and 600 miles beyond to the nearest habitation, the frozen rollers heaved across an expanse of desolation – a silver-grey desert furred by the softly hissing drifting snow. To the north lay my future – to the south my past.

I saw those years as paintings and uncompleted canvasses – pictures in a gallery – each one a different scene, all painted by the same unskilful hand. There were pictures of the desert there, the Andes and the Arctic, each one evoking memories of unfulfilled ambitions. Some excited new ideas – would there be time to paint them? I felt the need for three weeks at base to collect my memories before I could take up the brush and start another canvas. Every wasted hour thereafter would be time ticking faster.

The plane came like a noisy bird. We fed it with dogs and sledges and gear. In less than half an hour we were lifted into the air and comfortably droned northward.

CHAPTER TWENTY

Epilogue

Out of sight and earshot of Scott Base, below the ice cliffs caught by the evening sun, Pete and I pitched our tent. There we could reminisce in peace; and while the little primus purred and the candle flame played around the wick leaning from one man to the other, we talked. Our last few days in the South slipped by in ragged file, some rowdy, some painfully dull as we watched the new men fumbling with their unfamiliar way of life; and every evening we crept away without a word, back to our friendly polar tent.

Our shadows would stretch over the snow in grotesque, vague streaks, which shrank back to our size when they fell on the tent wall. Silent, black melancholy men they would become the moment before we crawled in through the sleeve entrance and rid ourselves of them. We could imagine them waiting outside in the sun, crouched and unseen – oppressive mimics of men heavy with the sadness of autumn. How different they were to the deep purple-blue shadows we had danced with in the spring. Sharp-cut images they were then; virile, hilarious, new-born after their winter's hibernation.

The Eskimos believe the shadow of a creature is the manifestation of its soul. On sun-less days, when the soul wanders from the body, the Eskimo succumbs to melancholy, for without the guiding influence of the soul, the spirits that inhabit every limb and organ of his body will engage in conflict one with the other. When the sun sinks and the grey-green curtain of winter descends on the Eskimo's world, a morbid sorrow thickens in their hearts, and the impulse to weep possesses the womenfolk. Such is the effect of darkness as it creeps into the void left by their 'departed' shadows.

We, with the superior intellect of Europeans, had built around ourselves a barrier of rational argument during our winters in the South to keep the fear of darkness at bay, and our aesthetic appreciation of the polar scene had stirred us. Were we not, therefore, psychologically m ore suited to the polar night and better trained to record the wonders of the polar world than the primitive peoples of the North? It was a temptation to think so! But I had begun to see polar men in a different perspective since my brief visit to Lapland, Spitzbergen, and Greenland.

What to a white man is an inanimate thing – a rock, a mountain, the sea, the air – is to a native of the Arctic a spirit in harmony or conflict with its neighbour. The Eskimos read oracles and histories in shadows; each phase of its length or tone of its colour has a special significance for them. To the Lapps, a boulder is a human soul that has found no peace – a symbol of unending doom. Even the trappers harbour superstitions, for they are men in deeper sympathy with nature than the exuberant explorers of the South. The polar Eskimos in particular are a part of their environment; born to it, perfectly attuned to it.

For six thousand years the Eskimos have been at grips with the implacable polar world. Their traditional techniques of travel, particularly in the kayak – that lightweight, fast, beautifully proportioned sealskin boat – and their ingenuity at fashioning implements for hunting from the few basic materials available in the Arctic, showed a degree of intelligence superior to most other 'primitive' peoples of the world. Physically the polar Eskimo is extremely powerful; physiologically he is completely adapted to the harsh environment: but psychologically he is incompatible with the ideal Antarctic explorer.

The spirit of adventure has no place in the heart of an Eskimo. He would consider it merely silly to risk his life to establish a theory or to make a map of unexplored country. He is by nature a hunter. The struggle for survival is his adventure. It is only in the higher civilizations that man, deprived of his natural adversary, goes in search of adventure as an outlet for his energy or to demonstrate his prowess. Nor could the Eskimo easily readjust to a womanless society, for in his world the man and his wife is a basic economic unit.

In the old Eskimo culture, man the hunter played the heroic role; on him depended the life of his family, and at times of his fellow villagers too, for meat was shared when it was scarce. He killed for food and skins; the hunt was his consuming passion and the function of his life. He was not an artist, a poet, or a musician; he had no commitments to a God. The witch-doctor Angakoks, who

like the Shamans of Lapp society were the intermediaries with the
spirit world, saved him the need to concentrate his vital energy on
pleasing or appeasing the Gods and left him free to hunt. The woman,
pillar of the home, scraped the skins the hunter brought in and sewed
them into clothes; she cooked, kept the house warm, dried the man's
kamiks, mitts and furs, and was his finest advertisement. Her size was
a measure of his prowess as a provider of food, and during the spring
hunting trips she was a travelling partner on whom he depended for
his physical well being. A world of men alone was inconceivable to
him.

An Antarctic man, unfamiliar with the mind of the Eskimos,
would at times have found them insufferable to live with; for there is
nothing more certain to cause friction among a group of Europeans
on an Antarctic expedition than conceit or sarcasm. These failings are
to an Eskimo a virtue. They take what we call sarcasm with an air of
serenity; conceit is to them a natural expression of pride; ridicule is
their form of punishment. Their capacity for humour and compassion,
their hospitality and discretion and all their other virtues would be
lost in the gulf separating the intellect of white man and Eskimo if
the native was plucked from his comfortable philosophy and dropped
amongst a small group of Antarctic explorers.

The world of men and the world of the Eskimos have few grounds
common to both. What my audience in Greenland had seen of the
Antarctic projected on the screen was as strange to them as the
expression I had seen in their eyes. They were the sons and daughters
of Eskimos. In each picture of a blizzard they had felt its energy.
They heard it cracking and moving the ice and snuggled in a white
man's tent, uncomfortably alien, but stoically resigned to wait for
better harmony between the wind which whined above the floe and
the waves which beat it from below. In pictures of cloudless days
with great mountains rearing out of the frozen sea, they had looked
for promising hunting grounds, but had smelt no tang of life on the
breeze. They had looked in vain for women and were puzzled. They
had seen only a cold desert, beautiful but barren. There was no
vegetation there; no gnats, mosquitoes, mice or hares; no musk-
oxen, reindeer, caribou, or polar bears. It was a weird world they
had seen in those pictures, desolate and pure – quite unlike their
living, breathing, hunting territory. They did not like the white

man's country. I had read in their eyes the creeping fear of foreign spirits.

What I had shown those Greenland audiences were pictures taken during my Hope Bay days in the South – how much farther from the Eskimo way of life was the modern rape of Antarctica! They would, I think, have thrown up their hands had I been able to show them pictures of Scott Base and McMurdo City, for they had seen the birth of a similar city at Thule and had heard aeroplanes in the north-west of Greenland. The inexorable march into their territory had long been under way by white man and his machinery.

The irony is that it was I who received the greater shock. The Greenlanders were already sceptical about the methods of white men in the polar world, whereas I was still living comfortably in the shadow of the illustrious Antarctic explorers like Nordenskjöld, Shackleton, Amundsen, and Scott, until I arrived amongst a new kind of Antarctic men.

Gone were the compulsive adventurers from the Antarctic scene; gone were the ascetics and self-provers and the 'characters' of old – men attracted by the challenge, by the beauty, by the rigours of the polar way of life. Most of the plums had been picked before the aeroplanes arrived. Now the windfalls are all rotten. Man the Scientist has come with his magnifying glass. Frontiers open up afresh. Man's ingenuity finds a continent waiting to be tamed. He burrows his new cities beneath the skin of polar ice; sets up atomic-power plants to distil fresh water from the sea, while women on the threshold wait to colonize the continent. This is progress. Who dares to scorn it? Man is proud of his machinery.

But the taste of modern exploration did not appeal to me. It was not the world of men I knew. My sympathy lay with those tough souls in Graham Land – men nearer in temperament to the hunter than to the polar explorer. I remembered them huddled around the bunkhouse fire; scruffy men repairing their gear, the atmosphere thick with sledging smells, the firelight glow warming their stories and their dreams of journeys that had yet to be done: journeys down the Blue Nile canyon, or into the basin of the Amazon; journeys along the old Inca trails or across the Arctic Ocean. The Antarctic to them was only one short stage of their restless journey through life. I had met none of their kind at Scott Base or McMurdo; but perhaps they had slipped away unnoticed in the roaring din of aircraft and machinery to seek out the quieter places where there is less glare or glory. The time surely had come to be on my way, for already there were forming once again those dreams of journeys that had to be done. I could hear the distant drummer beating – the drummer of ambition.

My sledging companion Pete Otway flew home to New Zealand; but the Antarctic is very possessive – I felt sure he would return. There will always be a few young men like him, experts in their field, honest and keen – men who will go South in search of adventure and be content enough to play a small part in a great endeavour. They will look nostalgically through their photograph albums in the years ahead and recall the faded names of men with whom they wintered, for it leaves its mark on every man in one way or another. They are a brotherhood of men, each with his own conception of what the Antarctic is like – memories unaffected by the opinions of his fellows or by the passing of time.

And so for two weeks I performed alone the nightly ritual of lighting the candle in a chill tent glistening with frost. The smells were there, the rustle of a breeze was near, but few clothes hung in the apex now to be cuddled by clouds of steam. My companions' space on the floor was bare. There was an abyss beyond the friendly primus – the tent, a vault of memories. In the silence of thought I talked with them all – the men who had shared my hopes and fears, short rations and feasts, long stories and laughter and miseries. They had all gone. We would meet again, older men, but not the same men I had known.